THE UNITED NATIONS UNIVERSITY
STUDIES ON PEACE AND REGIONAL SECURITY

LATIN AMERICA

PEACE, DEMOCRATIZATION & ECONOMIC CRISIS

THE UNITED NATIONS UNIVERSITY
STUDIES ON PEACE AND REGIONAL SECURITY

The United Nations University project on Peace and Regional Security was a special study carried out under the programme area on Peace and Global Transformation. Focusing on the Third World and Europe, the project attempted to analyse the trade-offs between the conflicting conditions in these regions of vulnerability and security and competition and solidarity. Five regional seminars were held in Africa, Asia, Europe, Latin America, and Oceania and the Pacific on themes related to conflicts over natural resources and security and human rights in determining global, regional, and national development. The results of these studies are part of the United Nations University's contribution to the United Nations International Year of Peace.

Project Co-ordinator: Janusz W. Golebiowski

TITLES IN THIS SERIES

Africa: Perspectives on Peace and Development
Edited by Emmanuel Hansen (1987)

Europe: Dimensions of Peace
Edited by Björn Hettne (1988)

Latin America: Peace, Democratization and Economic Crisis
Edited by J. A. Silva Michelena (1988)

Asia: Militarization and Regional Conflict
Edited by Yoshikazu Sakamoto (1988)

The Pacific: Peace, Security and the Nuclear Issue
Edited by R. Walker and W. Sutherland (1988)

Peace and Security in Africa: A State of the Art Report
Emmanuel Hansen (1989)

THE UNITED NATIONS UNIVERSITY
STUDIES ON PEACE AND REGIONAL SECURITY

LATIN AMERICA
PEACE, DEMOCRATIZATION & ECONOMIC CRISIS

EDITED BY JOSÉ SILVA-MICHELENA

The United Nations University
Tokyo

Zed Books Ltd
London and New Jersey

Latin America: Peace, Democratization and Economic Crisis
was first published in 1988 by:

Zed Books Ltd, 57 Caledonian Road, London N1 9BU, UK, and
171 First Avenue, Atlantic Highlands, New Jersey 07716, USA,

and

The United Nations University, Toho Seimei Building,
15-1 Shibuya 2-chome, Shibuya-ku, Tokyo 150, Japan.

Copyright © The United Nations University, 1988.

Cover designed by Adrian Yeeles/Artworkers.
Typeset by EMS Photosetters, Rochford, Essex.
Printed and bound in the United Kingdom
by Biddles Ltd., Guildford and King's Lynn.

British Library Cataloguing in Publication Data

Latin America: peace, democratization and
economic crisis. – (The United Nations
University studies on peace and regional
security. 3)
1. Latin America, Politics
I. Michelena, José Silva, *1934-1986.*   II. Series
320.98

ISBN 0-86232-722-9
ISBN 0-86232-723-7 Pbk

Library of Congress Cataloging-in-Publication Data

Latin America: peace, democratization & economic
crisis/edited by José Silva Michelena.
       p.   cm. — (The United Nations University
studies on peace and regional security)
    ISBN 0-86232-722-9.
    ISBN 0-86232-723-7 (pbk.)
      1. Latin America—Politics and government—
1980-   2. Latin America—Economic conditions—
1945-   3. Latin America—National security.   4.
Diplomatic negotiations in international disputes.
5. Latin America—Foreign relations—1948-   I.
Silva Michelena. José Agustín.   II. Series.
F1414.2.L3273 1988
320.98—dc19

Contents

List of Tables

Chart

IN MEMORIAM

The editor of this book, José Agustín Silva-Michelena, suffered a fatal heart attack on 8 December 1986. He was 52 and at the height of his creative capabilities. His sudden loss once again confirms what Albert Camus said: that 'death is the confirmation of the presence of an absurd element in the existence of human beings, which can only be conquered through their full realization of that humaneness as a species.' This is precisely the essence of the many things which Professor Silva-Michelena fought for during his life. And this is also the debt and the commitment to him of all of us who were his friends, comrades and colleagues.

This book presents one phase of Silva-Michelena's intellectual work; although it happened to be his last, he had perceived it as an opening towards new research fields, both for him and for the Centro de Estudios del Desarrollo (CENDES) at the University of Venezuela, an institute which was, truly and strictly speaking, his own. After retiring (by law, Venezuelan University professors have the right to retire after 25 years of uninterrupted service), freed from the burden of daily teaching, research and administrative chores, he devoted his full energies to a project on peace and global transformation, originally launched by the United Nations University and its active Vice-Rector Kinhide Mus koji, and now in progress in five countries. He was persuaded that this work was a widening and deepening of CENDES' research leitmotivs from its very beginnings: an empirical and theoretical investigation of the processes of social change and of the concrete possibilities for Man to intervene actively in them in order to guide society towards new, more humane and rational horizons and substance.

He soon became the co-ordinator of the Latin American sector of the project. His intellectual prestige, his capacity to convince, and his enthusiasm for a continuing exploration of the frontiers of knowledge persuaded many of his colleagues — those who have contributed to this book and many others whose contributions will be published in the future — to dedicate themselves to this research field and to its practical implications; that is, an attempt to contribute to the creation of new knowledge (and the synthesis of existing knowledge) in vitally important fields for a development process at the service of human beings and the vast majorities in our countries. He undertook his co-ordinating tasks guided by a sense of respect (for which he was so well-known) for theoretical and conceptual pluralism and for creative freedom among all those who participated in this new intellectual adventure.

Gradually, the field opened by José Agustín has been incorporated in CENDES. We are firmly convinced that it must be maintained and that our obligation is to continue the work he initiated. His physical absence will make it more difficult, but his intellectual presence will help us in fulfilling our commitment.

Preface

In commemoration of the International Year of Peace, the United Nations University launched a special study on Regional Peace and Security in the Third World and Europe as part of its international Project on Peace and Global Transformation. The study selected a number of regions plagued by chronic conflicts and tensions. Five UNU regional seminars were organized between November 1984 and June 1986 in Latin America, Africa, Asia, Europe, and Oceania and the Pacific. At each meeting, a UNU core group of experts interacted with a group of regional specialists.

Based on an in-depth analysis of the geopolitical, socio-cultural and economic realities of each region, made by specialists from each region, the project analysed the special sensitivities, the play-off between vulnerability and security, competition and solidarity which underlie and condition these conflicts. After identifying the major issues, the project attempted to explore the possibilities of creating regional mechanisms for resolving conflicts peacefully, in a way that precludes outside intervention and contributes to international peace and security.

The above remarks may help the reader understand the way articles are selected and presented in this book. First, it is important to remember that each of the regional peace problematique articles represents the analysis of regional realities made by a researcher of the region. Without any claim of representativity, we feel that many points made in them would not have appeared in an article written by an outsider, especially one who saw the problem from the point of view of the global actors and not of the peoples concerned.

Second, when we talk about the peace problematique, we mean not only the resolution of conflicts through peace-making and peace-keeping, but also the complex interaction of military, economic, political and socio-cultural factors which are at the roots of regional insecurity and that need to be dealt with in any attempt at peace-building. This is why the articles presented here combine ones on the regional military conflicts and ones on the broader context of regional security.

Third, it should be stressed that all the papers reflect the longer-range problems; hence, they are more analytical than short-term policy-oriented. The editors share the view of practically all the contributors to this volume that no easy policy solutions can be found to the complex set of problems constituting the peace problematique in today's world. The international community, and its global institution, the UN, will have to combine a variety of worldwide and regional measures, in collaboration not only with the member states, but with non-governmental groups and movements reflecting, often in a contradictory way, the needs and aspirations of the different peoples. The aim of this volume is to present a picture of the complexity of tasks the international community will have to face in the world of today and tomorrow.

The present volume is composed of three parts, the first dealing with the broader context of the contemporary economic crisis, within which regional peace and security in Latin America must be put in order to grasp the true nature of the conflicts. In the general literature on regional peace and security, the problematique treated in Part 1 is usually only cursorily referred to, if not completely ignored. It is thanks to the insistence of the Latin American researchers who participated in the project that the linkages between the economic crisis and the region's state of insecurity have been treated, as can be found in the four chapters comprising this first part. It is important for non-Latin-American readers to read attentively between the lines of the sometimes impassioned texts the deep concern of intellectuals of this region as to the *structural* causes of conflicts in this part of the world. This is an aspect of the problems of regional peace and security often overlooked by outsiders who tend to isolate these questions, hoping to handle them more easily on a military–diplomatic, institutional level, treating the economic crisis as a given. Seen from within, however, it is impossible to dissociate one from the other. This is an aspect to which the reader's attention should be drawn.

The second part treats the role of different states and geopolitical realities in the conflicts of Latin America as a whole and its different sub-regions. Here we find an approach to the problems of regional peace and security in Latin America which has been developed to the highest degree of sophistication and relevance in this region, i.e. a structural analysis of the actors in conflict from which are derived some striking conclusions opening new perspectives on the dynamics of the conflicts concerned. To give only two examples, we find this approach illuminating in the analysis of the authoritarian state as a key to understanding the Malvinas War, and in the analysis of the conflict patterns between democracy and dictatorship by looking at the various trends from populism to social democracy in the region.

The third part of the book studies the institutional framework. This includes, in addition to the inter-American system, the various aspects of human rights and the relevance of the UN model to the region. The reader will be interested, not only in the assessment of the relevance of the different institutions, but also in the attitude common to all the authors whose critical analyses of the institutional system show the strength of the long tradition of legal and institutional efforts which characterizes the Latin American regional peace and security approach.

In brief, the whole book is an analysis of the world economic crisis's impact on peace and security in Latin America analysed by Latin American specialists, using the powerful tools of analysis developed by them in pointing out the underlying politico-economic realities which characterize conflicts in the region and which have to be taken into consideration in building a Latin American system which might guarantee peace and security in this region.

While pointing out the importance of the fact that this book is the product of collaboration among Latin American researchers, we would like to pay a special tribute to the leading role played by the late Professor José Agustín Silva-Michelena as Editor of this volume. Co-ordinator of the Latin American Project on Regional Peace and Security, and as a Core Group member of the UN University Project on Peace and Global Transformation which provided the broader framework of the regional projects. His loss has left a great lacuna in the UNU international community of scholars. We miss his intellectual capacity to grasp the intricate interlinkages among different issue areas, which made his contribution especially precious in the preparation of the overall design of the project which gave birth to this book.

Finally, we hope that the readers of the present publication will also read its companion volumes on peace and security in the other regions of the world, as well as other related publications coming out of the UN University Project on Peace and Global Transformation.

We hope that the analysis of the regional peace and security issues in Latin America contained in this book will become a good entry point into the study of regional peace and security in all the Third World regions and the world at large.

Kinhide Mushakoji,
Vice-Rector,
The United Nations University.

1. Introduction

José Agustín Silva-Michelena

The present volume contains some of the papers presented at the United Nations University's international seminars on Peace, Security and Development in Latin American and the Impact of the World Crisis on Latin American Peace and Security.[1] As in most academic seminars, where a group of scientists meet to debate polemical issues, many ideas emerge which complement or contradict the arguments advanced in the written papers. The product of these debates is usually taken into account by those attending the seminar, in the sense that they may change some previously held points of view, or strengthen a given position, or define new lines of research. Nevertheless, the results of the debates remain unknown to a wider audience, because their publication becomes impossible owing to a series of reasons: transcription of the debates is too voluminous, and to edit them is a difficult and costly job; publishing both papers and debates is also too costly; and, last of all, it is very difficult to reproduce in written form the atmosphere of the discussions.

The purpose of the present introduction is to transmit to a broader audience, although in very summarized form, the central elements of the discussions during the seminars. In this way, we also hope to communicate some of the arguments presented in those papers not included in the present volume for reasons of space.

In order to do this, we have sought to link the central themes of the papers presented with the main issues debated during the seminar. Hence, not all the propositions contained in the papers or verbal interventions will be reported on in this Introduction.

During the debate, more importance was given to certain issues which, in fact, became a sort of organizing axis of the discussions. This Introduction takes this fact into account. In this sense, I am reporting on a collective effort, although the responsibility for errors and omissions is entirely mine.

Since it is a collective product, it would not have been appropriate to try to associate themes with particular authors, as is usual in introductions of this sort.

The Economic Crisis and the Need for New Proposals

The purpose of the debate was not to make yet another diagnosis of the world economic crisis, but to consider it in relation to peace and security. In this sense, it was strongly felt that the world is undergoing one of the most tense periods since the Second World War, not only by virtue of the depth and prolonged length of the economic crisis, but also because of the actual and potential dangers to world peace and security stemming from what has come to be called the Second Cold War.

As for perspectives on the crisis, there was a consensus that it is a profound, structural one to which no immediate way out may be seen. Some argued that a new long wave of prosperity might begin as early as the 1990s. Others indicated that the crisis could still last for some 20 or 30 years more since it is not clear what new permanent sources of accumulation could launch a new wave of prosperity for the world capitalist system. On the contrary, dangers of a new financial collapse, similar to that of 1929,* are present, in particular due to two inter-related factors.

The first and most dangerous are the huge and growing balance of payments and fiscal deficits of the United States, and the second is a possible cessation of payments owed on their external debt by the underdeveloped countries, a prospect which should not be discounted in spite of their manifest willingness hitherto to sign agreements with the International Monetary Fund.

The structural character of the crisis is revealed by the exhaustion of the post-war model of accumulation (basically of its consumerist and militarist character) and above all of its cheap energy base. The increasingly malfunctioning articulation of national economic systems with the international order is another sign of the depth of the crisis. The non-existence (already mentioned) of new sources of accumulation must be added to these factors. Even the rapid developments in electronics and micro-electronics, which are frequently mentioned as possible new sources of accumulation, are not having a significant enough impact on investment, employment and other key economic variables.

Turning to Latin America specifically, it is clear that its mode of insertion in the world economic system is exhausted and there are no clear signs that new ways of relating to the world economy are being established.

The world economic crisis seems to be having a contradictory effect on Latin America. On the one hand, it keeps on the agenda alternative options, but on the other, such options are being shut off by both the debt problem and the lack of political will to design, at a regional level, a new strategy of insertion in the changing world economy. In this sense, it was pointed out that such a strategy should take into consideration the strong tensions building up within the capitalist system. Even if these tensions among developed nations have not reached, as in the past, the point of actually leading to war, conflicts between the United States, Japan and Europe — and even within European countries — are becoming almost as acute as those which in the past led to a world war.

From the point of view of the world *political* crisis, it is clear that the main

---

* This was written before the great Stock Exchange nosedive of October 1987: *Publisher*.

conflict is still the East–West confrontation. Fortunately, there have emerged some signs recently that the situation may be changing towards a new detente. This, of course, would decrease the danger of a nuclear holocaust, but there are no signs that a new detente will exclude a reaffirmation of the traditional zones of influence of the Super Powers, and hence, to a 'new' Old World Order, instead of a New International Order where underdeveloped countries may have a better share. The possibility of a new and more favourable insertion of the underdeveloped countries in the world system has clearly been opened up by the relative military, political, and ideological weakness of the United States.

The crisis of hegemony of the United States has manifested itself in events such as the new wave of liberation movements, the post-Vietnam syndrome, the Iran hostage episode, the fratricidal war in Lebanon, the challenge of Libya, the inability to tolerate the revolutionary government of Angola, and so on. It is true that the Reagan Administration has defined a strategy to recover absolute American hegemony. This has implied abandoning former President Carter's human rights policy and action through the Trilateral Commission, concentrating instead on the US's bilateral use of force, militarism, political and economic pressures, and open intervention in other countries' affairs. This new policy is exemplified by the deployment of Cruise missiles in Europe in spite of the massive protest movements of the European population, and by the Strategic Defense Initiative (SDI), creating a new and more dangerous threat to world peace.

As is well-known, world military equilibrium used to be based on a strategy which, strangely enough, became known as MAD (Mutual Assured Destruction). It was based on the certainty that the destructive capacity of each Super Power was so big that nobody would 'lose' or 'win' in case of an outbreak of war. But if — contrary to the doubts of many specialists — total protection against a nuclear attack is achieved, as proposed by the SDI, an entirely new strategic situation would emerge. To put it in a nutshell, if the United States is 100% protected against a Soviet nuclear attack, then the Soviet nuclear arsenal would be completely obsolete. In such a situation the USSR would have the following options: (1) to build its own nuclear shield; (2) to launch a pre-emptive war; or (3) to accept the US as the global hegemonic power and try to adapt to the new situation. Since the first option looks the most likely, the nuclear arsenals of both Super Powers would be rendered obsolete. This is good, but the risk of their waging a conventional war would become much greater. The world would be back to the pre-World War II strategic situation, but at a much higher level of destructive capacity. Of course, the issues and alternatives involved are much more complex than just stated. One other alternative, for example, is that the nuclear arms race would continue, with each Super Power trying to develop new weapons capable of penetrating the opponent's shield.

Obviously, Latin American and other Third World countries would have very little influence on such a scenario. On the contrary, the Super Powers would prescribe a place for them. In the case of Latin America, the United

States has already designed a strategy to contain revolutionary movements. With some variants this strategy is applicable to any Third World country. It is based on the so-called Rapid Deployment Force which enables the US to place a significant force of combat-ready soldiers anywhere in the underdeveloped world, without warning and with the objective of annihilating insurgents. This military strategy is usually accompanied by a well-orchestrated ideological offensive to manipulate public opinion both at home and abroad.

Within this framework, the external debt appears to be one of the most serious obstacles to the development of Third World countries and one of the most salient aspects of the economic crisis. It was recognized by the participants at our seminars that the debt was the outcome of several factors: the long recession at the Centre, unforeseen events in the world financial markets (especially the sudden and steep rise in interest rates), a series of cumulative errors by both borrowers and lenders, and last but not least, the exhaustion of the transnational model of accumulation in Third World countries. Protectionism in Centre countries and deterioration in the Periphery countries' terms of trade have also contributed to the Third World economic crisis and particularly to a decrease in the capacity of the underdeveloped countries to cope with the problem of the debt.

What is the impact of this debt of nearly $900 billion (as of 1986)? In the first place, there exists the danger of a cessation of payments owing, which would result in bankruptcy for at least several important international financial organizations. This is no idle speculation. The case of Continental Illinois, the second most important US bank, which almost went bankrupt, is a good example of the dangers which the situation entails. A sudden fall in the price of exports of the underdeveloped countries, a not uncommon event, may trigger a world financial collapse.

Another consequence of the debt problem is the decline in political and economic capacity of underdeveloped countries, particularly of Latin America, which accounts for half the Third World debt. Economic self-determination has been significantly reduced owing to the need to apply IMF-'suggested' policies in order to be eligible for refinancing agreements. Politically, the room for manoeuvre has been greatly reduced by the Manicheist lens through which the United States judges political developments in Latin America. Without exaggeration, any unorthodox change is seen as necessarily related to East–West tensions and so stands a good chance of being considered a 'communist menace'. This results in pre-planned political, economic and military interventionist policies being put into effect. This potential danger, however, will never paralyse progressive social movements.

A close look at US–Latin American economic relations clearly reveals that, up to a certain point, there has been an increase in Latin America's bargaining power. Since the 1950s economic relations between them have been slowly changing in favour of the latter. Thus, the nature of commodities traded has altered, in particular, a shift from raw materials and labour-intensive manufactured goods towards fuel exports and capital-intensive goods. Middle-income Latin American countries now import more from other OECD countries and not just from the US. Moreover the debt itself has given Latin American countries a certain negative power. Fear of their going bankrupt is a bargaining factor. In addition, intra-Latin American trade has significantly increased. Wider South–South relations have also expanded, although to a lesser degree. All these factors have resulted in an objective change in Latin America's bargaining power.

Although no major collective effort has been initiated in order to take advantage of this new situation, some steps like the Cartagena Consensus or Argentina's trade with the Soviet Union have taken place, which would not have been possible were it not for the new bargaining power of Latin America.

However, since the crisis erupted in 1981, commerce between the US and Latin America is reverting to the 1950s pattern. In 1980 only 33% of Latin American exports went to the US, but by 1984 these exports had reached a level similar to the 1950s (44%). True, these exports are no longer labour-intensive goods but it is not very comforting to think that increased dependency on the US is now going hand in hand with renewed US efforts to recover its former position of absolute political hegemony as well.

It was pointed out at the seminars that there was an urgent need to produce intellectual tools to face this new situation, and in particular to produce alternatives to IMF policies and transnationalization, and to foster South–South co-operation. Some of the participants observed that Latin American socio-economic theory, particularly the theory of dependency, in spite of being a valuable intellectual product, had not reached the level of formalization necessary for drafting policy proposals which could be helpful at the negotiating table. This caused considerable debate. It was argued that even though formalization of theory was desirable, it could not be as determinant an influence over events at the negotiating table as other more real factors. For instance, it was mentioned that, even if it is true that the nature of trade between the US and Latin America has changed, dependence has in fact increased due to the transnationalization of the Latin American economies. The debt does represent a risk for the international financial community, but the truth is that it is imposing on Latin American countries its own terms for the negotiation of agreements, and Latin American efforts to change this situation are still ineffective. While various initiatives have been taken, there is not yet enough co-ordination and an agreed set of priorities has not been defined. One of the main reasons why not enough progress has been made on the Latin American side is because the dominant sectors in most of these countries, whether democratic or not, are closely related to transnational interests. Thus they have no interest in pushing for greater Latin American autonomy. Given this situation, what seems to be the dominant tendency in US–Latin American relations is bilateralism — i.e. the US relating to each country individually — which is what the US wants.

In spite of these contradictory points of view, there was a consensus that more detailed research was needed before reaching any conclusion. For instance, it is necessary to examine more closely the impact of exporting energy rather than other types of goods; no clear understanding of what is happening with investment exists; it is necessary to evaluate whether an increased South–South dialogue, given present trends, may not lead to a new regional disequilibrium in which Brazil, Mexico and Argentina would become hegemonic poles.

It was also mentioned that in Latin America there is no lack of rigorous proposals or initiatives; what is lacking is the necessary power or political will to make them effective. It was argued that what has really happened is that Latin America has lost power *vis-à-vis* the US's new exertion of its power. For instance, it has been proposed that the debt could be paid off with goods and services, which in turn could be a stimulus for Latin American development. However, this has not even been considered by international financial organizations. On the contrary, what is taking place is a huge flow of capital from Latin America to the developed countries, which is helping the latter to finance their own economic recovery while at the same time impoverishing the Latin American population.

There are factors in the Latin American situation which are an obstacle to devising common strategies. The most important of these is that Latin American economies are mostly competitive with each other; on top of which, many countries are not willing to give up the comparative advantages they now hold with respect to some products. Above all, as was mentioned, the socio-political bloc in power agrees with the transnational elites and is not interested in changing the present situation. Even the process of democratization which seems to be sweeping throughout Latin America will not significantly change this aspect of the internal correlation of power.

Thus, important as it is to devise rigorous policy proposals based on theoretically sound premises, it should be taken into account that the problem is not merely a technical one; it is also political. Ignoring this fact is as bad as ignoring assessment of the technical viability of the proposals.

Crisis and Democracy

One topic which frequently arose in discussion was the impact of the crisis on the democratization process. It was pointed out that the crisis pointed up the failure of military regimes and gave life to democratization efforts. However, by the same token, the crisis also increased destabilizing factors in the established democracies. Growing tensions due to economic shortages are making it very difficult to manage conflicts in a democratic manner.

Moreover, there seem to be several factors prompting the use of force and renewed militarization. In the first place, there is the growing autonomy of the armed forces, that is, their tendency to act without checks and balances from other institutions, even in the older democracies, and the propensity to repress public protests by means of military and paramilitary organs which could easily resort to the use of force. Since these protests are multiplying owing to the popular movements' opposition to IMF-recommended policies, resort to such repressive organs is easily justified in the minds of the bloc in power.

A second source which prompts the use of force and works in favour of authoritarianism is what may be called international financial violence. Systematic violation of international agreements on the social and economic rights of the people, in favour of restrictive policies which systematically undermine the living conditions of the popular sectors, increase unemployment and exacerbate social and economic discrimination, certainly create favourable conditions for the use of force and lead to the elite perception that authoritarianism is the ideal instrument to manage the crisis.

A third source encouraging the use of force is the US's political and ideological strategy towards Latin America and the Caribbean. This strategy can be seen in how the US has dealt with conflicts in Central America and the Caribbean. The Kissinger Report is a perfect example, and applicable not only to that region but to the whole of Latin America. It shows clearly that the US intervenes either indirectly, as with an economic blockade or aid to the 'contras' or, if necessary and the opportunity arises, directly as it did in Grenada. The question of the viability of such a strategy was posed at our seminars. Since the situation is complex and varies from country to country, there is no simple answer. More research is needed also to clarify recent tendencies in the global policies of the United States.

These three sources conducive to the use of force and encouraging authoritarian elements are resulting in a new legitimation of militarism. Hence the increase in military expenditures and military personnel, in the arms race, and in the growth of the arms industry. These tendencies are taking place in a situation where the previous security system in Latin America no longer operates effectively. Given this, latent conflicts among states — for instance between Venezuela and Colombia, Venezuela and Guyana, Peru, Bolivia and Chile — are more likely to be resolved by force. In other words, violent confrontation among States is becoming more probable. In addition, in order to confront the growing restlessness of the population due to economically restrictive government policies, regimes are increasingly falling into the temptation of confronting an 'external enemy', as a means of obtaining popular support. Not only authoritarian regimes may do this, as in the Malvinas (Falklands) War, but democratic governments may be similarly tempted.

Obviously, the possibility for military governments to apply internally the same tactics as they use on the international scene is greater than for democratic governments, not only by reason of their 'natural' inclinations, but also because there are no institutional controls to prevent such practices.

The situation is further complicated by a significant increase in arms going to paramilitary groups, added to the arms associated with drug trafficking. The parallel arms market has grown so large that it has created centres of semi-autonomous power.

But these are not the only dangers for the process of democratization in Latin America. The existence of an authoritarian culture is potentially more menacing. Institutions such as the Church or schools may in some cases generate a collective consciousness conducive to military solutions. In the case of Argentina, this is so pronounced that the term, civil militarism, has some meaning because even sports clubs adopt military forms of organization. However, it is evident that more research is needed on this subject in order to reach conclusions.

In short, urgent research is needed in order to design a policy to counteract the factors stimulating the use of force and authoritarianism. The overall aim should be demilitarization of the State and the political culture, and democratization of the armed forces.

Crisis and Geopolitics

The geopolitical role of Latin America is an ambivalent one, due to its dual character. On the one hand, Latin America is part of the Third World and, as such, participates in the North–South conflict. On the other, since it belongs to the security zone of the US, Latin American governments are expected to show some solidarity with the hegemonic power. This ambivalence has recently become more significant owing to the US's militarist and aggressive policy. In terms of this new policy, the US does not accept collective negotiations but only bilateral ones. This policy is supported by the transnational and national sectors constituting the bloc in power in most Latin American countries. However, the debt crisis may be creating circumstances favouring more concerting of policies by Latin American countries. The internal threat is so big that presidents themselves have participated in meetings such as the Quito Conference (January 1984) and the Cartagena Consensus. Even if these actions have not been very effective, they do show that there are cohesive elements which open up new perspectives for the international policy of Latin America. These elements, however, may not be sufficient to overcome the above-mentioned latent conflicts.

The growing East–West tension during most of the 1980s has increased Latin America's strategic importance. New strategic doctrines have upgraded the Latin American role as a provider of strategic and raw materials to the US. This upgrading of Latin America has not, however, influenced US policy toward the region in one sense; it still continues to consider Latin America as its backyard.

With respect to US interventionist policy, seen from a geostrategic point of view, the US is not likely to intervene directly in Nicaragua because that country does not represent a real danger. However, as was mentioned earlier, this is a matter open for discussion, and one which urgently needs more research.

One of the fields where Latin American foreign policy needs speedy definition relates to the necessity to break the financial siege and face up to international financial violence. New mechanisms must be created with sufficient power to induce international financial organizations to accept better terms.

Crisis and Human Rights

One issue which contributed to the originality of our discussions was the relation between the world economic crisis and human rights. There was serious evidence that international law, ratified through agreements and pacts signed by governments and aimed at defending civil and political as well as economic, social and cultural human rights, was being threatened by the crisis. It was pointed out that there were fundamental differences between these two sets of human rights as far as the relation with crisis is concerned. In effect, civil and political rights do not seem to have a clear, direct and unequivocal relation to the crisis. For instance, if it is true that the crisis has been a factor facilitating the ousting of dictatorial regimes, hence favouring respect for civil and political rights, it is also true that the crisis poses an equal menace to the stability of democratic regimes, increasing the temptation to use force to cope with mounting social tensions.

The impact of the crisis on economic, social and cultural human rights seems to be a more direct one. For instance, the policy package recommended by the IMF and applied by Latin American governments clearly violates economic and social rights. This package clearly contradicts legal rights such as employment, subsistence and other basic economic and social rights.

States tend to comply far more scrupulously with contracts signed with the international banking community than with agreements signed with international organizations, even where these unambiguously commit them to promote and protect economic and social rights.

Need for Changes in the Institutional Framework

The conclusion was that there was a need to re-examine the role which international organizations can play, in particular the global action of the United Nations, not only because its role has been occasionally positive, but also because of the possibility of introducing changes which might increase this eventuality.

As with all organizations, the UN has some built-in elements which lend weight to its actions. However, the UN also has some factors which tend to weaken it. A consideration of both aspects may throw light on the type of changes that it is necessary to introduce. There is no doubt, for example, that the UN has been capable of incorporating a growing number of States, and has enriched the content of their participation. Today, 'to be a member of the United Nations means not only to deposit, as other States do, some part of a State's self-interest, or of the alliance or region to which it belongs, but also to assume with solidarity the responsibility of the totality, not only of the States but also of the Nations and persons which form it.'[2]

Thus there is an internal tension in the United Nations Charter: States are the only members, but in practice, when it deals with human rights, for instance, the organization is also dealing with *persons*. This leads to the need to revise the concept of security in the sense that 'the primary security is that of persons, then of social communities, followed by the security of the State and, finally, the security of the community of States. This succession does not imply an order of importance, but a complexity of institutions.'[3] It follows that 'the security of the community of States, from which peace among them results, must first be secured through the mechanisms of the Economic and Social Council and then through the so-called Security Council.'[4] As a conclusion, in the case of the UN it is suggested that the Economic and Social Council should prevail over the Security Council.

As for the weakness of the United Nations, no reference is made to its well-known deficiencies, but rather to the principal cause which resides in the tension inherent to the dual concept of security. It is recognized that 'between the security of the community and that of persons, there is a dialectical tension which increases both as the social tissue and personal life thicken and become stronger. This tension is particularly delicate in the case of the constitutive elements of the State.'[5]

The conclusion follows that 'The great weakness of the United Nations model is its being unable to overcome national security doctrines or total security, and to have built upon them a Security Council where both conceptions clash, become closer and very laboriously seldom integrate themselves.'[6]

MacGregor further argues that 'the consequence of this weakness has been the strengthening of the Great Hegemonic Powers, the multiplication of States imbued by a National Security doctrine, and the confining of multilateralism to only those countries belonging to each one's own sphere of influence.'[7]

To summarize, the role of the UN can be more positive since it contains in its founding statutes certain principles which favour peace, such as the concept that security comes from justice and not from the force of an army. To the extent that these aspects are reinforced, the efficacy of its actions in pursuit of peace could be increased.

This appraisal of a global organization like the UN enhances the importance of a regional initiative like that of the Contadora Group. The novelty of Contadora lies in the fact that it is the first time that Latin American diplomacy has liberated itself from the OAS framework, and the first time that peace has been collectively sought through peaceful means. Contadora is also innovative because it uses the moral force of Latin American governments to induce those nations directly involved in the conflict to sit at the negotiating table. Obviously, if Contadora's efforts fail, then the road is open for a regional conflict which may even have implications for world peace.

To face this threat, there exist a whole range of institutional instruments and mechanisms, specially designed to seek peaceful solutions to international controversies. However, it is sobering to realize that, up to now, these instruments have failed notoriously in their task to solve disputes and conflicts.

Thus, there exists an urgent need to launch studies to provide a better understanding of the Latin American institutional framework for the peaceful resolution of conflicts. Studies of Contadora, of the Latin American security system and of initiatives such as the Cartagena Consensus are essential to face the present crisis and to design a strategy for peaceful Latin American development in the threatening years ahead.

Notes

1. These seminars are two in a series sponsored by the United Nations University, within the context of its major project: Peace and Global Transformation. The seminars were held in San José, Costa Rica (21–23 November 1984) and Caracas, Venezuela (25–28 March 1985). The complete set of papers is being published in Spanish in two forthcoming volumes.

2. MacGregor, 'The United Nations Model: Could it be a Road to Peace in Latin America?'; the essay, in a different translation, appears as Chapter 12 of this volume. p. 159.

3. Ibid., p. 163.

4. Ibid.

5. Ibid., p. 165.

6. Ibid., p. 167.

7. Ibid.

Part I
Economic Crisis, Peace and Security

2. The World Crisis and the New International Economic Order

Theotonio Dos Santos

All discussion of a New International Economic Order (NIEO) should begin from a conceptualization of the foundations of world power. According to Nineteenth Century thought, world power had its origins in the intrinsic superiority of the dominant countries, be it racial, climatic, its raw materials, culture, religion, etc. This point of view was based on an arbitrary view of causality which ignored the great historical differences between the colonizing nations and the colonies. Today it is not possible to accept such simplistic explanations.

It seems clear that changes in international power blocs are associated with the evolution of socio-economic relations which tend to concentrate power in specific regions as a condition of its own consolidation and ensuing expansion. Slavery concentrated itself in the city states of Ancient Greece before serving as a basis for the Madeconian Empire; and it was the full consolidation of slavery originally in the city of Rome itself which laid the foundations for the expansion of the Roman Empire. The Prophet Mohammed also developed mercantilism in Mecca before the colossal expansion of Islam. Capitalism concentrated itself in Portugal and Spain before subsequently passing on to Holland and finally triumphing in England where it found its true modern industrial basis — the factory.

This concentration–expansion dynamic seems to have been the way that the new forms of production emerged and advanced in an unequal and combined process; but it was only capitalism which ended with the conquest of territories on a world-wide scale and created an integrated international economy. From this moment on, unequal and combined development assumes a universal character. It is this universal character which opens its way through international economic relations: in the beginning of this century with World War I (or as the Asians call it, the Great European Civil War); then the anti-colonial struggles of the Turks, Chinese and Persians in the 1920s; followed by World War II, this time clearly a world war; and after it, the great anti-colonial liberation movements of Africa and Asia, the Latin American revolutions and the national democratic movements.

Evolution of International Contradictions: Socialism v. Capitalism; Nationalism v. Imperialism

The Non-Aligned Movement, preceded by the Bandung Conference, reflected the deep changes which were occurring in the world economy. Slowly the elements were being generated in the economically dependent countries for the formation of a more or less coherent anti-imperialist front.

This reality became more evident as the expansion of the socialist economies occurred with their growing identification with the anti-imperialist struggle. From 1917 to 1945, Soviet Russia had strongly supported the liberation movements of China, India, Turkey, etc. After World War II, the western frontier of socialism expanded with the installation of the 'people's democracies' of Eastern Europe and a new path to socialism emerged with the victory of the revolution of Yugoslavia in the Balkans.

Following these events, the revolutions of China, Korea, Indochina, Cuba and parts of Africa finally took on an openly socialist orientation. The cases of Algeria, Iraq and South Yemen also show a relation between a nationalist revolution and a socialist revolution.

We can therefore say that, starting in the late 1940s, and becoming stronger throughout the world, an intrinsic, complex relationship, contradictory in many respects, was established between the struggles for national liberation and socialism. For this reason the Non-Aligned Movement, as a result of the changes occurring within it, came steadily closer to socialism, in spite of serious tensions which may have taken place.

After 1945, the centre of international confrontation was located in Central Europe, the Balkans, Italy and Greece. In a complex process due to the Cold War, the cards of the European deck began to arrange themselves.

The Cold War got more tense with the victory of the Chinese Revolution in 1949, followed by the Korean War and the unsuccessful French attempt to recover Indochina. China, North Korea and North Vietnam (in spite of their counterparts, Taiwan, South Korea and South Vietnam) represented fundamental victories in terms of installing fundamentally different economic and social regimes. India, Indonesia and Ghana paved the way for other non-socialist movements of liberation. Egypt's anti-colonialist position under Nasser radicalized national struggles in the Arab world, and Iran experienced Mossadegh's (short-lived) victory. Only the intellectually blind refused to see in which direction the winds of history were blowing.

The late 1950s saw the dawn of the Algerian and Cuban revolutions. The consolidation of the latter led to the world passing through the danger of a possible nuclear war as a result of the famous Cuban missile crisis. Domestically, this almost catastrophic confrontation between the US and USSR combined with the socialist definition of the revolution to reveal the dramatic relation between these two poles of international contemporary politics: national independence and socialism.

The decade of the 1960s was dominated by the US's direct confrontation in Vietnam. The previous capitalist defeats had been attributed to a decadent

European colonialism; now, in Vietnam it was capitalism's leader, the US, which risked its own troops. The demoralization of its defeat, as a result, was very strong. Even more, in the 1970s, the liberation of Portugal's African colonies took a step further the consolidating of the relation between national liberation movements and socialism, a relationship which repeatedly reappears in many parts of Africa and Asia in recent years, radicalizing the confrontation between the developed capitalist dominant countries which make up the OECD and NATO and the socialist bloc united in COMECON and the Warsaw Pact.

In this context, Yugoslavia, the national democratic parties and some Social Democrats sought an equidistant position from the Super Power confrontation and supported intermediate solutions. On the other hand, China launched a ferocious anti-Soviet policy which led it to support NATO, the European Right (Thatcher, Strauss, etc.), and anti-Soviet militarism, thereby for a time increasing the dangers of a new world war. Only recently has Chinese foreign policy recovered its equilibrium and rooted itself in Chinese national interests.

The appearance of OPEC within this increasingly complex context of confrontation in the early 1970s brought up the issue of the underdeveloped world's negotiating power. However, the increase in oil output resulting from the rise in prices led to the subsequent weakening of OPEC.

These are factors which were responsible for the rise and fall of the North–South dialogue.

Changes in the International Power Structure and the North–South Dialogue

The central factors which led to the North–South dialogue were based on the following elements:

On the one hand, there was the weakness of North American imperialism after its military defeat in Vietnam. Politically, it was suffering the internal discredit caused by Watergate. Financially, the dollar had lost its strong and stable position in the world market as a result of the US's less dominant role in international trade and its increasing balance of payments deficit. Technologically, the US was losing ground to West Germany and Japan, while at the same time the USSR was growing stronger economically.

A second element was the fissures in the world capitalist front due to the aggravation of the global economic crisis. There was the increasing competition between the capitalist powers; the revival of economic protectionism; NATO's unsuccessful attempt to agree a united position towards the Middle East where oil was becoming a key matter affecting policy towards Israel; and the inevitable commercial integration between Western Europe and the socialist countries. All these developments threatened Western unity.

Then there was the growing importance which the Third World oil-producing countries were having on the world economy after the creation of the Organization of Petroleum Exporting Countries (OPEC). The capacity to co-ordinate a pricing policy through an organized and coherent cartel, together with the dramatic use of oil as a weapon in the Middle East crisis in 1973 increased the Third World's confidence as to its negotiating capacity. In the same way, the advance of the anti-colonial revolution in Africa and Asia permitted the expansion of the progressive forces within the Non-Aligned Movement, in turn inspiring and co-ordinating diplomatic action within international organizations and provoking the North American reaction which denounced the 'tyranny of the majorities' in the United Nations, withdrew from UNESCO and showed its disapproval of ILO resolutions.

At the same time as these changes were occurring in the capitalist international relations, there were speedy changes in relations with the socialist world. In the first place the Cold War climate was being overcome, giving way to so-called detente. In the second place, China's anti-Soviet position was utilized as an element of Western policy with Nixon's trip to China, and ultimately the recognition of the People's Republic of China to the detriment of Taiwan. These facts seem to support those who defended the thesis of a commonality of interests between the developed capitalist and socialist countries in relation to Third World countries.

These events and the new perceptions deriving from them eventually opened up a new dialogue between the developed countries of the North and those of the underdeveloped South.

Topics of the North–South Debate and Deceptions
This is not the place to draw up a detailed balance sheet of the discussions which took place between representatives of the North and the South, but it is necessary to summarize them briefly. During the North–South meetings, an exhaustive examination of the relations between the developed and underdeveloped countries was made.

The fundamental question according to leading Third World participants was that of unequal exchange. This is a much more complex topic than it seems. The central argument is that there has been a deterioration in the terms of trade between raw materials, which tend to become cheaper by the day, and manufactured goods, growing each day more expensive. But this argument was supported by insufficient facts, and in any case the terms of trade seem to vary according to the phases of the economic cycle. Moreover, attempts to explain those periods during which a deterioration in terms of trade can be observed, in terms of static factors related to the value of the products, are in theoretical terms simply ridiculous. What happens in the international market is influenced by differences in technology between sectors, general market conditions and monopolistic and monopsonistic behaviour.

The discovery of this latter fact occurred in practice as a result of research proving the existence of overpriced products imported by transnational corporations from their countries of origin. But these findings are not nearly as important as what OPEC signified. OPEC showed that the only way to achieve a just price for crude oil was through a producer's cartel (a typical form of monopoly behaviour), and this was only possible to the extent that the monopoly of the Seven Sisters (the companies which controlled the world oil market as a cartel) was broken. However, the Seven Sisters continued to control the marketing of refined oil products as well as important parts of production. With these resources behind them, they showed that they could far outstrip the earnings obtained by OPEC member states.

OPEC also uncovered another topic which had been theoretically debated before: the financial question. The enormous amounts of extra income which flowed into the petroleum-exporting countries as a result of the increase in the price of oil had to be managed through the capitalist international financial system. The petroleum-exporting countries immediately felt their impotence not only to apply their wealth internally in their own economies, which were too weak to absorb new investments, but also internationally since they lacked their own financial instruments to manage their new resources.

The increase in world liquidity which resulted from the appearance of the petro-dollars, increased the inflationary tendencies already existing before 1973 and consequently provoked an explosion of international private lending. Ironically, these credits were often used to cover the deficits in the balance of payments caused by the same increase in the prices of petroleum.

But this whole oil episode of the 1970s was only a demonstration of the dramatic character of the problems which derive from the structural forms which govern North–South relations.

The international division of labour between industrial producers of high technology goods and producers of raw materials (as well as, in recent years, of industrial goods of lesser technological development and value) limits the capacity to grow of countries appearing late on the world capitalist scene. The structures of modern global capitalism constrain the development of the middle class in these countries, as well as of the industrial proletariat, urban wage earners in general, and technicians and scientists in particular. Capitalist social relations are not sufficiently developed and therefore the productive forces in these countries are not used to their full capacity.

The transfer of capital and technology from the capitalist centre to the dependent capitalist periphery stimulates growing contradictions. Capital which moves to those countries must be analysed in two aspects. There is the physical aspect, which materializes itself in the transport of machinery to underdeveloped countries (which in itself embodies technology and demands a specific organization of production, social relations, and technical procedures). And there is the financial or accounting aspect under which the transport of machinery assumes the form of a direct investment, a movement of capital involving the right of property in those physical goods, the right to exploit local labour, and through the combination of both the means of production and labour, the right to obtain a new product of greater value which will be sold in the local or international market and generate a profit.

The recipient country will have to pay the real or inflated value of the imported goods (machinery and intermediate goods) and this is reflected in the increase in imports and in the growing tendency of a balance of trade deficit. At the same time, the recipient country will have to allow the remittance of the profits obtained from the capital, which in turn provokes another growing deficit, this time in the capital account, since the profits made will necessarily exceed the original fixed investments. If we add the payment of royalties (payments for the use of technology), rights for the use of brand names, licence fees, freight, insurance, technical assistance, etc., we have the structural explanation for the permanent deficits reflected in our balance of payments.

This complex combination between foreign investment, trade and the movement of services and capital correctly explains our commercial deficit, the consequent growing need for international credits, and the inevitable crisis of our external economic relations.

The present international financial crisis has made these mechanisms clear. Today we all know that the Third World countries are net exporters of financial resources. The remittance of interest and service payments on loans has dramatically increased the outflow of Third World financial resources, previously disguised under false capital entries.

In this way, traditional points of view have been overtaken by reality — whether it be those who see in underdevelopment a phenomenon of economic backwardness, independent of the relations between dominant and dependent countries, or those who seek the origin of the problem in commercial disparities such as unequal exchange and the deterioration of the terms of trade, or, again, those who pretend that such problems can be solved through the simple transfer of resources, capital and technology from the developed to the underdeveloped countries.

The complex relationship between the international division of labour, the movement of capital, and the inequalities in technology, development of productive forces and progress in social relations of production, oblige us to face these questions in all their complexity and demand an acceptance of the deep bond between the patterns of international economic relations and the internal socio-economic structures in both the developed and underdeveloped countries. The international movement of capital is merely the broadest and most sophisticated manifestation of the movement of capital in general, and more specifically of the capitalist mode of production and of capitalist socio-economic formations operating in a world where many components of other socio-economic formations act on the class contradictions and the interior of capitalist formations and the structures of national States.

The dialogue between the countries of the North and South could not go beyond what reality permitted. The conflicting interests sought ways of living together in a world of radical contradictions, and naturally failed to do so.

The appearance of the Trilateral Commission, sponsored by the Rockefeller brothers, was the response to the North–South dialogue. Here was developed capitalism or imperialism calling on its ranks to fight the dangers of the European socialist East and the underdeveloped South which was tending more and more to conflate its desire for economic development, nationalism and socialism as the only solution to its problems.

The response was to bring Europe and Japan together with the United States in a new pact which would take account of the changes in the correlation of world forces. This was the objective of the Trilateral Commission. Its history, with Carter in power in the US, Raymond Barre, Schmidt and Andreotti in Europe and Osaka in Japan, would require a separate account. Suffice it to say, it did not succeed in its intentions. The attempts to develop common economic strategies between the US, Japan and Europe did not come about despite the principles shared by some of the leaders. On the contrary, protectionism and nationalism became worse and the economic, political and military alliances of the developed capitalist world were weakened.

In the Third World, the US's attempts to regain its ideological leadership by means of Carter's human rights policy were not able to overcome the anti-imperialist feeling in these countries. Quite the contrary. In fact, anti-imperialist feeling grew precisely as democratic struggles in the Third World against military dictatorships advanced. As for the military, even their nationalism was accentuated since they felt abandoned by their previous tutors in the 'Western Christian world'. This feeling became even stronger in Latin America with the Falklands War episode (the Malvinas), where the right discovered that it could not even count on North American conservatives when a colonial matter was at stake. Consequently, the spirit of socialism, either as a solution to the problems of underdevelopment, or as a way of achieving real economic and military power, increased its presence in the underdeveloped world.

So the world became more complex and more dangerous. The capitalist crisis, with its millions of unemployed, absence of strategies to cope with the economic recession, and growing political despair created a very fluid, even unpredictable situation. It bore out another Trilateral thesis: that even the democracies are becoming harder to govern and it might be necessary to seek new democratic forms of government which could cope more effectively.

The Crisis, the Arms Race and the Question of Peace

In this context the threat of a nuclear war increases. This is because the capitalist world needs to appeal to armed confrontation in order to stop the advance of democratic and anti-imperialist forces. Also the solution to the economic crisis is helped by vast expenditures on military research and development. Developing the technologies which will control the world at the end of the Twentieth Century helps show that even a declining empire can hold back the factors which corrode its hegemony. The threat of nuclear war also grows because the economic crisis strengthens irrational factors in the cultural environment which becomes more and more charged with violence. Another factor in the mounting tension is the pressures exerted on the socialist countries and revolutionary movements in the Third World.

It was this moral, political, ideological and intellectual atmosphere which generated fascism in the 1920s and 1930s on the one hand, and Stalinism on the other. The one represented a radicalization of capitalist anti-communism; the other a harassed and blockaded socialism.

World peace is essential to pave the way for development and democracy. On the other hand, economic progress and democracy are the only way to assure world peace. This is an extremely dramatic dialectic. The economic deterioration represented by the long-term crisis in which today's capitalism is immersed also undermines democracy and an atmosphere of international collaboration. All previous periods of prolonged economic depressions (as envisaged in the Kondratiev cycle) have ended in armed confrontations.

There is no way of avoiding the fact that the world situation is deteriorating. Humanity's struggle to impose rational over irrational factors in history has acquired a uniquely dramatic character at the present time. This is the essence of socialism itself: man's dominion over his own history.

Humanity faces its planetary destiny. Man has mastered the power to destroy himself as a species. The survival of mankind now depends on how Man uses his own freedom. In this new reality the struggle for peace must be the first priority. There must be a global effort to protect human life. Here the exploitation of man by man, the expropriation of some nations by others, and individual, social or national oppression all become threats to the survival of mankind.

If socialism in the past was a superior moral aspiration to justice and democracy, today it is essential for the survival of mankind. But herein lies a tragedy. The very dullness of socialist thought and inadequacies of its practice, especially in Europe, have become the greatest obstacles to man's faith in the future and hope of survival.

Only reason can give rise to this faith. But in order to do this, reason must overcome the limits of current socialist practice and dare to imagine a future without the present obstacles. Only then can the social forces be mobilized for peace, which necessarily means socialism and democracy.

The values of reason, human rights, justice and freedom will become elements of a new civilization. To these must be added peace. A peace which can be constructed only as mankind overcomes the individualist struggle for survival and the antagonistic modes of production based on private ownership of the means of production.

The survival of national and international capital, and its political interest blocs, becomes therefore a threat to the survival of mankind. For this reason, the struggle for peace is located in the Centre itself. And for the same reason it must also become the central element of the struggle for socialism, adhering to a platform which first arose from the struggles of workers in the early Twentieth Century in the Second International. It cannot be forgotten that the first world peace movement began within the Socialist International. It was not liberalism, with its doctrine of the destruction of the weak by the strong, which generated a world peace movement. Only socialism as the dawn of a planet-wide communal civilization could generate a world peace movement.

Today, what started as a particular brand of political and economic doctrine, becomes an almost instinctive necessity for a confused and frightened humanity. In order to recover hope, it is necessary to establish that union between will and reason which only socialism can achieve as a global movement.

The Capitalist World: Economic Depression

1966–67 was the beginning of a new period of capitalist crisis. During the Twentieth Century, capitalism has already suffered one lengthy depression, beginning with World War I (1914–18) and only ending with the end of World War II in 1945. After this, a vigorous period of capitalist expansion started which awakened an enormous optimism among its ideologues. However, even during these years of expansion, there were small recessions in 1949, 1953, 1958 and 1961 while on the periphery of the capitalist system there occurred revolutions in China, Korea, Indochina, Algeria and Cuba, among others. There was clearly no solid basis for this optimism.

Beginning in 1966–67, the economic growth curve was broken. The rate of growth of the capitalist countries began to decrease and economic recessions became deeper, more widespread and more frequent. The stability of the dollar as an international currency collapsed, unemployment rates rose and a renewed revolutionary wave extended throughout the Third World and made significant changes in the correlation of power. The dominant capitalist countries began to question the optimism of previous decades and entered a period of social insecurity and political instability.

Economic Deceleration until 1990?
According to the most reliable economic estimates, the period of economic deceleration which began in 1966–67 will last until nearly 1990.

This period presents two aspects which are apparently contradictory. On one side, everything indicates that this will be the most severe stage of the general capitalist post-war crisis, resembling the decade of the 1930s. On the other, this crisis could generate the economic, social and political conditions for a new, long-term capitalist recovery and period of expansion starting in the 1990s.

These economic calculations are based on projections of several econometric models and the tendency for long periods (some 25 years) of prosperity to be followed by similarly prolonged periods of depression — a cycle which was discovered by the Russian economist Kondratiev. There is evidence that a recovery will be possible only if the system is able to decrease the present high rates of inflation, and this would be possible only after a long period of stagnation.

During this crisis, revolutionary situations may appear at the 'weak points' of the international capitalist system and these would lead either to victorious revolutions or to counter-revolutionary solutions strong enough to crush the social movements which always arise where the contradictions of the international system in crisis accumulate.

We have argued in our book, *Imperialism and Dependency*, that in the present crisis the weakest link in the chain would be the *developed* capitalist countries which are undergoing a very acute depression (like Britain), or those not able to break definitively with underdevelopment (like Italy, Spain or Portugal). Among the underdeveloped and dependent countries, those which have reached the greatest level of industrial monopolistic development — Brazil, India, Mexico, Indonesia and Iran — could be precisely those countries which present the most acute social and economic crisis with possible revolutionary or counter-revolutionary consequences.

State Capitalism

The only alternative to prevent this critical development would be a thorough expansion of state capitalism in these countries before the conditions of a general crisis develop within them.

The expansion of state capitalism is one of the ways to overcome temporarily a deep economic crisis. State intervention facilitates the survival of enterprises with low rates of profitability. It also liberates private capital so that it can operate in more profitable sectors. It fosters the development of new technology which private capital cannot risk experimenting with due to the enormous costs and risks which modern scientific research entails.

State intervention also assures and extends demand for important products. This stimulates investment and employs more labour. The State can also regulate the various markets. With its intervention, it increases the degree of socialization of the economy. In this way state capitalism can even prepare the conditions for a future socialist economy and become, in Lenin's word, 'the last step towards socialism'. At the same time, however, when the State puts this socializing force at the service of the monopolies, it strengthens capital, increases its rate of profit and guarantees a new period of accumulation.

In this sense, growing state intervention becomes state monopoly capitalism, thereby increasing the system's possibilities of survival and blocking in the medium term a socialist solution both in the developed countries and the dependent, underdeveloped countries.

The Phantom of Unemployment

The acute crisis we experienced in the early 1980s is likely to increase, at the same time as capital becomes more concentrated and monopolistic. In the coming years we will witness massive bankruptcies, not only of small and middle-size enterprises but also of large, less efficient companies (as happened in the case of Chrysler). This will provoke a massive depreciation of assets and lead to the absorption of firms with less resources by those which maintain a greater liquidity, especially the large financial groups which are the only ones able to make the gigantic investments required to stimulate a new period of capitalist growth.

The depreciation, added to the general decrease in demand, should, in the end, cause a drop in the inflation rate of recent years, as we saw in the last recession of 1981–83. The present recession will witness a slow recovery of business at the end of the decade.

But the price of recovery will be a long period of massive unemployment.

Unemployment rates which used to be around 3% in the 1950s went up to 5% and 6% in the 1960s and 1970s. In the decade of the 1980s, unemployment was near 10%.

Hitherto many countries were capable of paying unemployment benefit to workers who lost their jobs, and this mitigated the crisis. But it is very difficult to maintain this type of social security for the large mass of unemployed workers throughout the 1980s. The rights achieved by workers during the years of prosperity are now being threatened.

The social effects of unemployment are even more serious if we consider that the official statistics do not consider as unemployed those who stop looking for work — which can be twice as many as the openly unemployed. Enormous numbers of people are therefore unemployed or under-employed. They survive very precariously with odd jobs, public charity, begging, or simply crime.

But unemployment affects different sectors of the population unevenly. Racial minorities, legal or illegal immigrants, the youth, women and the most depressed and backward regions of each country have higher unemployment rates than the national average. Therefore, an increase in unemployment also intensifies racial, cultural and regional tensions, and threatens whatever gains particular minorities may have made.

Unemployment also affects the bargaining capacity of the unions which are the main workers' organizations in the advanced capitalist countries. The economic struggle is a fundamental instrument of the working class in periods of economic expansion and this is the social basis for the ideological and political hegemony of social democracy in Europe today. But in periods of acute depression, with their conquests threatened, the workers feel obliged to put their political demands first and their struggle for power becomes a priority in the class struggle.

The middle class reacts in a similar way during a depression. It develops a conservative line of thought and inclines towards the Right. It tries to create the political conditions for weakening the working class and tends to abolish the conciliatory mechanisms which have taken root in the capitalist countries since World War Two.

The National Question
Once the supremacy obtained by the US in World War Two is broken, its instruments will be, too. The supremacy of the dollar, US military superiority and the treaties which support it (NATO, the Treaty of Rio de Janeiro and the already extinct Asian military pacts, CENTO and SEATO), and the power of international agencies such as the IMF and GATT will constantly be put in question.

The struggle between the imperialist interests of the US, Germany and Japan, and between them and the other capitalist powers, will get even worse. This accumulation of contradictions as the crisis gets worse, makes it difficult to reconcile these competing interests in a uniform imperialist policy. Protectionism — that dangerous instrument of economic struggle between national bourgeoisies — will be used more and more as a defensive weapon to protect national interests. Consequently, world trade will decline, inter-imperialist conflicts will increase, as will the struggle between imperialism and the underdeveloped countries.

The struggle for control of energy resources, raw materials and agricultural production gets stronger every day. The movement of capital is affected by these phenomena. Disinvestment (the withdrawal of capital and the selling off of companies in the less stable countries), bankruptcies and possible moratoriums by the debtor countries are already on the way.

Recovery before the Twenty-first Century

However, those who see in the present crisis the end of capitalism are only fooling themselves. The crisis is a mechanism to correct the imbalances created by capitalist accumulation. It itself generates the elements for the future recovery of the system. In effect, industries going bankrupt eliminate the less productive sectors and permit a greater centralization of capital. This in turn generates the basis for a new stage of investments based on the new technologies.

Unemployment and the weakening of the trade unions also allows an increase in the exploitation of labour and so increases the rate of profit, which in turn stimulates new investments.

The destruction of the present international financial system, based on the dollar, will allow the recovery of gold as the universal measure of value. And this may create the conditions for a new financial stability.

Protectionism strengthens national markets and corrects in part the present excessive internationalization of capital. All these phenomena will pave the way toward a new phase of capitalist accumulation in the last decade of this century.

New Areas of Conflict

But, what will happen in these circumstances as classes and nations oppose one another? From similar historical circumstances, one can deduce that the system will suffer revolutionary fissures at its weak points, gradually working closer to the nucleus of capitalism at the Centre. In previous prolonged periods of depression, the exacerbation of contradictions resulted in wars like the 1871 Franco-German war and the two world wars. While renewed wars cannot be put aside, there is a new element which should be pointed out — the presence of a socialist bloc which focuses great strategic movements against it. Confrontation in the world today is polarized between the Soviet Union and the United States, and this is reflected in civil and regional wars.

The emergence of new right-wing regimes — authoritarian or totalitarian — may be countered by triumphant insurrections or advanced reformist regimes. However, the specific forms of this radicalization cannot be predicted.

In the Third World, it is necessary to watch particularly closely the violent crises threatening the three pillars of recent capitalist expansion: Brazil, South Korea and Indonesia. The most pivotal areas of the world in the next few years may be found in these countries. Such a situation would considerably increase the international tension already resulting from existing areas of conflict.

The Socialist World: Structural Changes

It is not possible to understand the present international situation without considering the effect that the countries with collective property and centrally planned economies will have on it. In contrast to the simplistic conceptions of the past, we can now see that these countries' experiences embody a variety of socio-economic forms and structures which reflect their different degrees of development, historical paths and particular geopolitical conditions.

Attempts to transform into models the concrete solutions experimented with by the different socialist countries now seem ridiculous. But some people still try to measure these experiences by some utopian yardstick that is supposed to represent what socialism should be. Such subjective analyses are still an obstacle in the examination of these countries' actual social and economic structures, the real tendencies of their evolution, and their impact on the international scene.

Contrary to what many Western commentators — both left and right — argue, there is a very vigorous social dynamic in these countries. It is accompanied by constant political crises, more or less in the open, which are expressed in changes in strategic guidelines, far-reaching self-criticism, and, at times, changes in leaders. That the top leaders are not changed for long periods of time should not be taken as an expression of conservatism or political and social stagnation. These personalities give continuity and unity to the revolutionary process. And, in any case, there occur frequent changes of middle and even senior leaders.

Scientific and Technical Revolution

From the socio-economic point of view, the changes are amazing. For example, the Soviet Union was until 1960 a predominantly rural society. Today only a little more than one-third of its population live in the country. During this same period, it became the leading world steel producer as well as of several important raw materials. It modernized a great part of its productive infrastructure and went from having in 1960 half as many scientists as the US to having twice as many in 1980.

The USSR's geopolitical situation has also changed radically, becoming a world power. In 1960 its military spending was half of North American military expenditure; now they are almost the same. Its military presence, besides assuring it a decisive position of superiority in Europe, now extends to the Mediterranean, the Indian Ocean and the South Atlantic.

At the same time, the development of a modern, predominantly urban society has taken place with a gigantic increase in the intelligentsia. Intellectual output has grown and become more sophisticated. Internal power centres have been diversified and the social structure has become more complex. All this only 60 years after having broken with a predominantly feudal society.

The Soviets call their new social structure advanced socialism. Its own laws of development derive fundamentally from the demands of the scientific and technical revolution. It sets the stage for the development of the productive forces which, while still in their beginnings, should serve as a basis for the communist future.

Social Mobility

As a result of these structural transformations, the social structure of the USSR is changing rapidly. Of the two basic classes — industrial workers and farm workers — the first is stronger. Technicians, skilled manual labour and the service sector (particularly education, science and communications) are growing in importance. In the managerial strata, besides the State, there are the military, the party and union bureaucracies, the scientists, intellectuals and enterprise managers who have a strong position in society. The consequent social differentiation stimulates the development of different interpretations of socialism. These range from orthodox Stalinism, which still prevails albeit in a modernized form, to important developments of classical Marxism, including expressions of socialist humanism which are quite close to Western social democratic thought.

The skilled manual workers and farm workers of state-owned companies and co-operatives have increased their organization and influence in the State. Planning has become more flexible and has delegated more authority to the level of the enterprise. New forms of self-management are being experimented with, including workers' brigades. The development of tourism has opened the country up to the outside world and the breaking down of the barriers put up during the Cold War are allowing diplomats, scientists and intellectuals to go abroad and obtain a more realistic and concrete view of the world.

The impressive recent development of the backward regions consolidates the rather problematic union of republics, languages and nations which make up this country–continent. At the same time national problems and cultural demands are being articulated, and people are regaining their cultural independence within the framework of the multinational society.

Internal Crisis

The internal crisis which these vast changes herald, remains hidden for several reasons. The fear that problems will be utilized by the enemy makes Soviet leaders and social scientists treat these subjects with pat formulae which make full comprehension of the phenomena occurring difficult.

Mysterious China

The great mystery is the People's Republic of China. Its nationalist behaviour took it along the blind alley of systematic anti-Sovietism and a system of alliances with the world's most reactionary forces. The development of new social strata in China was delayed because of the attempt to survive in isolation and because of the sectarianism of the Cultural Revolution.

The present reforms have moved the country away from its egalitarian ideology and collective forms of property and management. But they are opening the country up to technological progress, modernization, international economic relations and some degree of political freedom. This may introduce a healthy breath of fresh air in a society long assaulted by ideologues whose provincial totalitarianism was closer to a feudal community than to socialism.

The reappearance of the urban petty bourgeoisie and the nationalist bureaucrats thrown out during the Cultural Revolution does not guarantee a progressive or internationalist political direction. But it at least opens the way for workers (who are still a minority in China), the most able intellectuals and scientists, military personnel and state officials to create a political bloc whose strength will increase with the modernization of Chinese society.

There still exist forces in this society strong enough to guarantee the survival of collective property and planning, and to prevent the ideological hegemony of a form of socialism which would damage the progress of world socialism.

Yugoslavia after Tito

Yugoslavia is undergoing serious external pressures during its first decade of the post-Tito era. However, this ought to push the different social forces into building an even stronger unity.

The working class, which is growing in line with the country's economic progress, the mass of rural and urban workers in self-management enterprises, the executives with their strong technocratic orientation, the party bureaucracy whose expansion is limited and subjected to effective social control, and the state bureaucracy all maintain the fundamentals of the socialist state in the country. Self-management, respect for the nationalities, the policies of self-determination and non-alignment are historic facts which will be difficult to remove from the social and ideological principles of Yugoslavian socialism.

This does not mean that political crises will not arise. The society embraces a complex balance of forces which emerged from the devastation of the Second World War. Their determination to be independent demanded an enormous political, ideological and diplomatic effort. Paradoxically, it was its flexible opening towards the outside world which guaranteed it its internal autonomy, creating a complex balance of forces and a skilful diplomatic posture which assures it of a role in international affairs without falling into anti-Sovietism or the kinds of right-wing alliances which the leaders of the Chinese Communist Party made.

The Third World: Mobilization For Common Interests

In this complex international situation, the emergence of the underdeveloped countries is an irreversible political fact. The greater the anti-imperialist contradictions and the importance of the socialist countries, the greater is the field of action for national liberation struggles.

The intensification of the capitalist crisis stimulates national liberation movements which no longer accept the norms of the capitalist system. There is also a mass participation by industrial and agrarian workers in the struggle for democracy. These forces point towards Third World capitalism either evolving towards a strong state capitalism (with a doubtful possibility of survival except in very exceptional situations of economic wealth) or towards a radicalization that could proceed to socialism.

This does not mean that capitalism does not have ample reserves in the Third World. The bourgeoisies can hinder democratic progress. They can use force. They may stabilize themselves through state capitalism, allowing some social progress — but always subject to their own interests. Where they achieve this, they will consolidate themselves during the possible global economic and political recovery of the 1990s.

Modernization

This recovery would mark a new phase in the international division of labour. A new space will be opened up for the industrialization of the dependent countries. They will produce those products which are being outdated by the technological revolution in the developed countries. This revolution is making vast productive sectors obsolete. These sectors will be displaced to the Third World, including the production of traditional machinery, the manufacture of parts for durable goods, electronic and chemical products, and the processing of raw materials and agricultural products. In this way, the areas of modernization of the underdeveloped countries will be expanded. There will be a growing demand for technicians, scientists, engineers, intellectuals, etc. The rural sector will see the transformation of the traditional latifundia into modern agricultural enterprises. The State will have to become more efficient and public utilities expand.

These developments will generate a renewed faith in the potential of dependent capitalism. However, it is necessary to stress that the economic recovery which will occur in the 1990s, and the new international division of labour, will only be possible through an enormous internationalization of capital of the imperialist countries. This would mean a violent transfer of the resources accumulated during the 1980s by the national bourgeoisies and a new stage in the submission of local bourgeoisies to international capital.

Modernization would still only be for a small part of the population. Marginalization and impoverishment would still be the fate of most poor people in the dependent countries. And so a new phase of contradictions would begin, rather than a stage of independent, integrated and stable countries, as many think today.

The Semi-Developed Countries

In the international field, a contradictory phenomenon has occurred. On the one hand, the differences between the semi-developed dependent countries — Brazil, Mexico, Argentina, Venezuela, Iran, India, and Indonesia — and the less developed Third World countries increased. The former sought to profit by the weaknesses generated by the world crisis in the developed capitalist countries. On the other hand, those same semi-developed countries are propelled to unite the whole Third World in a common front against the great powers. This is so that they can strengthen their negotiating capacity, create space for their investments and open markets for their products.

The North–South dialogue will be able to begin once again, but this time with the underdeveloped countries having a greater bargaining power. The UN will become more and more an instrument for the consolidation of the Non-Aligned Movement, in spite of the internal differences within it. What our countries will desperately be searching for is to consolidate, rather than extend, their bargaining power in a situation where the prices of raw materials, the volume of world trade and the international financial system will be in permanent crisis. Their stance will, therefore, be primarily a defensive one.

The only countries which will be able to advance substantially are those which, instead of using the capitalist crisis to increase their bargaining power, will try to take advantage of it in order to change their internal structures substantially. Only these countries will be able to resist the subsequent imperialist pressure. For the imperialists will attempt to recover during the new phase of economic expansion the advantages they lost during the crisis of the 1980s.

Who Will Hold Power?
Our warnings of the precarious character of the apparent achievements of organizations like UNCTAD, UNIDO and other similar bodies, seem to be disregarded in the interests of maintaining the peace of mind of the popular movement in situations which constitute only superficial victories for the Third World. We do not deny that steps like the nationalization of enterprises, the support received by liberation movements, guarantees and protection given national industries, do not signify important advances. But the effectiveness of these measures depends fundamentally on who holds power in these countries. The crucial question is whether the popular movement will be able to create its own state or will remain subject to the middle-class nationalism of the petit bourgeoisie which in recent years has revived and is certain to develop owing to the growing international contradictions.

These tendencies will be the result of the intensification of the capitalist crisis, not of the end of the system. They will result from the way the system recovers and initiates a new stage of capital accumulation, technological innovation, economic growth and political and ideological co-operation.

In this context, revolutionaries will struggle so that the anti-imperialist and democratic forces do not remain half-way, but become the dawn of a new society, ending imperialism and assuring for mankind the real democracy for the great popular majorities — socialism.

3. Peace, Security and Development in Latin America

Pablo González Casanova

Limitations of the Post-war Ideological Schema

I would like to point out the limitations of a general perspective which prevents the understanding of some unexpected problems related to peace, security and development in Latin America.

It is a fact that social scientists as well as many of our present-day leaders have not broken with the dominant post-war ideological schema. Ever since 1945 there has existed globally a certain official line of thought relating to science and culture which embraces certain attitudes — objectivity, optimism — a particular vocabulary — technical, scientific — and certain concepts — world order, development — which are quite contrary to the historical reality in which we find ourselves several decades after the founding of the United Nations and the Bretton Woods Agreement. But neither actual history nor particular circumstances, nor the true structures and orientations which during these years have affected the problems of peace, security and development, have led us to depart from this official line of thought and change our vision, our symbols, our national or international public preoccupations.

If we take the concept of development prevalent in the late 1940s and early 1950s, we see that in those days the existence of economic cycles and the possibility of a new crisis were discarded. The orthodox position held that the European post-war recovery and Third World economic, social and cultural development would follow the formation of a relatively rational world order more or less in accordance with the United Nations Charter.

It is true that when the Cold War began in 1947, conflicts arose between what was known as the free world and the socialist countries. But the idea remained that, in the 'free world', the concepts, language and spirit of the United Nations Charter would still be valid.

The Organization of American States was founded in 1948. Its founding constituted an acknowledgement of the structure of the United Nations world order. Moreover it acknowledged on behalf of all the signatory states (the United States among them) the principles of non-intervention and self-determination which had been defended for more than a century by the most outstanding Latin American internationalists, the most progressive Latin American Foreign Affairs Departments and by the Latin American people.

Today the concepts of the 1940s and 1950s not only confront historical circumstances which contradict them, but the very concepts conceal patterns of historical behaviour and of present-day social and economic structures which consequently we do not notice. We continue to use the same concepts, and this intellectual and emotional rigidity prevents us from contributing to the solution of problems which may occur, not only at a regional level, but also world-wide, and not only in the medium term, but more immediately.

None of the predictions embodied in the great orthodox hypotheses have been fulfilled during the past four decades and today we find ourselves in a crisis which we can neither understand nor express. Nor do we have reasonable technical or theoretical arguments to convince others of the correctness of certain measures, of the urgency of others, and of the vital need of still others for peace and security. This is all because we insist on maintaining the overly optimistic post-World War II concepts.

The New Colonial Multi-system

Foreign credit is the new colonial system at the international level. It is complemented by the transnational corporations and involves both international financial firms and the governments and armies of the post-industrial countries. All these elements constitute a colonial multi-system which benefits from the unequal exchange of goods, from the production of raw materials and industrial goods, based on differential costs of production rooted in local Third World wages and the labour of migrant workers, which are very favourable to the metropolis and to capital. All of this is complemented by high rates of interest and commissions on loans which are renewed and increased as a form of tribute. And there are systematic and increasingly unfavourable relationships entered into by the weaker and more dependent regions, countries and enterprises. The new colonial multi-system works in terms of a geography of negotiation and repression, where the latter is much greater in the dependent countries and regions and in moments when the economic cycle is going through its recessionary and critical phases. In such times, the decrease in the demand for the goods and services from the dependent areas and their enterprises is added to the decrease in their prices and the increase in tariff and customs barriers, as well as the expulsion of the migrant workers who remain in the metropolis.

The multi-system has gained so much strength during the post-war period that in the present crisis it is able to regulate quantities and prices of merchandise, services and labour. Its strength is even greater in its capacity to increase the rates of interest, almost without any economic, political or diplomatic restriction or control.

The combination of financial capital and transnational companies permits these companies to continue their intra-company commerce. This involves over- or under-pricing, and combining it with unequal and manipulated billing practices with their sister companies in other countries according to the requirements of the transnational market.

The strength of the multi-system is also revealed in its capacity to use whatever energy resources it needs, controlling the increase in its prices, and promoting a consumer society by means of its advertising and the mass media. All this without any great care for the pollution and ecological destruction it wreaks. The best scientific and technological know-how supports its activities and the social sciences contribute their rationalization techniques. And when necessary military and police controls back up their operations when ethical, historical and religious arguments fail to sustain their legitimacy.

The problems arise because the neo-colonial multi-system does not correspond to the types of unit (nation states) envisaged by the United Nations. Nor is it consonant with human rights or the solution of the problems of international peace and security. Moreover, the neo-colonial multi-system is manifestly incapable, from a historical or structural point of view, of promoting the economic, technological and cultural development of countries. It tends naturally to a situation of transnationalization which, with the return of the current economic and financial crises, takes on characteristics tantamount to economic, ideological, and cultural war. The social democratic governments of the post-industrial countries feel obliged to collaborate in these processes more or less reluctantly, while the neo-conservative and neo-liberal governments of course collaborate in a much more coherent and enthusiastic manner. The strength of either of them relative to the multi-system is, in any case, too small to be able to insist on the primacy of the public interest internally, let alone internationally.

The system may achieve in the metropolitan countries a certain degree of energy conservation and protection of the environment. It may respect the rights of employees and workers and decrease internal tensions. It may, through making technological advances, permit the more powerful poles of the multi-system to reduce production costs and defend themselves from a fall in the average rate of profit. But even in these advanced countries, the problems of irrational fuel consumption, destruction of the environment, declines in investment, reduced social spending and the bankruptcy of some large-scale industries are problems which cannot be ignored. When turning to dependent countries and production or service units which are not part of the multi-system, the situation is far worse. In fact, the metropolitan governments may themselves engage in a sort of economic, ideological, cultural war against these dependent countries and violate the provisions of the United Nations and its organs, and international civil rights in general.

To the industrial ruin of the dependent nations and the counter-development resulting from the profit transfers in favour of the hegemonic units of the multi-system, we must add interventions in the affairs of the debtor countries — either by the subservient armed forces of these peripheral states or, when these fail, by agencies and even armies of the metropolitan countries themselves.

Interference in the economy is not only intended to prevent competition with the Centre units of the multi-system. It also intends to place the government of a peripheral State in a condition of growing economic, financial, political and military dependency. This ranges all the way from growing dependency on food imports to dependency on metropolitan military support for the very continuation of these regimes in office. There is always the threat of destabilization by the Centre in cases of disobedience or defiance on important issues. In such cases, the peripheral governments are overthrown through the use of the very contradictions generated by the multi-system for its own benefit. Military interventions can be produced via local forces or by means of programmes specially designed for each country or region.

Theoretical Contradictions

Few of the aforementioned phenomena are taken cognizance of by the present-day United Nations, or in universities and institutes of higher research, or most progressive political parties and movements. Economic and financial analyses of the crisis do not in any way take into account this multiple reality of transnational companies, banks, financial organizations and nation states with their different governments. Economic problems continue to be seen as problems which must be analysed from a monetary or structural point of view; juridical and diplomatic problems from a governmental point of view. The rest of the units of the multi-system are simply ignored.

The problem becomes even more serious if the political–economic and military character of the crisis is misunderstood. We do not seem to understand how a global crisis can derive from local interventionist wars and escalate into a third and last world war.

Seeing everything in East–West terms makes the neo-colonialist crisis all the more incomprehensible. Ideological differences in the interpretation of the crisis stem from the contestants' different positions in the world's political geography. Of course, the Reagan Administration sees the crisis in sharply distorted terms. But even those who fight against neo-colonialism do not always perceive the universal importance of comprehending and solving the problem.

The East–West confrontation is one of the most significant struggles of our times. Neo-liberals and neo-conservatives see it as the struggle between the 'free world' or 'Western civilization' or 'democracy' against 'totalitarianism'. Marxist–Leninist ideology sees it as a manifestation of the class struggle and the contradiction between capitalism and socialism. But even though that struggle is so important in present-day history, it is occurring simultaneously with another for the abolition of neo-colonialism. Neo-colonialism denotes a dependency mediated by local governments and armies which, in the former colonial world of Africa, Asia and Latin America, play the roles which in earlier times used to be played by colonial viceroys and armies, though today allowing greater negotiations and concessions to certain sectors of the middle class, and even industrial workers and some agrarian workers.

The neo-colonialist crisis throws up local problems which can become universal and which can give way to the creation of new economic, juridical, political and military structures in which the relations of the great powers and the small nations are rebuilt on a less unequal and less dangerous basis for world peace and security. But to reach these objectives, it is essential to recognize: (1) the existence of neo-colonialism; (2) the existence of its crisis; (3) the political and military impossibility of continuing neo-colonialism where countries develop their consciousness and strength and seek to end all trace of it, as has happened with the People's Government of Nicaragua and the People's Front of El Salvador; (4) the need to confront the global multi-system of domination by promoting peace and security at the level of nation states and the effective self-defence of all aspects of their economies; (5) the need to design policies which confront the problem of peace and security not only in the immediate areas of conflict which provoke the peripheral neo-colonialist crisis, but similar policies to prevent political, military and ideological intervention by the metropolis itself. Today, more than ever, these metropolitan forces threaten peace and security in the peripheral regions of the world.

Ideologization of Politics

Unfortunately, not only President Reagan and his advisers, but a great number of US politicians and diplomats and the great majority of the North American people still see Central American problems through the lens of the strong colonialist ideology which allowed them to conquer the West and structure inter-American relations as one of the most efficient neo-colonial systems. At a time when the inter-American neo-colonialist system has entered a state of crisis in Central America and the Caribbean, many US leaders hold to the old ways of solving problems, without even noticing that they don't understand the new world that is emerging.

The problem of the lack of understanding of the real world by the leaders of the multi-system, as well as by the institutions which systemize knowledge, is made worse by two equally significant phenomena: neo-colonialist prejudice and political and diplomatic lies. The huge impact of these factors on social science, diplomacy, and military circles results in initiatives and responses far removed from reality.

The relation between the dominant concepts held by the hegemonic powers (concretely, the United States) and the most common prejudices is very clear. The thinking of many people is governed by the power established by the US's way of thinking and acting in Latin America and the Third World. This has been proven by research. John Crothers Pollock[1] confirmed the 'persistence in the main media of at least three perspectives on Latin America which seem to be linked to the great basic orientations of hemispheric relations.' He called the first perspective colonial, the second technocratic and the third hegemonic. Pollock writes:

In contrast to the *colonial vision* which mocks Third World governments, or the *technocratic vision* which considers the others capable of reaching political and economic maturity if they follow the example of the industralized countries of the West, the *hegemonic perspective* takes away legitimacy from the attempts at transformation which threaten the leadership of the metropolitan countries: the leaders are denigrated by propaganda which accuses them of not responding to the demands of the majority, and what is worse, they are slandered as inhuman, greedy, dishonest; the political institutions are charged with being inaccessible, inflexible and dictatorial, without the least respect for civil liberties; the efforts to decrease national dependency are also denigrated in two ways — suggesting that the attacks on dependency and the efforts at self-government cause internal economic and political chaos, and the leaders are accused of being bad examples which threaten the industrialized countries.

Moreover, today's hegemonic perspective considers that: 'strong political protests against United States influence are in themselves a threat, independent of the presence or absence of the influence of the socialist countries.' The US accuses them of being a threat and necessarily influenced by the socialist countries. The author concludes that this perspective results in 'an even bigger obstacle than the cold war, implying a general hostility to political, economic and social changes, with or without the assistance of powerful extra-continental countries.' From its numerous official declarations, one can see that this is the prevailing perspective of the present US Administration.

Its biased interpretative framework and stereotypes complement one another, and are supported by the large newspapers and the media which report on Latin America. But these biases and stereotypes are not confined to the press, television or radio. They can also be found in academic circles and scholarly books. One can often perceive in them a subtle mockery of nationalism and populism; or a certain condescension towards the modernizing and democratic efforts of South American 'amigos'. They contain slanderous criticisms of Central American and Caribbean revolutionary leaders as tyrants, power hungry or dishonest. In truth, the studies of the structures of social change by these experts at the service of North American hegemony suffer from the same intellectual limitations as the media. And they are as opposed to any change which is not favourable to the reproduction of dependency and the neo-colonialist multi-system.

If one studies the results of most US research on Latin America, it is easy to discover that the majority of its hypotheses, variables, definitions and conclusions conform to the limits officially prescribed by each US administration. So, when the Kennedy Administration in its early days demanded changes in fiscal and agrarian structures, these were faithfully reflected in the recommendations and findings of empirical research. Later, when US politicians openly placed their hopes on the military in Latin America, the researchers forgot all about the reforms or relegated them to second place. And when the politicians forgot the ideals of the Alliance for Progress, North American researchers did so too. Since then their praises of militarism and dictatorships have been a constant refrain; today they even laud these authoritarian regimes as defenders of liberty and democracy against socialist 'totalitarian' regimes.

Social Science as an Ideological Instrument

US social science with its apparently objective language justifies, rationalizes and legitimizes authoritarianism and militarism, and so reinforces the prejudices of US politicians and the media. In a book on US policy and the Third World, for example, Charles Wolf,[2] an expert of the Rand Corporation, tried to demonstrate 'empirically' that in Latin America 'military assistance has a positive effect on political development', that 'per capita military expenditures are higher in countries which have a higher political order', and that the 'greatest military projects do not seem to be associated with movements which originate in more authoritarian political institutions'. According to Wolf, it is a completely false hypothesis that, in order to wage successful counter-insurgency, the United States and its allies should win popular support. In other words, this expert from the Rand Corporation says that the United States does not even have to bother to seek popular support. With 'empirical arguments', Mr Wolf argues in favour of political and military intervention. But he does not do so in too obvious a manner. As a man of science, he asks his readers to keep a healthy dose of scepticism with respect to his conclusions.

Besides the existing misunderstanding of the world today and sophisticated prejudices, there is the serious problem of the 'docudrama'. This dresses up the lie as political reality with a dynamic which is in part theatrical. The problem of the docudrama is not only a moral one, it is also political.

Eldon Kensworthy[3] has defined the docudrama as a reality processed in images which the public can absorb easily while the government proceeds to act in exactly the same way that it planned beforehand. Moreover real decisions are justified by imaginary arguments. The distance between decisions and the reality on which they claim to be founded grows not only for the masses but also for the decision-makers.

Kensworthy himself analysed, in a rigorous and precise manner, the political 'theatricality' of the Grenadian invasion, a theatricality which not only disguised the reasons for the invasion, but its effects and scope.

This trivialization of current history and the puerile way of presenting it are combined with very sophisticated intellectual resources where the interventionist discourse takes hold of the people's language of liberation. This can be seen in President Reagan's message of 19 July to the Heads of the independent Caribbean Countries. His message was that of the liberator who does not declare the just war of the traditional empire, or of the Western democracies, but that of the oppressed peoples themselves.

The whole new paraphernalia at the same time projects an image of efficiency and audacity, of justice and decisiveness, and in general, of being able to win not only in a war against an army of only 1,000 men — as in Grenada, whose leaders had just assassinated the people's highest dignitary, the leader of a population of no more than 60,000 people — but able to win against any other nation of any size, against any army, whether or not led by its best leaders and allied with great forces.

This is what we are up against today — the limits of non-comprehension, the limits of colonialist and hegemonic prejudices which cannot be rooted out, and the limits of docudramas and political theatricality. Yet, for all these conservative and interventionist leaders' misapprehensions of the world, their useless prejudices and TV docudrama lies, they still cannot act as their colonialist and interventionist ancestors did in the past. In fact, those self-same leaders would not consider acting in the same way in relation to other larger and more powerful countries.

In these conditions, the only feasible way to maintain peace and security is for the democratic and social democratic forces of the hegemonic countries — especially the United States and Europe — to question their own colonial psychology and ideology. They must then present a more consistent alternative to the ideological threat posed by neo-conservatism's aggressive policies. But even this could prove to be insufficient.

In the countries of the periphery, where the social movements which are only just struggling for democracy, or to increase their democracy and define an alternative model of accumulation which would contribute to the consolidation of democracy, they must not limit themselves to these democratic or social democratic aims. Rather they should relate them to the struggle against the neo-colonialist multi-system in its different manifestations: the neo-colonialist crisis; the absurd increase of the foreign debt and rates of interest and the defence of the production and consumption of the great masses of the periphery.

It seems improbable that there is another way to formulate a true alternative to the present crisis and to the threats to peace and security implied not only for Latin America but for the whole world. If the balance of terror between the Super Powers may lead to nuclear war, however, one way of breaking it would be to promote a global decolonization. This would not mean going from colonialism to neo-colonialism, but from colonialism to real sovereignty. The only alternative for peace seems to be to support the nations which are involved in this struggle to destroy the neo-colonialist multi-system, starting at its weakest points.

Notes

1. John Crothers Pollock, 'The United States press and political change in Latin America: An anthropological approach to mass communications research', in *Latin American Research Review*, Vol. 13, No. 1, 1978.

2. Charles Wolf, *United States Policy and the Third World*, Boston, Little, Brown & Co., 1967, p. 204.

3. Eldon Kensworthy, 'Grenada as theater', in *World Policy Journal*, Spring 1984, pp. 635–51.

4. Transnationalization and Political Change

José Agustín Silva-Michelena

Introduction

In 1982, for the first time after 40 years of growth, the combined GNPs of all Latin American countries decreased by one per cent. According to the Inter-American Development Bank, in 1983 continental GNP fell by more than three per cent.[1] Although in 1984 and 1985 there was a slow growth, it was mostly due to a high rate of growth of Brazil. The remaining countries grew very little or continued to decline. The most commonly accepted explanation for this phenomenon is that offered by the United Nations Economic and Social Council:

> The single most important and general factor explaining the region's crisis was the unexpectedly long and pronounced recession at the centre (i.e. in the developed countries).[2]

To be sure, other factors internal to the region were also mentioned as also having contributed to the crisis:

> Unsatisfactory management of fiscal and exchange policies or internal and external conflicts accounted for most of the large declines in product in several countries of the Southern Cone and Central America and for the stagnation of economic activity in countries such as Mexico.[3]

If we examine the GNP trends of Latin American countries in the early 1980s (see Table 4.1), it is clear that until 1982 those countries with bureaucratic and oligarchic dictatorships — where socio-political conflicts are in general more acute — had growth rates below the average for Latin America as a whole, while the majority of those with democratic and revolutionary governments experienced above average economic growth. In 1983, however, as the crisis deepened, more democratic governments also experienced below average growth rates.

It is certainly true that the global crisis in the developed countries has negatively affected the Latin American economies. The recession in the Centre:

Table 4.1
GNP Trends by Types of Political Regimes

Political Regime and Countries	Year 1980	Relative to Regional Average	Year 1981	Relative to Regional Average	Year 1982	Relative to Regional Average	Year 1983	Relative to Regional Average
Bureacratic Dictatorships								
Argentina	1.4	(-)	-6.1	(-)	-5.0	(-)	2.8	(+)
Brazil	8.0	(+)	-1.9	(-)	0.5	(+)	-3.3	(-)
Chile	7.5	(+)	5.3	(+)	-14.1	(-)	-0.8	(-)
Panama	4.9	(-)	3.6	(+)	0.5	(+)	0.2	(+)
Uruguay	3.7	(-)	-0.7	(-)	-9.5	(-)	-4.7	(-)
Oligarchic Dictatorships								
Bolivia	0.6	(-)	-0.6	(-)	-7.5	(-)	-7.6	(-)
El Salvador	-9.6	(-)	-9.5	(-)	-4.5	(-)	0	(+)
Guatemala	3.5	(-)	1.0	(-)	-3.5	(-)	-2.0	(+)
Haiti	5.7	(-)	-3.0	(-)	-2.0	(-)	1.3	(+)
Paraguay	11.4	(+)	8.5	(+)	-2.5	(+)	-3.7	(-)
Democracies								
Columbia	4.0	(-)	2.5	(+)	1.5	(+)	0.8	(+)
Costa Rica	0.6	(-)	-3.6	(-)	-6.0	(-)	0.8	(+)
Dominican Rep.	5.6	(-)	-3.4	(-)	1.5	(+)	3.9	(+)
Equador	4.8	(-)	4.3	(+)	2.0	(+)	-3.3	(-)
Honduras	2.5	(-)	-0.4	(-)	-1.5	(-)	-0.7	(+)
Mexico	8.3	(+)	8.1	(+)	0	(+)	-4.7	(-)
Peru	3.8	(-)	4.0	(+)	1.0	(+)	-11.8	(-)
Venezuela	-1.2	(-)	0.6	(-)	0	(+)	-3.0	(-)
Revolutionary Regimes								
Cuba	1.4	(-)	12.0	(+)	2.5	(+)	5.2	(+)
Nicaragua	10.0	(+)	8.9	(+)	-1.0	(-)	5.3	(+)
Latin America	5.9		1.5		-0.9		-2.9	

was, in its turn, due to the persistence of deflationary policies in the developed world, which relied mainly on monetary instruments, thereby increasing international interest rates, real and nominal, to unprecedented levels, and negatively affecting current and capital accounts of the Periphery (developing countries). The reduction in the demand in the Centre decreased the volume of exports from Latin America, at the same time as the high rates of interest and the recession led to the further deterioration of the terms of trade. Correspondingly, the high rates of interest inflated the payments for debt services of the region, while the necessarily poor performance of the export sectors and the high levels of debt discouraged the flow of capital into Latin America.[4]

Notwithstanding the correctness, empirically verifiable, of the preceding explanations, they are not sufficient for the purpose of this study, which aims to analyse the relationships between peace, security and the process of economic development.

The crisis in Latin America began to manifest itself towards the end of the 1970s, and per capita income only started to decline in 1981. By contrast, the economic crisis in the developed countries began to manifest itself as early as the closing years of the 1960s (1967), when the rate of profit started to fall and the level of unemployment began to rise. Nevertheless, initially, Latin America's economic growth kept up at fairly high rates. However, despite this, the problems of mass impoverishment continued to worsen, particularly in relative terms, and the level of social conflict reached such heights that internal peace was seriously threatened and grave political crises ensued.

These political crises took various forms. In the Southern Cone countries, the most advanced of the continent, extremely repressive bureaucratic and authoritarian regimes emerged, and violated the most basic human rights of the people. These regimes adopted the so-called national security doctrine,

> with its vision of a bipolar world where a total war rages between the capitalist and Christian West and the threat of Communist subversion emanating from the machinations of the USSR.[5]

Notwithstanding these military regimes' ideology of 'modernization' and adherence to a neo-conservative ideology and economic policy, the logic of concentrated power led to an aggravation of international conflicts, for example, that between Argentina and Chile over the Beagle Strait, until they reached an agreement with the Pope's mediation in 1984; and Argentina's war over the Malvinas, in which a regime totally bereft of any semblance of legitimacy exploited — in an extremely irresponsible way, to say the least — legitimate historical claims in a desperate bid to acquire legitimacy for itself.

In Central America, on the other hand, the political crisis takes on the form, as we shall see, of an organic crisis of the State, giving rise to revolutionary processes which are seen by the United States as threats to its own security, inasmuch as it regards such processes as front lines in the East–West global confrontation.

In order to understand better the relationships between peace, security and development, at least in the case of Latin America, it is necessary to explain in a more specific way the nature of the development process, in terms of an exclusive capital accumulation model that is excessively vulnerable to changes in the Centre economies and that, having exhausted itself, gives rise to a generalized economic crisis whose political expression varies according to the concrete socio-historical process of each sub-region or country. The first section of this chapter tries to describe, against the background of the diversity of socio-historical processes, the general characteristics of this model of accumulation and its concrete expression in specific countries. The second section briefly sketches the various political forms in which the crisis is expressed.

The Socio-Historical Process: The Diversity of Accumulation Models

To understand Latin America today, it is necessary to indicate, even if briefly, the essential elements of its historical formation. Latin America's under-development is characterized by structural diversity because the different sub-regions of the continent underwent distinct types of insertion into the capitalist world system, thereby giving rise to a double structural heterogeneity. There is, firstly, the heterogeneity across countries, where diverse models of accumulation were transplanted according to the historical period; and secondly, the structural heterogeneity within each country, as a consequence of the coexistence of distinct types of relations of productions. It is not our task here to review the socio-historical process in Latin America. It is enough for us to point out certain historical facts which are especially relevant for our understanding of the present.

(1) Those sub-regions of the continent where a large indigenous population existed, with a highly developed culture and rich in gold and silver, constituted the centres of power (*virreinatos* or viceroyships) of Spanish domination. The political organization and system of military control by the Spanish Crown were designed to maximize hegemony. Thus was created the system of *virreinatos* — Nueva España (Mexico), Peru, Nueva Granada (Colombia), and later that of Río de la Plata — which impeded trade between the provinces, and consequently ensured that the territorial identities, expressed in the new nations, would follow both the pattern of administrative division of the colony as well as the commercial isolation in which they remained for a long period.

(2) Primary products (minerals and agricultural crops) were the principal sources for surplus extraction. The surplus was for the most part destined for the Spanish Crown and unproductive use (churches and luxury items). The little that was reinvested went into export-oriented production, so that the economies were forcibly converted into mono-producers and mono-exporters. With the exception of Mexico and Bogotá, the main cities and communication networks were oriented towards trade with the metropolis.

(3) After independence, with Great Britain having replaced Spain as the

Great World Power, English investments in Latin America were oriented principally towards the Southern Cone, where raw materials needed by Great Britain (meat, wool, wheat, etc.) were already being produced and where, thanks to the type of cultivation which promoted a transportation and communication network, a market for British products had already been created. Between 1830 and 1930 the countries of the Southern Cone became the most developed in Latin America while the old colonial centres stagnated and the rest of Latin America remained only marginally linked to the global market. In these zones, the agro-export model remained predominant and state power was monopolized by dictators dependent on an oligarchic system of domination.

Towards the end of the last century, and coinciding with the ascendancy of the United States to Great World Power status, a process of industrialization by import substitution began in the Southern Cone, which gave rise to the formation of an industrial bourgeoisie. During the crisis of 1930–45, the process of import substitution was accelerated. This coincided, in the Southern Cone, with the rise to power of charismatic leaders of populist persuasion. For the first time in the history of Latin America, the urban masses played an active political role, as distinct from being nothing but cannon fodder, although it was still a subordinate political participation. During the 1950s, coinciding with the post-war boom, the developmentalist ideology, spearheaded by ECLA, became the official policy of almost all Latin American States, with the exception of the oligarchic dictatorships of Paraguay, Haiti and Central America.

At the beginning of the 1960s, it nevertheless became evident in the most advanced economies of the Southern Cone that the developmentalist model of accumulation was exhausting itself. During this period, the tendency towards the transnationalization of the economies of the Third World was imposing itself within the context of a new international division of labour.

In the Southern Cone, where the process of import substitution had been most advanced, the transnationalization process occurred more rapidly. But it also proceeded quickly in Mexico, Venezuela, Central America and in the rest of Latin America.

Transnationalization

The model of transnational accumulation spread to almost all the Latin American economies, although with different political effects on the distinct sub-regions. This model permitted the accelerated growth registered by all of Latin America in the 1960s and the mid-1970s, when it began to show signs of exhaustion and eventually ended up in total crisis in the current decade.

Our argument here is that the particular mode of functioning of this accumulation model leads inevitably to the worsening of problems of fiscal deficit, balance of payments deficit, foreign debt, greater and intolerable inequality in the distribution of income, greater external vulnerability of the economy and, finally, exhaustion of the basis of growth itself.

There is no doubt that the dynamic source of growth has been the industrial sector. As can be appreciated in Table 4.2, between 1950 and 1978 industrial production grew at an average annual rate of 6.5%. The growth was greater in the bigger countries, but in all of them was at a high rate.

Table 4.2
Growth in Industrial Output, by Size of Country
(Average annual growth in %)

Country	1950–65	1965–73	1973–78	1970–78	1979–82
Big	6.3	9.9	4.5	6.8	–0.6
Middle	6.4	5.1	3.7	5.6	
Small	5.6	7.7	6.7	6.5	
Latin America	*6.3*	*8.2*	*4.5*	*6.5*	*2.1*

Source: Juan Carlos Bossio, 'Amerique Latine: Desindustrialisation précoce et re-primarisation Larvel,' CREDAL-IHEAL, Document de Recherche No. 15. October 1983. Paris. p. 8.

This industrial dynamism was due to a large extent to transnational capital, whose share of industrial output rose from 16.2% in 1966 to 19% in 1975. The origin of the investments was primarily North American, whose share of manufacturing output alone rose from 9% in 1966 to 11.2% in 1975.[6]

What were the effects of this type of growth? In the chart we try to synthesize, in a general way, the process which can be described as follows:

(1) The national economy integrates itself more fully into the circuit of international accumulation and, at the same time, the process of disintegration of the national economy speeds up, not only because of the necessity to import raw materials and capital goods so as to be able to assemble goods locally, but also because of increasing imports of new kinds of consumer goods (electronic gadgets, etc.). All this exerts a negative pressure on the balance of payments, which tends to go chronically into deficit, even if exports increase.

It is interesting to underscore the fact that this extraversion goes together with an increase in the coefficient of imports of manufactured products while the *trade deficit* of the industrial sector remains particularly high, which has in fact not decreased ever since 1960. This evolution is one consequence of the lack of integration and development of the productive system; the exporting of manufactured products requires capital goods and raw materials which are not locally produced. In other cases, exports of these products presupposes the importing of manufacturing materials.[7]

(2) Transnational corporations intervene principally in the so-called high technology industries — those sectors producing intermediate goods as well as

46

The Transnationalization Accumulation Model: Adverse Consequences

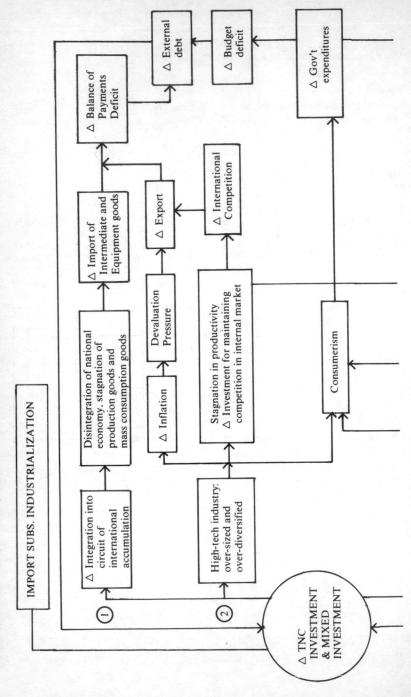

47

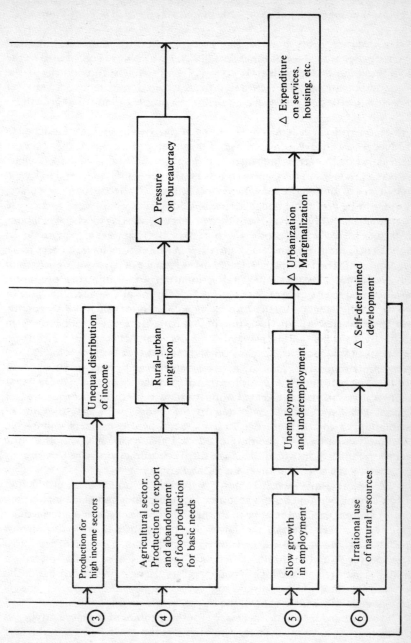

Note: Numbers refer to explanation in the text.

durable goods. These are industries requiring a high degree of entrepreneurial organization apparently not available in Latin America. To quote Fajnzylber:

> The clearest expression of the precariousness of national industrial enterprises in the face of other social forces which have contributed to the formulation of the industrial policy of Latin American countries is the indiscriminate presence of foreign firms which dominate a wide range of sectors, particularly those which define the profile of industrial growth.[8]

These industries are generally over-extended and over-diversified. Designed to produce for vast markets, like those of the developed countries, they find the local market to be narrow but still demanding the whole range of models which are being produced in the Centre countries. Consequently, they tend to have a high degree of unused capacity. From this follow two effects. In the first place, in order to be profitable under such conditions, they are obliged to increase prices immeasurably. This is one of the reasons why, despite much lower labour costs, the cost of the final product is equal to or even higher than that produced in the Centre countries. This also helps explain why exports have not been more dynamic, which fact is in turn reflected in the balance of payments deficits, and why structural pressures intensifying inflation are continually produced. Inflation and the balance of payments deficit chronically weaken the value of the national currency, usually provoking a chain of devaluations. Secondly, another characteristic of this kind of industrialization is weak growth in productivity, which hardly reached 1.7% per year between 1968 and 1979, despite the rapid industrial expansion and the fact that the technologies used were capital-intensive. This, of course, damages export possibilities. Low productivity is due to the underutilization of installed capacity and the fact that the new investments are oriented almost exclusively to the incorporation of technological innovations generated in the Centre with the sole aim of maintaining a competitive edge in a market where consumers imitate the consumption patterns of the developed capitalist economies. In effect, the incorporation of industries designed to satisfy consumerism in the Centre ends up installing the same consumerism in the Periphery.

(3) As can be clearly seen in Table 4.3, between 1950 and 1975 the production of non-durable consumer goods accounted for the greater part of manufacturing output, but has declined relative to the production of capital and intermediate goods. As is well known, the latter are the industries with the highest productivity, and on whose expansion national economic growth depends to a large degree. But the products of these industries are geared towards a capitalist market and the high-income sectors. Hence, on the one hand, the dominant position of the transnational corporations in the local economies is strengthened, since these control the key sectors in an oligopolistic way,[9] and on the other hand it becomes necessary for the incomes of the more privileged social groups to grow much faster, since they are the ones who have the highest propensity to consume these kinds of products. It follows that policies for concentrating income are adopted openly or covertly in order to expand the

internal market, given the fact that, as mentioned above, the possibilities to export — apart from exceptional cases — remain limited. In a word, as Ikonikoff puts it, 'The concentration of income becomes a necessary condition for growth to take place within the framework of this model.'[10]

Naturally such concentration of income distribution exacerbates consumerism, a propensity which is continually reinforced by advertising, thereby implanting in the minds of a majority of the people a consumption pattern without any correspondence to the level of development of the country. Through demonstration effects, this stimulates rural migration to the towns and drives up unproductive expenditures and waste by governments.

Table 4.3
Structure of Industrial Output by Size of Country (%)

Size of Country	Year	Non-durable Consumer Goods	Intermediate Goods	Durable and Capital Goods
Big[a]	1950	64	24	12
	1975	35	37	28
Medium[b]	1950	66	28	6
	1975	48	35	17
Small[c]	1950	85	14	1
	1975	66	26	9

[a] Argentina, Brazil, Mexico.
[b] Chile, Columbia, Peru, Uruguay, Venezuela.
[c] Bolivia, Costa Rica, Ecuador, El Salvador, Haiti, Honduras, Guatemala, Nicaragua, Panama, Paraguay, Dominican Republic and other Caribbean countries.
Source: Juan Carlos Bossio, op. cit., p. 19.

(4) One of the most negative aspects of transnationalization is the tendency to devote resources to agricultural export production, to the detriment of the production of food for the mass of the population. Table 4.4 shows how growth in production for export was the principal source of agricultural growth in Third World countries.

This concentration on the production of certain products for export, a process wherein transnational firms intervene significantly,[11] takes place to the detriment of basic food crops. As a result, there is a scarcity in food which hits mainly the mass of the population, and an increase in imports of staple foods, which in some cases like Venezuela may reach 60% of national consumption, thus further aggravating balance of payment problems. It is thus perfectly logical to speak of a serious problem of food security.

To the extent that the balance of payments deficit increases, recourse to external borrowing also becomes greater. However, once high levels of indebtedness have been reached, and an ever growing volume of foreign exchange is required to service such debts, the possibility of importing food

Table 4.4
Food Production and Exports, by Continent
(Average Annual Growth, 1970–77)

Region	Food Production	Food Exports	Fodder Exports
Africa	1.3	10.6	8.5
Latin America	3.4	17.3	30.9
Far East	2.9	20.4	19.2

Source: Kostas Vergapolous, '"La Periferia" en el Sistema Internacional Agroalimentario,' in *La Question Agraria*, No. 11, 1983, p. 34.

becomes more difficult, at the same time as production for export has to continue undiminished precisely because of the overbearing necessity to increase foreign exchange earnings.

> The immediate effects of this induced food penury and of the reduced purchasing power of the marginalized, whose number keeps growing all the time, make us think that the problems of urban hunger which become more acute every day, are in fact only the beginning of what could occur in the future.[12]

The deterioration of traditional agriculture, which is the sector that employs the greater part of the work-force, stimulates rural-to-urban mass migration, thereby aggravating the problem of food scarcity, employment, marginalization (particularly in the large cities where between 40 and 60% live in slums or *favelas*), and other related urban problems such as personal insecurity, degradation of social services and conditions of life, including deterioration of the environment.

> In 1950, 55% of the total work-force in Latin America was rural; in 1980 only 35% remained so. This rapid displacement of the active population from the rural areas to the cities has simultaneously brought about, even in those modern sectors of the economy that have absorbed much labour power, a transfer of rural underemployment to urban underemployment.[13]

As can be expected, these urban masses, particularly in the democratic countries, exert permanent pressure on the government to employ an ever growing number of people, which in turn increases considerably current government expenditures and aggravates the problem of the budget deficit, which is serious enough already owing to growing state expenditure aimed at valorizing private capital, mainly national, as well as other financial demands of transnationalized industrial development. In particular, one must stress the mechanisms of transfer pricing (or disguised subsidy) which compel State joint enterprises with private firms, to act in favour of the latter's profitability.[14]

(5) It is true that the industrialization process increases employment (4.5% annually on average, well above the total economy's average of 3.2%). But this rate of increase was below the rate of growth of the urban population, and the increase in real wages was only moderate, even in the period of fastest industrial growth. Thus there followed:

> a great uncertainty in employment, the proportion of temporary workers being at times very considerable even in the most advanced industries and in public enterprises. This proves that the instability of employment is not just a phenomenon affecting unskilled workers, but skilled ones as well.[15]

For this reason, the growth of industrial employment does not constitute a market for modern industrial production; so long as industrial growth continues to be held back, it contributes instead significantly to the aggravation of the problems of unemployment, underemployment, and marginalization.

(6) Also typical of the transnationalization process is the transfer of those industries from the Centre which are heavy consumers of energy and destructive of the environment. Indeed the use of natural resources is so irrational, even by the standards of capitalist development, that it ends up endangering the future possibilities of self-determined growth, which therefore makes the economy even more dependent on foreign investments.

To sum up: as the process of transnationalization advances, the budget deficit and balance of payments deficit also increase. To solve these problems, Latin American governments resorted to external debt as the instrument *par excellence*, since it was believed to have only slight inflationary effects and supposedly permitted the adjustment of internal (budget deficit) and external disequilibria, without imposing the necessity to take measures such as tax reforms which were likely to evoke opposition from powerful sectors.

This attitude was encouraged by the huge surpluses accumulated in the international private banks following 1974, as a consequence of the recycling of petro-dollars and the decline in economic activity in the Centre countries brought about by the recession.

Thus the foreign indebtedness of Latin America accelerated, particularly of the largest countries, exactly as happened in all the so-called newly industrializing countries (NICs). At the same time, the structure of indebtedness changed, in the sense that the majority of loans were contracted with the private sector and on a short-term basis.

In Table 4.5 we can see the high level of indebtedness of all Latin American countries, and the extremely high rates at which debt grew between 1979 and 1981. Afterwards, with the crisis, the rate of growth diminished. Already towards the end of the 1970s, at a time when Callaghan's Labour government in Britain, Carter's Democratic administration in the USA and the Social Democrats in Germany were still in power, a monetarist and neo-liberal policy was adopted at the Centre. This was seen as providing the appropriate ideological justification for reducing costs of production and thereby solving the crisis. This policy was taken to extremes during the period of Mrs

Thatcher's government in Britain, Kohl's in the Federal Republic, and Reagan's in the United States. As a consequence:

> In 18 months, Thatcherism wiped out all the industrial growth of Callaghan's Labour government (15%), and in three months Reaganism did away with that of Carter's (10%). What remained of economic growth in the Centre took place in the more social democratic countries and the more competitive exporters (Japan). This generalized recession led in only a few months to a drop in the demand for raw materials, including oil. In this manner, the surplus of OPEC was reduced, and the rise of interest rates prevented the oil importers from benefiting from the drop in the price of oil, thus accentuating the recession in the United States.[16]

In short, the Latin American countries were strangled by, on the one side, the decrease in foreign exchange earnings due to the decline in exports and the deterioration in the terms of trade; and, on the other side, by the outflow of foreign exchange due to the rise in interest rates, the appreciation of the dollar and the impossibility of reducing imports in the short term. In this manner the crisis was generalized, which in turn led to a situation where there emerged the danger of an international financial crash stemming from the impossibility of the developing countries, particularly the Latin Americans, cancelling their foreign commitments, now that these obligations had reached an extremely high proportion of their export earnings.[17]

For the renegotiation of debts, the international financial institutions turned to the IMF. The IMF, in turn, demanded that the debtor countries swallow its bitter medicine for the adjustment of balance of payments deficits. As is well known, this consists of a devaluation of the currency, a contraction of aggregate demand, the opening up of the country to foreign trade and the 'liberalization' of market forces (with the sole exception of the price of labour, over which price control is permitted).

Naturally, aside from limiting national sovereignty by reducing the alternatives open to States, this aggravates the recession, thus creating a situation which — in the case of Mexico — was described as follows:

> The country entered completely into a vicious circle: in the past, in order to grow it had opted for a strategy which led to its excessive indebtedness; today and in the immediate future, in order to pay back its debts, it seems to have no feasible option but to give up its economic growth.[18]

Another consequence of IMF policies was a deterioration in the living conditions of the poor, intensifying the problem of hunger and accentuating social conflicts in a way that could lead to serious political crisis, whose consequences for peace and security would vary according to the type of political regime.

Table 4.5
Latin America: Total Gross Disbursed External Debt ($ millions)

	Total External Debt ($ m)						Rate of Increase of the Debt (%)		
	1978	1979	1980	1981	1982	1983	1979–1981	1982	1983
Latin America	150,893	181,978	221,059	275,422	308,336	332,279	22.2	12.0	7.8
Oil exporting									
Countries	64,390	77,585	92,324	118,963	128,657	137,387	22.7	8.1	6.8
Bolivia	1,762	1,941	2,220	2,450	2,373	2,780	11.6	-3.1	17.2
Ecuador	2,975	3,554	4,562	5,868	6,187	6,689	25.4	5.4	8.1
Mexico	33,946	39,685	49,349	72,007	78,000	82,000	28.5	8.3	13.9
Peru	9,324	9,334	9,594	9,638	11,097	12,418	3.4	15.1	11.9
Venezuela	16,383	23,071	26,509	29,000	31,000	33,500	21.0	6.9	8.1
Non-oil exporting									
Countries	86,503	104,393	128,735	156,459	179,679	194,892	21.8	14.8	8.5
Argentina	12,496	19,034	27,162	35,671	43,634	45,500	41.9	22.3	4.3
Brazil	52,285	58,907	68,354	78,580	87,580	96,500	14.5	11.5	10.2
Columbia	4,247	5,117	6,277	7,930	9,421	10,740	23.1	18.8	14.0
Costa Rica	1,870	2,333	3,183	3,360	3,497	3,848	21.6	4.1	10.0
Chile	6,664	8,484	11,084	15,542	17,153	17,454	32.6	10.4	1.8
El Salvador	986	939	1,176	1,471	1,683	2,000	14.3	14.4	18.8
Guatemala	821	934	1,053	1,409	1,504	1,766	19.7	6.7	17.4
Haiti	210	248	290	372	410	446	21.0	10.2	8.6
Honduras	971	1,280	1,510	1,708	1,800	2,000	20.7	5.4	11.1
Nicaragua	961	1,131	1,579	2,163	2,797	3,385	31.1	29.3	21.6
Panama	1,774	2,009	2,211	2,338	2,820	3,275	9.6	20.6	16.1
Paraguay	669	733	861	949	1,204	1,469	12.4	26.9	22.0
Dominican Rep.	1,309	1,565	1,839	1,837	1,921	2,000	12.0	4.6	4.1
Uruguay	1,240	1,679	2,156	3,129	4,255	4,509	36.1	36.0	6.0

Source: CEPAL, *Estudios Económico de América Latina y el Caribe*, 1983, vol. I, Santiago de Chile, 1985, Table 30, p. 56.

Economic Crisis and Political Crisis

From the preceding discussion we can conclude that the economic crisis affecting the Latin American countries is intimately linked to the global crisis. This derives principally from the exhaustion of the transnational accumulation model, which is brought about by the impossibility of sustaining growth within the narrow limits of the market and by the very nature of the process of import substitution.[19] Although it is a generalized phenomenon which clearly explains the crisis of Latin America, the political manifestations stemming from it vary according to the geopolitical context of each sub-region and the socio-historical process of each country.

Obviously, it is not possible to examine in this chapter political changes in each Latin American country. A detailed analysis of the cases of Mexico, Central America and Venezuela is provided in other chapters. Nevertheless, it is worthwhile identifying some common political situations in Latin America, which imply similar strategies for determined social forces, and which may have similar consequences for regional or sub-regional peace and security.

There is no doubt that, in the present decade, the dominant political tendency in Latin America is towards democratization. A decade ago, most Latin American regimes were dictatorships; in 1986, only Paraguay and Chile remained governed by dictators. Social democratic or Christian democratic tendencies now dominate social movements and political parties. However, within this general tendency, it is necessary to distinguish two types of process.

The first type is taking place in the Southern Cone. Here, on the one hand, a struggle for democratization and human rights and, on the other hand, the failure of the neo-liberal economic policies carried out by dictatorial regimes, magnified by the world economic crisis, have determined the advent of democracy in Uruguay and Argentina. In the latter, democratization was also stimulated by the defeat of the Argentinian army in the Malvinas.

Brazil followed a rather different economic policy, fostering a vigorous process of industrialization, including the arms industry, and gradually and consciously advancing towards democratization. However, it shares with Argentina and Uruguay a situation where the main objective of social movements is to consolidate representative democracy and to block conservative forces struggling to return to power.

The economic crisis magnified the economic policy failures of the dictatorships and, eventually, helped the move towards democracy. However, if the economic crisis continues and, particularly, if governments continue to apply IMF-recommended policies, there is no doubt that social tensions will mount to a point where democracy certainly will be endangered. A return of conservative forces to power, and a new period of massive violation of human rights, are possible under the circumstances of a continuing economic crisis and the implementation of restrictive economic policies which place the burden on the popular sectors.

The second type of situation is that confronted by 'old' democracies such as Colombia, Costa Rica, Mexico and Venezuela, which have more than 25 years of democratic regimes. If the economic crisis helped to bring down dictatorships in the Southern Cone, there is no doubt that it also endangers the older democracies. In these countries, the challenge facing social and political movements is that of deepening social democracy and defining new accumulation models which may provide a true solution to the crisis. But these objectives are being hindered by, on the one hand, the reluctance of the bloc in power to open new spaces for participatory action and, on the other hand, by the restrictive economic policies being applied in order to be able to renegotiate the external debt. Since these policies hit the popular sectors hardest, social tensions are building up to form an immense social volcano.

Countries like Bolivia, Peru, Ecuador, Dominican Republic, Panama and others with democracies newer than Venezuela, but older than Argentina, face the double challenge of consolidating democracy and deepening social participation. Both are basic objectives of significant social and political movements. Since these countries also confront the same restrictions as the other types of countries discussed above, one may conclude that democracy in these countries faces still greater dangers.

Paraguay and Chile are the only two remaining dictatorships. Although they are not similar, social and political movements in both countries have a common goal of struggling for democracy. One can expect an indefinite prospect of conflict in these two countries.

The Central American situation continues to be the most dangerous one for regional peace and security, not only because of the threat of a regional war, but also because this conflict, for the first time in Latin America has, at least subjectively, acquired an East–West conflict dimension.

Notes

1. *El Nacional*, Caracas, 25.3.84, p. D-4.
2. United Nations, *Economic Survey of Latin America, 1982*, 20 May 1983, p. 2.
3. Ibid.
4. Ibid.
5. Jacques Chonchol, *Pour une nouvelle coopération française en Amérique Latine: Quelques orientations pour l'action*, mimeo, IHEAL, January 1984.
6. Juan Carlos Bossio, op. cit., p. 29. For a broader and more detailed documentation, see *Industrialización e Internacionalización en América Latina: Recopilación de trabajos sobre distintos paises y sectors, selección de Fernando Fajnzylber*, Mexico, FCE, 1981.
7. Ibid., p. 33.
8. Fernando Fajnzylber, 'Intervención, Autodeterminación e Industrialización en América Latina', in Pablo González Casanova (coordinador) *No intervención, autodeterminación y democracia en América Latina*, Ed. Siglo XXI, Mexico, 1983, p. 18.
9. Suffice it to mention as an indicator that a quarter of the North American transnational firms operating in Brazil and Mexico controlled more than 50% of the respective national markets in 1972. Half the firms declared that they controlled at least 25% of their markets. Chudnovsky, *Report to the US Senate*, quoted in J. C. Bossio, op. cit., p. 28.
10. Moisés Ikonikoff, 'Tercer Mundo: Modelos y Opciones. Los Interrogantes', mimeo, 1984, p. 1.

11. Gonzalo Arroyo, *Les Agents Dominants de L'Agrocapitalisme*, Credimi, Dijon, 1983; 'Les Firmes Transnationales et L'Agriculture en Amérique Latine', *Anthropos*, 1980.

12. Pierre Salama, 'Endettement et Dissete Urbaine?', CEP No. 25, 1983, p. 17.

13. Jacques Chonchol, op. cit., p. 4.

14. Juan Carlos Bossio, op. cit., p. 27.

15. Ibid., p. 24.

16. Alain Lipietz, 'Le fordisme périphérique etranglé par la monetarisme central', paper presented at the Colloquium Vers.

17. Alexander Schubert, 'Misión Imposible: servir la deuda external', *Neuva Sociedad*, Sept.–Oct. 1983, pp. 44–5.

18. Rosario Green, 'La experiencia mexicana: 1970–1982', *Gaceta Internacional*, July–September 1983, Vol. 1, p. 68.

19. See Moisés Ikonikoff, 'Tercer Mundo: modelos y opciones', op. cit.; and Ricardo Hausmann and Gustavo Márquez, 'La crisis económica de Venezuela', *Cuadernos del CENDES*, No. 1, Sept.–Dec. 1983.

5. Foreign Debt and Regional Security

Augusto Varas

Introduction

The insertion of Latin America in the international political and economic system typical of the pre- and post-World War II periods has changed substantially in the last two decades. Likewise, its position by the end of the century will be very different from its historical insertion in the world. The reason for this change can be found in the long-term structural crisis which the Latin American countries have entered as a result of the critical situation generated by the enormous external debt.

In this context of political and social tensions and a middle- to long-term recession, it is necessary to mention the process of militarization of local political systems and economies. The economic crisis and its social and political effects will tend to stimulate the militarization of the Latin American societies. This reality pregnant with conflict at a local and international level contrasts with the lack of collective and consensual efforts which may help to solve it. Instead of generating efforts within each country or the hemisphere, it is producing increasingly acute levels of conflict. The explanation of this situation lies in the magnitude of the economic contraction which the region is undergoing, as a result of the response to the debt crisis.

These middle- to long-term economic tensions have generated dysfunctional reactions to solve them, including authoritarian forms at both a local and international level. They tend to legitimize the use of force domestically and consolidate the repressive role of the armed forces as a resource in case of need. As a result, the adequate control of military expenditure is prevented, the local production of arms continues as does the growing importing of military technology.

Recently, three principal sources of authoritarian solutions have emerged. The first is the economic crisis itself; the second, the inevitable social polarizations which result from it; and the third, the authoritarian conjuncture of the international private and multilateral financial system as well as the irreconcilable policy of the Reagan Administration.

Foreign Debt and Authoritarianism

The historical tendency during the recent past has been the growing gulf between the rate of development of the region compared to the developed capitalist countries, with the sole exception of Brazil. Latin America has had a smaller share both in the flows of direct international investments and in world trade as a whole. Yet owing to the world recession, the region has become increasingly dependent on foreign trade and on foreign financing in order to try to overcome its crisis.

The important role of the US in direct foreign investment, at first in the extractive sector and afterwards in manufacturing, has notably decreased. Its investments now are focused on only a few countries — Brazil and Mexico — each of them highly transnationalized, constituting (with Argentina) the most important economies of the region. These investments are oriented — in some cases associated with local state and private capital — towards specific industrial sectors, such as electronics, metallurgy and petrochemicals. The rest of the industrial sector tends to remain in the hands of local capital, being of a more traditional nature. In this way, the structural heterogeneity which marked the Latin American economy in the 1960s is characterized in the 1980s by a greater degree of regional heterogeneity.

The negative effects of foreign investment stand out in the Latin American economies' new commercial and economic relations, which tend to reproduce the general recessive conditions. A recent ECLA report indicates that the principal transnational investors in Latin America show little or no increase in their traditional or non-traditional exports and they continue their role as capital exporters to their head offices.[1]

The economic aspects of greatest relevance at the present time are the high level of foreign debt, the vicious-circle tendencies limiting exports, and the scarcity of new direct investments coming into the national economies. This is what distinguishes Latin America from the rest of the Third World, as it is the only region which has to devote more than 60% of its exports to pay its foreign debt (see Tables 5.1 and 5.2).

This situation is characterized by the doubling of the foreign debt in the last 10 years to reach almost $400 billion in 1984, or half the total debt of the underdeveloped countries.[2] The debt amounted to 12% of Latin America's GNP in the 1970s; in 1982 it reached almost a third. In 1970, service payments on the debt represented 7% of total exports; today, as we mentioned, it exceeds 60%. The nature of the debt itself has also changed. During the 1970s it tended to be contracted on medium- to long-term periods; now, however, those periods are shorter. In the 1970s, 80% of foreign financial resources were obtained from government and multilateral financial sources; now it is essentially private (see Table 5.1.). As for interest rates, which in the 1970s were fixed, these are now variable. All this, together with the decrease in direct foreign investment, has greatly increased the economic and financial instability of the region as a whole.[3]

This continent-wide economic reality consequently generates a structural tendency to recession, generating growing tensions as a result of the contradiction between the need to convert into cash the financial resources committed to the region and the inability to service the foreign debt. The use of foreign financial resources for non-productive consumption, which we will comment on later, has strengthened this tendency to recession.[4]

For these reasons, the Latin American balance of payments crisis is the most important factor determining both intra-regional relations and relations with the rest of the world, as well as internal developments, during the next two decades.

Socio-Political Polarization

The region's great financial error is generating an explosive situation within each country. Wage workers — the sector which has been most affected by the prolonged recession — will tend to show their discontent and protest at the lack of satisfaction of their vital needs, either peacefully or by means of armed mass movements. This situation can already be seen in countries such as Brazil, Bolivia, Peru, Uruguay and Colombia. In each, popular discontent reaches levels of mobilization which are a constant threat to the stability of democracy. These tensions obviously will affect the political future of the countries of the region. Right-wing maximalist reactions are generated which promote an increasing state of repression against the whole population. Examples include the new growth of the extreme-right PAN in Mexico and the increasingly aggressive Costa Rican right wing.

However, resorts to authoritarianism have not been able to control the crisis produced by the prevailing high international rates of interest. Indeed these very rates of interest were a factor in the processes of transition to democracy in Latin America. Even though it is not possible to isolate this element and single it out as 'the' explanation of these democratization processes, it is true that it did play a role in the removal of the authoritarian governments of Argentina, Brazil and Uruguay.[5]

Even though authoritarian governments were the principal recipients of the enormous flow of external finance, they are incapable of managing the crisis which this situation has unleashed. They are unable to create that general will capable of mobilizing national energies in pursuit of the enormous effort which the payment of the debt implies, evenly sharing the load. The very nature of authoritarian governments involves a lack of mechanisms for political participation in the decision-making proces, thus impeding any national effort like the one needed for the payment of the debt. It is not strange then that it is precisely those countries which have had democratically elected governments which, in spite of internal conflicts, have survived the debt crisis in better shape, as the cases of Colombia, Mexico and Venezuela illustrate.

On the other hand, this situation is accompanied by additional complications when we observe the problems inherent in a process of democratic negotiation over the foreign debt and its cancellation. Countries which have changed from military governments to democratically elected ones, can also be destabilized by the economic and social crisis and by the social protest which is generated in the period immediately following democratization, as occurred in Argentina, Brazil and Uruguay.

As a result, the authoritarian alternative, in spite of its original sin in having contracted the debt, sometimes appears as the best option for the managerial sector, as in the case of Chile at present. In other countries, there is the temptation to maintain the military option in case the situation gets out of control, as in the case of Bolivia and Peru.

This highly unstable configuration leads to a political polarization, with its resulting authoritarianism in the national political scene and, once more, the armed forces stand out as the last bastion against the attempts by wage workers to win a greater priority for their interests in government.

International Financial Authoritarianism

There exists another source of authoritarianism which supports the one we have just analysed. It is the 'heavy hand of the IMF and its ideological rigidity'.[6] The short-term recessionary policies of the IMF and the parallel policies of the World Bank for the medium term, through the imposition of their structural adjustment loans,[7] also generate a situation tending to a unilateral imposition of conditions, and constitute, in the final analysis, a resort to force — albeit non-military force — which is almost as effective.

This tough position towards the debtor countries is explained by the enormous importance of the North American banking system in the North American economy. The 'pivotal position of the banks'[8] seriously affects Washington's policy in these matters.

The importance of the US banks can be seen in Tables 5.3 and 5.4 where the proportion of assets abroad held by the whole US banking system can be compared with the exposure of the principal North American financial institutions in their operations in Latin America. The weighted average of US bank profits generated in operations abroad reached 44% in 1983, an amount which is even higher if we discount the recently bankrupt Continental Illinois bank. Indeed if we examine the exposure of the nine so-called money centre banks (Bank of America, Citibank, Chemical, Chase, Morgan, Manufacturers, Continental Illinois, Banker's Trust, and the First National Bank of Chicago), it appears that, as of 30 June 1983, their operational risk level in the Third World reached 62%.

In the case of Latin America, the greater part of the exposure of the main North American banks is concentrated in Mexico, Brazil, Venezuela, Argentina, Chile, Colombia and Peru. Consequently, the political character of the regional foreign debt is totally irrelevant.

To the extent that this situation is a highly critical matter for the whole US economy, it has become the most controversial point in hemispherical relations.[9] 'Hawks' and 'doves' dispute forms of solutions which in the end are decided by a US administration of highly conservative orientation in monetary matters. Not being able to create new international monetary instruments capable of solving or even acting as a palliative for the crisis, the Reagan Administration has opted for the hard hand of the IMF, even though in critical cases it has given emergency aid, as in the Argentinian or Brazilian cases during 1984.

Since no Latin American country can survive an international financial blockade without serious internal disturbances, the Reagan Administration has left them with no other alternative than to pursue recessionary policies. The Argentinian experience is an illustration of one of the most autonomous positions in the region.

One of the consequences of this strong pressure are the evidently disadvantageous criteria used to protect the Latin American economies from uncontrolled external investment. The cases of Mexico, which changed its terms on which foreign capital could collaborate with local capital, and more recently Venezuela, where the terms of the Andean Pact were practically nullified in the request to modify Decision 24, are examples of this situation. All of this is taking place in a situation where regional direct investment has decreased and the North American companies are showing a decreasing interest in investing in the area. According to the Council of the Americas, 52 of the largest North American companies operating in Argentina, Brazil, Mexico and Venezuela show their operations in those countries making a decreasing contribution to their total profits, and making small efforts to remain in those markets. The contribution of sales in those countries dropped from 7.5% in 1981 to 5.2% in 1983 and 3.8% in 1984. According to the Council, behind this decrease lay the regional balance of payments crisis.[10] In this way, the US business community shows an over-protected position in Latin America. On the one hand, it has been able to divide and conquer with respect to matters relating to the payment and renegotiation of the debt. On the other hand, it has reduced the importance of its operations during the current period of high risks and at the same time obtained much better conditions to remain. All of this under the surveillance of the IMF, the World Bank and their recessionary recipes.

The consequence of this ideological rigidity and over-protected US interests will be a new wave of Latin American nationalism. If it is not channelled within a regional institutional framework, it will end up in a rhetoric which will prevent any improvement of the region's bargaining position with the US.

Because of this, even though the effort to solve the crisis demands consensual solutions both at a local and an international level, there exist strong pressures to impose solutions by force as a last resort. In all of these, the armed forces appear, once again, as the most obvious institution to carry out this repressive task. Even in those countries which have recently undergone democratization, the effect of this economic and political situation is a renewed legitimacy of both the repressive functions of the armed forces — as exemplified by the recovery of the military's political initiative in Argentina — as well as of the high levels of military expenditure in all of Latin America.

The Political Intransigence of the Reagan Administration
All of these tensions are generating a series of ideological–political alternatives, much more extensive than those that existed in the region during the last two

decades. Consequently, the presence of extra-continental forces supporting one or another sector will increase.[11] In certain regions of the hemisphere as well as in the whole of the continent, as in the case of Grenada, Central America and the pressure which Cuba has had to resist, the internal political effect of these actions is none other than to strengthen the authoritarian military sectors.

After the Report of the US Bilateral Commission on the Central American situation, this attitude became a doctrine.[12] In it, the ideological diversity which emerged from the economic and social Latin American crisis is interpreted as a threat to US strategic security.

This explains how and why US military aid has been oriented in this direction. The increase in US military aid to the underdeveloped countries is justified in terms of developing security forces in those countries which 'are struggling to maintain or develop democracy, [thereby] alleviating the US Armed Forces in their global responsibility'.[13]

This perspective is evident in US military operations in Honduras and in its support to the armed forces of El Salvador, as well as in the assistance which was offered to Peru to solve the political problem raised by Sendero Luminoso by military means. The same approach can be observed in the Brazilian–North American Agreement of 1984, as well as with the aid requested of the US Congress for Costa Rica and the joint exercises of North American and Venezuelan naval units in the READEX-84 operation (where for the first time a foreign naval unit, *El Almirante García*, participated in joint exercises in the Caribbean).

The same approach governs North American ties with the Central American countries and has used their big foreign debts to align them behind its interventionist policy in the region.

All this shows the excessive emphasis which the Reagan Administration puts on military ties, over and above political and diplomatic ones. It makes abundantly clear the militarized fashion in which the United States intends to solve the social and political problems of the region. The US faces the hemispheric crisis with a perspective which promotes solutions of force in Latin American countries. For this reason during the past few years the White House has developed strong bilateral military relations in the hemisphere in the belief that the continent's armed forces continue to be a barrier to the internal political changes which it considers strategically unacceptable.

This excessive importance given to Pan-American military ties coincides with the downgrading of multilateral forums, where the US tends to prevent the creation of coalitions for negotiation which may restrict its room for manoeuvre. The strategy of divide and rule has clearly been successful in the past few years, especially with respect to the Latin American foreign debt. Faced by attempts at collective negotiation by Latin American governments and their politicization of the issue, the US has put forward a counter-strategy aimed at the protection of the North American banking system in spite of the precarious economic situation of its Latin American counterparts.

At the same time, this tendency to bilateral action has been expressed in the

US's withdrawal from UNESCO, its flouting of the International Court at The Hague, and its threats to do the same thing at the United Nations and the ILO.

As a result, its policy has succeeded in weakening the multilateral organs of the hemisphere, such as the OAS, the Andean Pact, the Interamerican Treaty for Reciprocal Action and regional consensual initiatives such as Contadora. It has been able to alter the usual procedures of organs such as the Interamerican Development Bank, where the US vetoed a credit for Nicaragua! As for the Contadora process, this is facing serious problems due to the US determination to undermine its mediator role and align it instead with Reagan policy.

The Latin American governments, for their part, have not been able to go any farther than their proposals to renegotiate the debt, obtain 'adequate grace periods and amortization and a reduction of the interest rates, commission margins and other financial charges'.[14] Their Ministerial Meeting in the Dominican Republic in 1985 reflected the same lack of any imaginative and active response to this serious regional problem.

This priority given to hemispheric military relations over regional political realities[15] was made evident during the visit of the US Assistant Secretary for Latin American Affairs, Nestor Sanchez, to some Latin American countries as well as numerous delegations from the US Navy and the Congress Armed Services Committee. On his visit Sanchez met the various military chiefs of staff. In these meetings they discussed the need to standardize military equipment and to co-ordinate defence plans, as well as strategy and logistical support.[16]

It is clear, therefore, since the episode of the Falklands (Malvinas), that the US's military interventionist policy has been complemented by the first attempts to reorganize the whole Pan-American security system and change its obsolete structure. The effect of these efforts has been none other than to stimulate those local elements which see in this association with the US an opportunity to legitimize growing military expenditures. In this way, there have appeared proposals advocating higher levels of military integration with the United States. These ideas are occurring in the midst of a growing international polarization and White House aggressiveness towards Moscow. They can have no other intention than to increase the levels of militarization of the continent.

It has actually been argued that 'new military policies and the insertion of South America in the East–West confrontation as a military actor with higher relative weight could improve relations between the Super Powers.'[17] This line proposes the operational integration of up to 20% of Latin American armed forces with US forces. In the same way it suggests integrating the continent's arms industry in joint projects.

This return to outmoded conceptions of belonging to one or other bloc contrasts with the actual experience of Latin America of not becoming involved in the strategic bipolar confrontation. The new strategies are supported from both the North American and the Latin American side by the non-ratification of the Nuclear Non-Proliferation Treaty by Argentina,

Brazil and Chile and nuclear developments in Peru and Colombia.

The pressures to increase the levels of continental militarization as a whole through its insertion in the US–USSR confrontation, only legitimize the already high levels of military expenditure, arms imports and armaments production in the region. At the same time any greater integration of Latin America in the Super Power conflict will bring direct nuclear insecurity to all parts of the hemisphere.

Militarism

One of the reasons which helps to explain the Latin American debt crisis was the existence of authoritarian governments in a majority of the principal indebted countries — Argentina, Bolivia, Brazil, Chile, Ecuador, Paraguay, Peru, Uruguay and the Central American countries — at the moment of the international boom of financial flows. In the case of Mexico, its (in effect) single party system with restricted political competition had much the same consequences. The net result was the dictatorial allocation of resources to consumer goods (see Table 5.5 for the increase in consumption by the armed forces) rather than satisfaction of basic needs of the people. In contrast, those countries where there were democratic regimes, for example Colombia and Venezuela, showed a lower debt servicing/export earnings ratio (see Table 5.2).

One of the consequences of this dictatorial use of internationally acquired resources was to increase the stock of armaments belonging to the armed forces, as well as the development of local arms industries and the expansion of the number of military personnel (see Tables 5.6, 5.7, and 5.8). And military expenditures and arms imports far surpassed whatever growth there was in GNP in the years 1975–85, thereby in part explaining big growth in the foreign debt.

The international financial flows which had begun to enter the region in the mid 1970s coincided with the Carter Administration's new Latin American policy, epitomized in its slogan of Human Rights. The Carter Administration suspended military ties with the principal military powers of the hemisphere as a consequence of the strong deterioration of the human rights situation existing in those countries where repressive military dictatorships existed. The sanctions taken against Chile in 1976 and 1979, and exclusion of Brazil from the US Military Aid Program in 1977, and the pressures on Argentina in 1976 were the principal episodes in the already prolonged crisis of the Pan-American security system. Ironically, the net effect of all this was to allow the military establishments of the various countries to diversify their sources of supply and to obtain the necessary fiscal resources by other means. Even those few countries which did not directly use the new loans for the purchase of armaments took away important fiscal resources from the areas of social investment, in the context of neo-liberal, anti-statist policies.

Carter's Human Rights policy ended up, however, being sidetracked into unimportant corners of his Administration owing to the important ties which grew between the Latin and North American bankers and businessmen. His Administration was unable to establish a coherent policy which would allow at one and the same time a maintenance of the moralizing aims of his regional policy and the broadening of the operations of US financial capital in the region.

The end result has been a sustained increase in military expenditure, expansion of the region's armaments industry and the importing of modern military technology. Many examples of this could be mentioned. Colombia has modernized its armed forces by means of a multi-million programme of arms purchases. Its armed forces have recently allocated $247 million to the purchase of corvettes from the Federal Republic of Germany, using a credit granted to them by the German company FEROS in December 1980. They have also spent an additional $150 million on the purchase of submarines and missiles. And there is an agreement with Sweden for the construction of a naval base in Bahía Málaga at a cost of $150 million. The army and air force have similarly been given large resources for their modernization.

The new Colombian purchases were quickly followed by Venezuela, whose air force will receive 16 General Dynamics F-16-A Fighting Falcons ($30 million each) as well as eight two-seater F-16-B's. Twenty-four Argentinian FMA LA-58 Pucaras ordered in September 1983 were received. A second shipment of 19 CF-5's was also due, as was a consignment of four G.222 light transports ($14 million each) together with four Augusta H-3 helicopters. The Army Air Force will receive eight Augusta R.109 helicopters. There then followed a strong devaluation of the Venezuelan currency and a major economic recession, which compelled the Venezuelan armed forces to make their last large purchase. This was to equip the newly formed La Concepción Missile Artillery Group on the coast of Lake Maracaibo at a cost of $52 million. Each one of the Israeli missiles of this system cost $6,000.

In the case of Brazil, the most important aspect has been the incredible development of its arms industry (see Tables 5.5 and 5.6) and its new military agreements with the US. 95% of Brazilian armaments production is exported. During 1984 Brazilian arms exports reached almost $3 billion with shipments to some 33 countries, giving work to 400 factories employing 100,000 people. The abnormal development of the Brazilian arms industry reflects the major distortion of the country's entire economy which is reorienting itself more and more towards exporting, at the expense of other areas of civil consumption, despite the fact that these use more manual workers.

The Brazilian arms industry has recently been strongly stimulated by the Brazilian–North American Agreement signed in February 1984 which has enabled Brazil to produce conventional arms using North American technology and selling them to other Third World countries with Washington's prior agreement. This renewal of bilateral military relations following their interruption in 1977 under the Carter Administration has converted Brazil into the US's only Latin American partner in these types of activity. These agreements with the US also extend to nuclear, scientific and space collaboration. In return, Brazil will cede to the US certain facilities in the

Atlantic, notably a prospective US naval base on the Brazilian island of Trinidad.

As for Argentina, recent years have witnessed a massive process of rearmament, particularly after the War of the Falklands (Malvinas). Following its military defeat and before the new civilian government took over, the air force bought 200 planes to replace the 109 which had been lost in battle. The navy purchased new Super-étandard planes ($12 million each); replaced and increased its stocks of Gabriel and Kfir C.7 missiles ($6 million each) and bought an unknown number of Exocet AM-39 missiles. The navy also bought AWAC early warning planes, four German 4,000 ton MEKO 360 H-2 frigates, five 1,800 ton MEKO L-40 corvettes and placed purchase orders for six conventional TR 1700 submarines. The Argentinian armed forces bought seven Lockheed L-186 Electra planes, 18 Lynx HAS8's and 12 Embraer 325GB Xavantes ($60 million).

The Peruvian case is interesting because it illustrates the relation between military expenditure and the foreign debt contracted during a period of military rule. According to the former Minister of Finance, Javier Silva Ruete, who held the post from 1978 to 1980 during the military government of Morales Bermúdez, Peru spent $850 million on arms in 1982. This represented 30% of the $2.8 billion which the Peruvian Government received as loans.

This explains how the Peruvians were able to buy four unloading barges, 20 Mirage 2000's ($25 million each), 12 Mi-24 Hind helicopters, 40 to 50 light assault one-seat MB.339K Veltro 11 planes (manufactured by INDAER-Peru under licence), 30 Mirage 50's ($7 million each), 12 Bell 214ST helicopters and an unknown number of Sikorsky UH-60 Black Hawk helicopters. All this, in addition to the production of naval materiel under licence.

Other countries have also participated in this military spending spree. Bolivia, in the midst of one of the worst political crises of its history, has ordered 12 Mirage 50's ($7 million each) and 2 LAMA helicopters; Chile, submerged in a chronic economic crisis, has bought 21 CASA Aviojet planes and 6 CASA 212 planes ($2.1 million each); and Mexico has ordered 45 Ultralav armoured cars from Panhard.

Countries like Cuba and Nicaragua also have had to increase their military expenditures by large amounts, in order to face the dangers of US aggression.

Economic and Military Consequences

Many arguments have been put forward against increasing military expenditure, both world-wide and in the Latin American region.[18] However, the situation we face in the middle of the present economic crisis renders these consequences even more serious.

On the one hand, one of the most obvious consequences of the current high levels of military expenditure is going to be the enormous obstacle they pose to the region's economic recovery. On the other hand, this disproportionate expenditure will prevent easing the social and economic consequences of repaying the debt and even more dramatic situations of confrontation. Even more importantly, acceptance of high military expenditure levels — fuelled by the increase in personnel, the transfer of military technology and the development of a local arms industry — will have as a consequence a more permanent presence of the armed forces in the national life, in spite of the destabilizing element which their presence implies for democratic development in Latin America.

To the extent that state companies may be the most energetic sources of local economic recovery, the local arms industry will be seen as more sensible and positive economically than ever before. Thus the co-operation agreements, for example between the arms industries of Argentina and Peru, which have an evident geopolitical implication, would be supported as a possible means of substituting locally produced for imported arms on the one hand, and on the other, by the mirage that they will generate export surpluses. In this way there will appear a halo around these local arms industries, with all the positive memories of the import-substitution industrialization era. The arms industry will appear invested with all the positive attributes which presently encourage the Brazilian case. All the negative elements associated with it will be passed over, as well as the mortgage which it implies for a balanced middle- to long-term economic development.[19]

Associated with this problem is the false perception that military expenditure and the arms industry support national development. Even though it might have a positive effect for private companies in some developed countries, it is not the same situation in Latin America. Here the surplus capital which has been invested in the arms industry only appears productive, given two assumptions. One is the unequal income distribution, which apparently makes these investments the only feasible thing to do. To the extent that a very different investment strategy — for the production of goods for civil consumption — would demand a drastic change in the distribution of income, and considering that this would demand a drastic change in the prevailing conditions in Latin America, this type of military use of resources is at least consonant with existing social inequalities and contradictions.

Secondly, the existence of an arms industry which has apparently positive economic effects for the country as a whole, does not take into account that this is possible and appears to be internationally competitive only because of the high levels of domestic military expenditure. This latter phenomenon is crucial for subsidizing both the national and international arms supply industry, as well as the controversial regional arms industry programmes.

Consequently, to the extent that the economic crisis is reflected in the large foreign debt which in turn has its roots in the authoritarian allocation of those financial resources to the military and the arms industry, continued high levels of spending on the latter will reproduce the crisis on an amplified scale. The serious thing about this is that, in order to solve this critical situation, it will be necessary to submit to firm democratic control armed forces which are growing more autonomous from the civil power.

It will therefore be necessary to reverse these tendencies whereby the military are becoming an ever more dominant institution, not just politically but also economically. We have to conclude that the Latin American recovery must also involve the democratization of the armed forces and demilitarization of the State.[20]

Table 5.1
Latin America's Foreign Debt, Selected Years ($ millions)

	1975	1983	1984 (estimated)
Argentina			
Total	6,026	40,718	45,000
Public	3,121	18,590	
Private	1,193	12,353	
Short-term	1,712	9,775	
Brazil			
Total	23,344	91,613	100,000
Public	13,751	54,312	
Private	9,593	24,700	
Short-Term	n.a.	12,602	
Colombia			
Total	3,572	10,500	10,000
Public	2,348	6,701	
Private	297	822	
Short-Term	927	2,978	
Chile			
Total	4,854	17,654	20,000
Public	3,731	7,619	
Private	536	8,335	
Short-Term	587	1,700	
Mexico			
Total	16,900	86,516	96,000
Public	11,540	67,783	
Private	5,022	8,738	
Short-Term	338	9,994	
Peru			
Total	4,066	11,592	12,500
Public	3.021	8,113	
Private	230	2,304	
Short-Term	815	1,175	
Venezuela			
Total	5,700	32,804	35,000
Public	1,262	12,000	
Private	995	13,810	
Short-Term	3,443	6,994	
Latin America			
Total	75,393	336,230	
Public	44,956	204,871	
Private	19,340	80,265	
Short-Term	11,097	51,094	

Sources: Lagniappe Quarterly Report 31 January 1985; BID. *The Foreign Debt and Economic Development in Latin America.* Washington D.C., January 1984.

Table 5.2
Foreign Debt Service and Interest Payments as a % of Exports

	1975	*1983*
Latin America		
Service/Exports	26.6	64.6
Interest/Exports	13.0	37.8
Argentina		
Service/Exports	31.9	149.4
Interest/Exports	13.3	56.9
Brazil		
Service/Exports	40.8	82.4
Interest/Exports	19.4	40.7
Colombia		
Service/Exports	20.9	42.9
Interest/Exports	10.9	24.3
Chile		
Service/Exports	36.2	62.5
Interest/Exports	15.5	48.8
Mexico		
Service/Exports	38.6	59.3
Interest/Exports	21.1	42.4
Peru		
Service/Exports	31.6	66.2
Interest/Exports	14.6	31.8
Venezuela		
Service/Exports	10.2	26.6
Interest/Exports	4.3	25.0

Source: Ibid., Chart 1.

Table 5.3
International Profits of 10 Leading US Banks, 1979 and 1983

	1979		1983	
	(US$ m)	*(% of Total)*	*(US$ m)*	*(% of Total)*
Citicorp	355	65.3	468	54.8
Chase Manhattan	146	46.9	181	48.3
Bank of America Corporation	225	37.4	185	49.7
Manufacturers Hanover	103	48.7	164	51.7
J.P. Morgan & Co.	150	52.2	250	54.2
Chemical New York	43	31.7	129	42.7
Continental Illinois	32	16.6	8	8.0
Bankers Trust New York	59	51.6	101	39.2
First Chicago	4	3.5	22	12.1
Security Pacific	18	10.9	46	17.4
Total	*1,136*	*42.4*	*1,554*	*44.0*

Table 5.4
Exposure of 12 Leading Banks in Key Third World Countries, 30 June 1983

	Total Capital	*% of Risk*
Mexico	44.4	54.9
Brazil	44.0	64.7
Venezuela	25.1	67.9
South Korea	20.9	59.4
Argentina	17.3	62.1
Philippines	13.1	67.1
Chile	10.2	54.6
Taiwan	9.3	66.2
Indonesia	9.0	84.3
Colombia	7.5	67.9
Peru	4.8	55.7
Yugoslavia	4.8	62.5
Total	*210.4*	*62.0*

Table 5.5
Foreign Debt and Militarization in Latin America, 1975–82

Latin America	Annual Average Rate of Growth (%)
Gross National Product	2.7
Military Personnel	4.1
Military Expenditure	4.5
Debt	19.2
Arms Transfers	24.10

Sources: BID, *The Foreign Debt and Economic Development in Latin America*, Washington, D.C., January 1984; ACDA, *World Military Expenditures and Arms Transfers 1972–1982*, Washington D.C., April 1984.

Table 5.6
Arms Production in Latin America: War Planes

Country	Helicopters	Training	Cazas	Transport	Light Planes	Missiles
Argentina	CK-1 Cicare 500-M[2]	ARROW-3[2] LA-58A Pucara Cessna-A 150[2]	LA-58B Pucara LA-62[1]			
Brazil	As-332[4] AS-350-M[4] SA-315-L	A-132 Tangara EMB-312 Tucano UIR/PURU-122 A Universal 1 y 2 EMB-326 Xavante[6] S-10[7] S-12[7]	AMX[6]	EMB-110 Bandeirante EMB-110 A " EMB-110 B " EMB-110 K1 " EMB-110 N " EMB-111 " EMB-111 N " EMB-120 Brasilia EMB-121 Xingu EMB-121 Xingu-2	IPAE-26 EMB-Piper	MAA-1 Piranha MAS-1 Carcara SAM BRA Cobra 2000[1]
Chile		PA/28[2] T-Pillan[2]	T-36 Halcon[8]			
Colombia					Cessna[2]	
Mexico		EMB-326 GB[9]		EMB-110 MEX[9]		
Peru		MB-339 A[6]				

Source: Stockholm International Peace Research Institute, *World Armaments and Disarmament 1980–1984.* Taylor & Francis. London.

[1] FRG; [2] USA; [3] UK; [4] France; [5] Switzerland; [6] Italy; [7] Netherlands; [8] Spain; [9] Brazil.

Table 5.7
Arms Production in Latin America: Military Vehicles

	Obus Launcher	Heavy Tanks	Light Tanks	Personnel Transports	Middle-Sized Tanks	Infantry Transport	Anti-tanks	Light Cars	Blinded Cars
Argentina	Model 77 155 MM	Nahuel D1-43 Bonanza V-35B	AMX-B(4)	VAB (4) Roland (5)	TAM (1)	VCTP (1)			
Brazil	TM BRA 105 MM	EE TL X-30		EE-11 Urutu	MT-X X1A2 Carcara		EE-17 Sucuri	EE-3 Jararaca	EE-9 Cascavel
Chile				Alacran Carancho Orca Escarabajo Piranha (5)					
Mexico				Azteca Class (3)					DN3 Caballo

Source: Ibid.

Table 5.8
Arms Production in Latin America: Naval Vessels

	Patrol Craft	Transports	Tank Transports	Research Vessels	Frigates	Submarines	Destroyers	Mine Sweepers	Rapid Attack Boats
Argentina	Kebir Class (3)	Costa Sur Class	LST Type C 42	Puerto Deseado	MEKO-40 (1) Type 21 (3)	TR-1700 (1) TR-1400 (1) Sauro Class (6)	Type 42		
Brazil	Anchova Class Itaipu				Bra 82 Niteroi (3)	Type 209/3 (1)		MSC-Bra	PB CHE 77 (2)
Chile			Batral (4)						
Mexico	Azteca (3)								
Peru					Lupo Class (6)				

Source: Ibid.

Notes

1. See CEPAL, 'The transnationals and Latin American foreign trade', LC/1.322, 2 November 1984, Santiago.

2. See Luciano Tomassini, 'The international scene and the Latin American foreign debt', *CEPAL Review*, No. 24, December 1984; Ricardo Ffrench-Davis, 'Debt and external crisis', *Cono Sur*, June–July 1984; Roberto Devlin, 'The renegotiation of the Latin American Foreign Debt', ibid.; Samuel Lichtenstein, 'From stabilizing policies to adjustment policies', in *Economía en América Latina*, No. 11, 1984; Armando Arancibia, 'State and economy facing the present Latin American Crisis', ibid.; Ricardo Ffrench-Davis, 'The foreign debt and development alternatives for Latin America', *Estudios*, CIEPLAN, December 1984; Giles Couture, 'La responsibilité des banques américaines dans le surendettement du tiers monde', *Le Monde Diplomatique*, February 1985.

3. See Lars Schoultz, *Human Rights and United States Policy Towards Latin America*, Princeton University Press, New Jersey, 1981. Different causes have been used to explain the disproportionate flow of foreign finance and its unproductive utilization in the last 10 years. However, all of them are based on the irresponsibility of both the lending banks and the recipient groups in each Latin American country which was ruled by authoritarian regimes at the time those international resources were received.

4. This has been well demonstrated by Alejandro Foxley, *Latin American Experiments in Neo-Conservative Economics*, University of California Press, Berkeley, 1983.

5. See Augusto Varas et al., *Transition to Democracy: Latin America and Chile*, ACHIP-Ainavillo, Santiago, 1984.

6. See Richard Feinberg and Valeriana Kallab (editors), *Uncertain Future: Commercial Banks and the Third World*, Transaction Books, New Brunswick, 1984.

7. See Stanley Please, 'The World Bank: Lending for Structural Adjustment', in Richard Feinberg and Valeriana Kallab, *Adjustment Crisis in the Third World*, Transaction Books, New Brunswick, 1984.

8. Richard E. Feinberg, 'Restoring Confidence in International Credit Markets', in Richard E. Feinberg and Valeriana Kallab (editors), *Uncertain Future: Commercial Banks and the Third World*, op. cit.

9. See Inter-American Dialogue, *The Americas at the Crossroads*, The Wilson Center, Washington, D.C., 1983; and *The Americas in 1984: A Year of Decisions*, Aspen Institute, Washington, D.C., 1984; Riordan Roett, 'Prospect for Atlantic Area Political and Security Relationships in the Wake of Economic Upheaval', presented at the Atlantic Conference of Chicago on Foreign Relations, in Iguazú, Argentina, 8–11 November 1984.

10. *Journal of Commerce*, 7 November 1984.

11. In this respect, see Wolf Grabendorff, 'The Transnationalization of the Central American Crisis', in Wolf Grabendorff, Heinrich W. Krumwiede, and Jorg Todt, *Political Change in Central America: The Internal and External Dimensions*, Westview Press, Boulder, 1984.

12. Kissinger Commission, *Report of the National Bilateral Commission on Central America*, Editorial Diana, Mexico, 1984. These ideas are taken up again in 'Report of the Secretary of Defense Caspar W. Weinberger to the Congress', 1 February 1984. On the relation between political crisis and security in Central America, see José Agustín Silva-Michelena, 'Latin American Peace, Security and Development,' presented in the meeting of the United Nations University, University of Peace, San José, Costa Rica, November 1984.

13. 'US Considers Giving Developing Nations More Military Aid', *New York Times*, 18 November 1984. Also see 'Statement of Stephen W. Bosworth, Principal Deputy Assistant Secretary of State for Interamerican Affairs', *Proposed Transfer of Arms to Uruguay*, US Government Printing Office, Washington, D.C., 1981; and Michael Klare, *American Arms Supermarket*, University of Texas Press, Austin, 1984.

14. See Riordan Roett, 'Latin America's Response to the Debt Crisis', *Third World Quarterly*, Vol. 7, April 1985.

15. See Eugenio Rivera, 'Strategic Consequences of the Latin American External Debt: The Central American Case', presented at the International Studies Association, Washington,

D.C., March 1985. Also see Paul Vinelli, 'Honduras' Economic Development and Productivity', and Ernesto Paz Aguilar, 'Recent Evolution of the Foreign Policy and the National Security Policy of Honduras', both presented to the Conference on Honduras: An International Dialogue, Florida International University, November–December 1984. On military policy in Central America and the Caribbean, see Ricardo Córdova, 'Evaluation of the North American Military Strategy in Central America (1980–1984)'; and Peter Bell, 'The Search for Peace in Central America: To Strengthen Contadora', *Relaciones Internacionales*, 8–9, 1984.

    16. See *El Mercurio*, 19 March 1985.

    17. Daniel Prieto Vial, 'Chilean–Argentinian Military Co-operation.' *El Mercurio*, 14 December 1984.

    18. See United Nations, *The Economic and Social Consequences of the Arms Race and of Military Expenditures*, New York, 1978.

    19. For a discussion of the Brazilian case, see Renato Dagnino, 'O papel do Estado no desenvolvimento e a competitividade das importacoes do sector de armamento brasilero'; Peter Lock, 'Arms production in Brazil'; Clovis Brigagao, *O mercado da segurança*, Editora Nova Fronteira, Rio de Janeiro, 1983; by the same author, *A corrida para a morte*, Editora Nova Fronteira, Rio de Janeiro, 1984; Amilcar Herrera, et al., *O armamentismo e o Brasil: A guerra deles*, Editora Brasiliense, São Paulo, 1985.

    20. See Augusto Varas, 'Demilitarization of the State and Military Democratization: An Alternative Military Policy', *Documento de Trabajo*, FLACSO, Santiago, 1985.

Part II
The State and Conflicts

6. Forms of State, Peace and Security in Latin America

Heinz R. Sonntag

Nature of the State in the Periphery

During the long period of world-wide capitalist expansion which took place between the beginning of the post-World War II period and the end of the 1960s, the role of the State was fundamental, more important than perhaps in any other historical period. This role was manifested, on the one hand, in the greater significance and relevance of its 'traditional' functions, guaranteeing the general productive and reproductive conditions for the relations of capital as a dynamic axis in the organization of men's lives in capitalist society. On the other hand, there emerged new state functions, which demanded the great expansion of that period in two basic respects.

Firstly, as a result of the permanent interventionism which was made necessary by the 1914–45 capitalist crisis which reached its apogee in the Great Depression of the early 1930s, the State became a powerful agent in the economy, and in many social formations it came to be a fraction of capital as a state producer, for example, in Germany, Britain, Italy, etc.

Secondly, the new mechanisms for integrating and controlling of citizens made the State become a more active entity in society, establishing and assuring internal peace and security (for example, mitigating class struggles and contradictions) and, consequently, external security as well. To do this, it not only made use of new legitimation mechanisms but also of other non-traditional forms of language and communication.

In addition, the Great Capitalist Crisis which lasted from 1914 to 1945,[1] and the subsequent expansion caused a transformation in the 'State System' (to use Wallerstein's phrase) which affected each one of the nation states which composed it. The emergence of the Soviet Union initially, and of the whole socialist bloc afterwards, and the establishment of US hegemony in the capitalist bloc caused basic redefinitions of the concepts of internal peace and security in each State. Those redefinitions in practice implied modifications in the behaviour of States with respect to their societies and individual citizens, emphasizing still more its transformations.

In other words, the capitalist State reached its maturity as a 'condensation of a correlation of social forces' (Poulantzas) in each of its concrete historical moments. This resulted in modifications in the forms of States,[2] which often occurred behind an unchanging façade. As an example, consider democracy, which in appearance remained the same as in the previous period but not in its way of operating. It brought about mutations in the political parties and other organizations which served as mediators between the individual citizen and the State. These affected both ideological and structural aspects, where the changes were more obvious than in the forms of the State.

The reason for these changes resided in the new social and economic obligations of the State, as well as in the redefinitions of peace and security which upset the traditional relationship between it and civil society, which had been silently penetrated by the State, or in any case, more than in normal periods of capitalist development. That penetration occurred ideologically in the process of carrying out the State's objectives and those of its favourite form: democracy (the welfare state) and, with it, not as a perturbation of civil society but as its climax. In other words, the anti-communism of the 1950s and the exacerbated consumerism of the 1960s, as transmission belts of the dominant consciousness, camouflaged this invasion and imposed an upside-down perception of reality, since its material substrata, for example, the industrial–military complex and capital's compulsive need to grow, would not have been possible if the State had not assumed its new obligations.

Transformations in the forms of the State, even those which are not quite visible, are always the result of changes in the composition of the dominant forces and social class alliances, according to the previously mentioned definition of Poulantzas. The institutional and constitutional structure of the State and its *modus operandi* are intimately linked to the 'movements' within the social forces and the dynamic of class struggle, especially in the changing requirements of the domination process. This is particularly clear in a period of expansion where there occur important changes in the middle class and its supporting classes. This explains, this time from the point of view of the dynamics of society, the great scale of transformations which occurred in the forms of the capitalist State.

Due to this circumstance, internal peace and security in the developed countries was particularly well cared for during the expansion, at least in comparison with previous periods of capitalism. This guaranteed a growing well-being for broad sectors of the population, and tended to decrease the importance of conditions which at other times had disturbed internal peace and security. In addition, transformations within the dominating classes and the changing alliances with their supporting classes also contributed to mitigate class struggle, becoming more latent than manifest, and therefore eliminating the dangers for peace and security. Finally, even though this might only be in the eyes of the citizens — and therefore subjective — the modifications in the internal nature of the State took away its character as an instrument of class domination and allowed a high degree of identification with it, with large groups adopting the capitalist State ideology and having consequently been oriented by it in their behaviour with respect to it.

External peace and security in the Centre States were assured by the balance of terror which prevented the Cold War from becoming hot. In spite of the emergence and growing strength of the socialist bloc, the global State system acquired characteristics of stability and coexistence, which became known by the name which Khruschev gave it in the late 1950s, peaceful coexistence.

In Latin America, that expansion ensured that, in the majority of social formations, capitalist relations of production became dominant, which created a great change in the structure of society. This happened during the twenty or so years during which the expansionary phase lasted, under the more or less open control of the development-cum-democracy formula. This embodied two of the aspirations of the emerging dominant classes, which were also shared by the theorists of the Economic Commission for Latin America (CEPAL)[3] and other regional and international bodies. On the one hand, they hoped that the conversion of Latin American countries into capitalism would imply a development like that which had been experienced by the societies of the Centre. And on the other hand, they believed this process would work out in such a way that democracy as a state form would become a permanent feature. In this way, both internal peace and security problems would have been solved with the passing of the chronic instability of state forms so characteristic of all the post-independence period of the nations of the continent. In short, the States would come to acquire the nature of the Western societies, and would continuously mature until they reached the most advanced forms of democracy which some of them had progressed towards during the expansion.

As early as the beginning of the world capitalist structural crisis and its first manifestations in the Latin American countries, it was realized, however, that the democratic forms of the State in the Central capitalist social formations were historically specific and not necessarily permanent. Also, that the economic and socio-political evolution in the Latin American peripheral countries had not kept up with the original assumption that development and democracy would go hand in hand. Once again, instability in the forms of the State prevailed in the Latin American political scene. Even if Brazil's 1964 *coup d'etat* could initially be interpreted as the exception to the rule of continental development and Bolivia's periods of military rule as part of the unique idiosyncracy of that country, this was no longer possible after the coups in Argentina, Ecuador, Uruguay, Peru, Panama and Chile, and the new state forms which emerged. The undoubtedly strong economic development of the 1950s and 1960s had not made democracy the prevalent state form, nor had it solved the problems of internal peace and security for the great majority of societies. It had not even been able to avoid serious threats to the external peace and security of several nations. This implied the existence of deeper, structural problems which we have to analyse in order to examine Latin American peace and security in relation to the forms of the State.

The problematic of the underdeveloped countries has been under analysis during approximately the last 40 years. This analysis had for many years an economistic bias based on the simple-minded conviction that economic growth and the modernization of production and distribution would generate development and thereby resolve social and political problems. But in the last 20 years there has been a change in the analyses and an acceptance of a more political point of view. The institutional locus of this new approach was CEPAL; and, as time went by, many other institutions, academic or non-academic, came to share this point of view and accept the ideas of CEPAL.

From the first formulations of the group around Raul Prebisch, there has been a minimum consensus over one undeniable fact: the capitalist system has developed in an unequal manner; the progress generated in the countries of endogenous capitalist development did not spread throughout the entire world (as postulated by the classical theories of foreign trade put forward by Adam Smith and, above all, by Ricardo). Two clearly differentiated poles had been generated in the system: the Centre and the Periphery. This new consensus implied acknowledging the existence of an international division of labour whose dynamic was determined by the economies of the Centre, which only granted the countries of the Periphery a subordinate place in the *structure* of the system. This subordinate place permeated and determined the internal economic and social relations of the Periphery countries and prevented them from reaching the developed position of Centre countries.[4]

Consequently, from early on, the notion of dependency played a very important role in research and reflections. For CEPAL it was merely a case of external dependency. This was characterized by the fact that the Periphery countries depend on the Centre countries in order to sell their products and increase their capital. At the same time, they have to import from the Centre manufactured and capital goods (including technological knowhow).

In the mid 1960s the dependency approach appeared[5] and defined this situation as structural dependency. In other words, dependency is not only a relation of economic and political domination externally exercised by the Centre countries. It is also deeply established within the structures of the Periphery countries in such a way that these countries reproduce it in their activity. Consequently, the agents of dependency are collective actors within the dependent countries, classes and class fractions which mobilize structures, including economic structures, in pursuit of their interests and by means of a system of domination. Their interests are determined in alliance with the dominant classes of the Centre countries.

With this new definition of the concept of dependency, the emphasis of analyses was transferred to the domination systems themselves and their collective actors, namely, social classes. This gave way later to the first attempts to conceptualize the nature of the capitalist Periphery state, an analysis which has been considerably extended during the last ten years.

At the risk of generalizing from the point of view of the *whole* of the Periphery rather than emphasizing the *diversity* of the concrete situations of underdevelopment and dependency, it can be said that peripheral capitalism is characterized by two intimately related facts. One is its dependence on the world system for its reproduction and functioning. In other words, the mode of production of structures in the Periphery is determined by the dynamic of the world system which, in turn, is determined by that of the Centre countries. This is particularly true for the economic structures, generating 'extroverted' (Samir Amin) or 'bidirectional' (Sonntag) capitalist accumulation. It means that one part of the surplus created flows towards the Centre countries, and this 'extroverted' accumulation predominates over the 'inner' accumulation, subordinating it to its rhythm and volume.

The other fact which charaterizes peripheral capitalism is structural heterogeneity. This means the coexistence of social relations of production and forms of labour organization belonging to different modes of production. Wage labour exists side by side with other diverse forms of labour, often stemming from small-scale mercantile production. As the capitalist development of the peripheral economies increases, due to changes in the international division of labour and these economies' changing positions within it, so typical capitalist relations and forms of organization begin to prevail. But this does not mean that the other relations and organizational forms disappear. It merely means that they are subordinated to the capitalist ones, which put them at the service of the particular operational rationality of peripheral capitalism.

Both facts make the economic sphere particularly weak in relation to the global reproduction of society. In the conditions of Centre capitalism, control over some of the important mechanisms of society reside in the economic 'instance', or sphere, precisely because accumulation is 'self-centred' (Samir Amin) or 'unidirectional' (Sonntag) and the social relations of production and organizational forms tend to become homogeneous.[6] Under these circumstances the State complements the economic control mechanisms. This role can increase in situations of crisis and generate new state forms, as it did after the Great Depression. However, the evolution of the State in the societies of the Centre is 'normal' and parallel to that of the economy. This means that the changes occur behind a façade of relative stability; in other words, changes *in* and not *of* the state forms.[7]

The weakness of the economic sector as a determinant in peripheral capitalism cannot be overcome except through strengthening the State (or the political instance of which it is expression). As a consequence of this weakness, the global society's mechanisms of control have to operate at a political level. That is why the State is internally strong in peripheral social formations and solutions to all conflicts are channelled through it. Precisely because of that power of the State, it is almost impossible to maintain a determinate form of it. It is the State of peripheral capitalist formations, the 'State of permanent exception' (Sonntag, Evers).

This argument is also relevant to understanding the collective actors, that is to say, the social classes (particularly the dominant classes). Each of them has to penetrate the State in order to make the control mechanisms function according to their interests. The class struggle, or the struggle of any class fraction for hegemony, becomes a struggle for the State, and modifies its form. Usually it is not enough to make limited changes in the form of the State, but necessary to change that form more fundamentally. In other words, precisely because the State is in each historical moment the condensation of a correlation of social forces, a change in that correlation imposes a change in the form of the State, given the conditions of peripheral capitalism and the weakness of the economic sphere to regulate social life. Only in rare historical circumstances due to special circumstances of the moment, is a limited change in its forms sufficient.[8]

According to the dependency approach, dependency reproduces itself in the underdeveloped countries through the system of internal domination, and not merely as a reflection of imperialist domination exercised by the particular hegemonic Central State acting on behalf of the whole global system of States at any one moment. The system of domination is the arena where political struggles take place to build alliances which allow a class or fraction of a class to achieve hegemony. Hegemony cannot be practised if it does not extend to the State. Dependency and structural heterogeneity cause internal heterogeneity in classes in a way that is often difficult to establish, for example, a consensus between the different fractions of the dominant classes respecting the overall project of society. The fulfilment of specific class interests is subordinated to the changing internal material conditions which result from the functioning of the international division of labour. As we tried to show before, it is only possible to manage these conditions if the State is the main regulator of life in society.

Before concluding this point by looking at the consequences for internal and external peace and security, one other thing must be said. The more or less prolonged existence of a particular form of State regime confirms in the case of dictatorships, what has been said. When it is the democratic representative form of State which survives, it is possible that, behind the façade of permanence, there do occur changes in the form of the State. It would be interesting to clarify this point through empirical research in the four Latin American peripheral States which are democratic — Colombia, Costa Rica, Mexico and Venezuela. In any case, the survival of representative democracy (even though formal) as the form of a State demands very specific conditions which are often directly related to the State's role as regulator of social life (and its resulting 'persuasive capacity' in the class struggle for hegemony).

Internal peace and security of the individual citizen in such regimes are almost exclusively guaranteed by the State. But since the State changes with relative frequency its form of regime, the maintenance of that peace and security becomes rather arbitrary. This is because in each form of State, peace and security are defined in a different way. Besides, in some forms of State they tend to be conceptualized in ways contrary to the interests of citizens when this suits the social force which has imposed its hegemony. This has obvious consequences for the relation between State and the civil society.

Turning to external peace and security, these are guaranteed exclusively by the State. Its capacity to maintain them seems rather small, however, owing to the subordinate position which it occupies in the system of States, in spite of each State's formal independence. This also has its structural causes. The dynamic of 'bidirectional' or 'extroverted' accumulation which makes the State in peripheral countries the regulator of internal social life, makes it its keeper abroad.

The Collapse of Old Models and Implications for the State

The evolution of Latin American social formations in the last six decades provides practical illustrations of what has just been argued.

The analysis, however superficial and abridged, cannot be limited to the expansive phase of capitalism on a world level, and its repercussions on Latin America. During the Great Crisis (1914–45), there also occurred processes similar to those which followed in the post-war period. The Crisis destroyed the basis of an export system oriented to primary products in the majority of peripheral societies owing to the transformations which were taking place in the international division of labour. Some of them embarked on an industrialization process relying on import substitution. This went quite a long way in those countries which experimented with it for several years (Argentina, Brazil, Chile, Mexico, Uruguay). Others had only just started and still a third group of Latin American countries only began much later, owing to their particular structural place in the international division of labour. The process of industrialization via import substitution implied changes in class structures, both the dominant and the dominated classes, and therefore the system of class domination. The political power of the traditional land-owning oligarchy was broken more or less decisively and that of the commercial (import–export) middle class decreased. There emerged new fractions in the midst of the dominant classes; these middle sectors increased in numbers and power. And those proletarian groups organized in political parties and trade unions also entered the political scene. The subsequent struggles within the system of domination led to changes in the forms of the State, in particular the emergence of the populist and nationalist state (*Portantiero*), camouflaged as representative or plebiscitary democracies.

The same thing happened twenty years later, when the economic strategy of these countries became a model approved of by CEPAL and was applied in almost all the countries of the continent. In this way import-substitution industrialization, which had started as a consequence of changes in the international division of labour system, was converted into a project for the whole Latin American continent, and generated the same transformations in class structures and forms of the States as had occurred in the original countries. During the 1950s and 1960s the struggles within the system of domination led to the establishment of representative democracies as forms of the State in many Latin American countries. In this sense, the hopes placed on the development-cum-democracy 'double act' were apparently being fulfilled.

There is no doubt that internal peace and security for individual citizens were particularly well assured under this form of State. The fact that representative democracy (and its plebiscitary forms as well) was the typical form of national populist State implied that the class alliance which underpinned it was able to offer the subordinate sectors a certain degree of economic well-being and political participation, conditions which are the material basis for internal peace and security.

From the point of view of external peace and security, the structural weakness of the State together with US hegemony over the system as a whole explains why Latin American countries abided by the security system proclaimed by imperialist post-war policy with its premise of anti-communism. Later, as we will see, a new concept of external security, which came to be formulated in the struggle against insurgency, was adopted and eventually led to state terrorism. This, however, produced a certain resistance in some Latin American armies, leading to a new relationship between security and economic and political development.

However, the economic development which was taking place in Latin American peripheral societies was not able to eliminate the circumstances which had made these countries 'permanent states of exception'. Neither the reproductive dependence of the economy on fluctuations in the world system nor its structural heterogeneity could be overcome. Moreover, as the import-substitution strategy advanced, those features became stronger. The reason was simple: this project was inscribed within the changes that had occurred in the international division of labour which in practice had been responsible for its implantation in the first place. In this way the project was carried out with the growing participation of foreign capital, free from any conditions being placed upon it, and also implied the maintenance of increasingly important non-capitalist relations of production and forms of social organization, even though these were subordinate to and had their place prescribed by capitalist ones. Consequently, the state remained the *locus* of social regulation since the persistence of the 'bidirectional' accumulation model maintained the weakness of the economic factor as regulator of life in society.

With the passage of time, euphoria over the development-cum-democracy model made it possible to forget the reality of the structure of peripheral capitalism. But sooner or later it had to materialize itself again in changes in the forms of the State so well known from previous periods in its development. These changes had to occur to the extent that the import-substitution industrialization model did not resolve the contradiction inherent in peripheral capitalism.

It was not a coincidence, therefore, that the euphoria was first shattered in Brazil with the 1964 *coup d'etat*. In that country import-substitution industrialization had advanced more than in most other Latin American societies, in part because it had started there earlier. It has also had a socio-political history, albeit not without accidents, marked by a rather long period of democracy which was an expression of the national popular nature of the State. Therefore the changes implied for class structures by the new trans-nationalization of industrialization model were felt earlier in the struggles within the system of domination in Brazil. This led to the rupture of the democratic form of the State and the installation of a regime that became in the end the epitome of what some scholars called 'technocratic–authoritarian'.

For the other Latin American peripheral societies (with the exception of those which maintained patrimonial forms of State such as Nicaragua and Paraguay), the internal and world economic crisis precipitated changes in state forms at a moment which did not correspond to their degree of transnationalization and the installation in each of them of the import-substitution model. With the exceptions of Colombia, Costa Rica, Mexico and Venezuela,[9] the countries which maintained a democratic–representative form of State seem to confirm the rule, since behind the appearance of maintaining the form there occurred in the 1970s highly significant changes within it. In almost all the countries of the region, there occurred a process of 'expropriation of decisions on public affairs'[10] through the transformation of the forms of the State which reaffirmed the characteristics of the State of permanent exception of peripheral capitalism.

In all the social formations, the transformation in the forms of the State signified a serious threat to the internal peace and security of individual citizens. This threat was expressed in different forms: State terrorism in Argentina after 1976, the minimal protection afforded to the classes exploited by the State in Chile after 1973, and the attempt to install fascism in Bolivia with Banzer's military coup in 1971. All these transformations had a common denominator, even where they attempted a modernization of society and promoted development processes geared to greater equality (as did the dictatorship of Velasco Alvarado in Peru and Torrijos in Panama). This common denominator was a new conceptualization of internal peace and security. In other words, when talking of internal peace and security, the focus became not the individual citizens but the State itself.

The new period did not herald significant changes in notions of *external* peace and security, and the place of Latin American peripheral countries in the global system of States remained largely unchanged. There were isolated attempts to defend Latin America's external peace and security more effectively through the constitution of movements of underdeveloped nations in order to be able to promote more powerfully their common interests *vis-á-vis* the system's hegemonic powers. There also occurred occasional and temporary affiliations to a Third World movement in order better to defend the economic and political sovereignty of peripheral societies. All this, however, did not lead to greater independence, even though it did lead to a stronger awareness among some social sectors and political organizations of the importance of the issue. In any case, the United States tried to impose its hegemony once again, with the political support of some other Centre States. The return to bilateralism in the 1980s from the multilateralism of the 1970s eloquently confirms this.

In the present decade so far, there have occurred new processes of democratization in some countries of the region. This certainly does not mean that the structural circumstances which caused the state of permanent exception to be typical of peripheral capitalism have been overcome. It means that, owing to the crisis, there have occurred important changes in the class structures and the forms of struggle in the political system. I believe that it is too soon to prognosticate on the future of democracy in Latin America and, therefore, on the prospects for internal peace and security of the individual citizen. I also believe that it is indispensable to deepen our analyses of the changes occurring in our societies in order to discover the dynamic which may make life more peaceful and secure in the Latin American peripheral social formations. I haven't the least doubt that the State plays a very important role, provided we are able to make it more efficient and put it at the service of the great majority. It is in this sense that democracy, probably a new democracy which implies a total transparency in decision-making processes, must be the objective of our theoretical and practical struggles, even in the conditions of peripheral capitalism, so that we may overcome the structural circumstances which are so dangerous for the internal and external peace and security of our societies.

Notes

1. For those who use the concept of crisis in an apocalyptic or fatalist sense, the results of that crisis should be revealing. It should teach them that the crises of society in capitalism are more or less prolonged periods of modifications and adjustments in the structures and mechanisms of the social system. Only if these readjustments fail does the social system tend radically to change its structures. In other cases, and certainly the immense majority of the crises up to now, the social system remains the same and takes on new expansive force.

2. A current of contemporary political science has tried to conceptualize the transformations referred to with the notion of mass democracy which places importance on their substance, unless referring to the existing dialectic between what is quantitative and what is qualitative.

3. Acknowledgement of the relative failure of the CEPAL proposals by these same theorists has meant that today, once again, CEPAL plays an important role in the discussions of Latin American development, as does the new body, SELA, since its creation in 1975.

4. As can be seen, I am making a very brief summary which does not take into account the political propositions contained in CEPAL's line of thought. The reason for this is my interest in pointing out a certain continuity in the reflections on development.

5. I don't want to discuss here whether it constituted merely a new methodological approach to the development problematic, or was a full blown new theory of dependence, namely a coherent body of concepts and assertions.

6. It is clear that most of the time they are not so homogeneous, but the existence of other relations and forms is marginal and doesn't have as high a quantitative or qualitative importance as in peripheral capitalist social formations.

7. The rise of fascism in Italy and national socialism in Germany constitutes the exception to the rule and corresponds with very particular characteristics of the capitalist development of those social formations, on which I cannot elaborate in this work.

8. This is the case of the more or less prolonged permanence of a form of State as a representative of democracy. I will come back on this point.

9. For reasons of space, I cannot enter into details respecting those changes. However, some symptoms were the permanence of the state of emergency in Colombia, the new attempts at militarization in Costa Rica, and State modifications by Echeverría and De la Madrid in Mexico.

10. This happy expression was used by Augusto Varas when discussing my suggestion during the Seminar in Costa Rica.

7. The Impact of the World Crisis on Geopolitical Conflicts

Edgardo Mercado Jarrín

The need to think about the impact of the world economic crisis on Latin American peace and security is more urgent every day, particularly since there is no agreement about the regional crisis and Latin America is the only continent which does not have a regional instrument of co-ordination where essentially Latin American matters can be discussed outside the inter-American context.

Here we will analyse the impact of the crisis on geopolitical conflicts; notably the role of Latin America in a world context; the specific forms taken by the disputes; the significance of Latin American conflicts in terms of a possible indirect confrontation between the Super Powers; and the relation between economic crisis, political vulnerability, military dependency and its impact on strategic considerations.

The Geopolitical Role of Latin America in a World Context

Geopolitically Latin America forms part of the southern hemisphere, the Periphery, the underdeveloped world, the poor countries. Latin America does not have the basic elements which contribute to powerful international status, including the necessary military resources. Nevertheless, in today's world, influence does not come only from power, but also from economic, social, political and psychological factors, as well as the ability to influence the conduct of other spheres. Latin America makes up part of the Third World and, as such, will demand international justice together with those countries and will react against the prevailing pressures of the world's dominant power centres. This attitude and co-ordination with other Third World countries becomes more urgent as a result of the crisis which the continent is undergoing.

At the same time, Latin America belongs to the western hemisphere, is located within the USA's sphere of influence, and together with it constitutes the inter-American system which has the OAS as its organ, but which also includes a series of other treaties and agreements. The system constitutes in economic, social, political and military matters the field of multilateral relations between Latin America and the United States. At present the OAS is going through a critical stage due to its having been largely excluded from the process of seeking solutions to the problem of the debt. Also, it has not been able to become an instrument of moderation of North American political power, as was shown in the crisis of the Malvinas (Falklands) and the present Central American crisis.

Geopolitically and strategically, Latin America is situated in a dual position: as part of the Third World and as part of the inter-American system. This puts it in a complex international position. But it does not imply that it has to accept an unjust international order which the Great Powers perpetuate. Beyond geopolitical considerations and relations deriving from the systems and spheres of interest particular countries form part of, their positions are the result of their internal situations.

Latin America is one of the main actors in the present North–South conflict because, in spite of its growing foreign debt, the region has an even greater potential for growth than the rest of the South due to its mineral, forest, water and energy resources. Its population is rapidly growing and is already more than 360 million people. Its combined GNP exceeds 600 billion dollars, which is large enough to ensure it plays a significant role in the future development of the Periphery. Besides, Latin America, unlike South Asia or Africa, has a predominantly Western culture. Its dual position does not only make it a principal actor in the North–South context, but also, as a nexus between the Third World and the dominant world, it should serve as a bridge between the Third and the First and Second Worlds.

Its socio-economic structure and state of development make Latin America part of the Third World. On the other hand, its geographic and geopolitical situation locate it within the Inter-American system and place it in the direct security area of one of the Super Powers. This dual situation makes our region have peculiar characteristics since it is in a position where it would be actively affected by conflicts in the present quadripolar world: the First World, Second World, Third World, and People's Republic of China. Latin America is drawn into the two principal confrontations currently possible: the classic bipolar East–West conflict (the US v. the USSR) which entails a possibly violent use of power; and the new North–South conflict between the industrialized countries — rich nations — and the developing countries — poor nations, where the conflict implies only a peaceful use of power. The fact is that belonging to different fields in both confrontations causes a great part of the contradictions and paradoxes which we see in the daily politics of our countries. At the same time, this contradiction affects the strategic position of the Inter-American system in a global situation where the United States is the dominant power, but whose hegemony is continuously decreasing.

From the point of view of international politics and the world context, the principal Latin American characteristic during this century has been its geopolitical marginality. The region does not have any influence on international affairs. The technological progress of the Great Powers in the military field, despite its accompanying and growing economic and social crisis, have also made Latin America lose any global relevance.

However, today, and to a great extent due to the new North American conflict strategy, there now arise new factors which make Latin America's strategic role more important again. These factors include its mineral resources, the importance of its maritime communications, and the active Soviet presence in the oceans around it. In the event of conflict between the Super Powers, these factors will make the region more important as a provider of raw materials to the United States.

Nevertheless, Latin America continues to be regarded as unimportant by US public opinion. President Reagan's declarations, as well as those of the press, are directed exclusively towards the Central American crisis, though even this problem in relation to the others is less important. The geopolitical reality, as a result, is that Latin America is a continent located in the southern hemisphere and its strategic importance is marginal since world affairs revolve around the East–West conflict.

To maintain this geopolitical marginality and in order to subordinate Latin America to its global strategy, the United States regards it as necessary to prevent regional concertation by Latin America as a whole, emphasizing instead a bilateral policy towards each country as a separate entity. Such bilateral negotiations make possible a careful gradation of incentives or coercive threats which lead to immediate results. Bilateral relations give the US a large degree of flexibility in its regional foreign policy. In this way, for example, it managed for a long time to postpone approval of the revised Contadora Treaty. The US also refused to accept the collective criteria proposed at Cartagena for the treatment of the foreign debt and instead promoted separate refinancing agreements for the Mexican, Venezuelan and Argentinian debts, and later Brazil's. The situation would be different if relations were formulated between the United States and the region as a whole in a coherent and multilateral way.

Therefore, the evolution of the region towards playing an effective and unbiased geopolitical role in the consolidation and maintenance of world peace and security will not be an easy task. Certain powerful sectors of US society still believe that Latin America is their hinterland. The elites, the transnationals and the monopolistic circles will persist in using their influence to weaken the process of Latin American integration and the strengthening of institutions which incarnate the regional idea. They will try to focus US relations on the petroleum-producing or key countries. But in the next century, Latin America's growing regional capacity in the international sphere, in the mobilization of resources and the solution of global problems — that is to say, in its new geopolitical role as 'bridge' — will render Twentieth Century neo-colonialism obsolete and direct interventionism difficult if not impossible.

Our countries have a cohesive power which propels them into the world, to feel and act daily as members of a region. This vitality may come both from its relative geographic isolation — 3,000 miles to the West and 6,000 miles to the East of other continents, and its nearness to a hegemonic power. Today that potential strength is increased by a unique factor: the pressure of the enormous foreign debt and of the economic crisis and the struggle for a New International Economic Order. If this cohesive force is adequately handled in the interactions generated by Latin America's dual situation (being within the US security zone and part of the Third World), its regional position and geopolitical role will become stronger. As a consequnce of this dual situation geopolitically, the continent can constitute on the one hand a 'bridge' across which the interchange of new economic and political relations flow, and on the other, a 'barrier' facing up to the pressures from the US with its immense concentration of military and economic power.

In this prospect of the consolidation of the region, there do not appear to be obstacles such as its geopolitical location, ideological differences, or particular local conflicts. Nevertheless, in Latin America's relations with the rest of the world in recent years — for example, the Malvinas (Falklands), Grenada, the Central American crisis, and the foreign debt — there has not prevailed a common sense of purpose overriding local differences. But an agreed Latin American foreign policy over the debt and the North–South dialogue would guarantee the value of the region to the world in the coming decades and so its geopolitical role.

But in order to reverse the tendency to international marginality and ensure its geopolitical role, it is necessary that the Latin American countries take the regional 'scenario' more seriously. The truth is that it hasn't happened that way. Above all, it is necessary to find a way to project a geopolitical presence through concerting policy on a regional basis. We have to face together neocolonialism, dependency and unequal exchange, and reach the objectives of peace, security and development.

An important step would be the constitution of a new co-ordination mechanism based on a Council of Foreign Affairs Secretaries, including Cuba. This would be separate from the OAS which would continue to carry out its functions. The new Council could also take advantage of the infrastructure of the Economic Council for Latin America (SELA). It would meet annually or, in case of emergency, when requested by a member country. The economic and social crises which Latin America is going through emphasize the need for new machinery like this. What is essentially regional should be treated separately from the whole of Inter-American affairs.

On the occasion of the crisis of the Malvinas (Falklands), Latin America lost an opportunity to institutionalize this mechanism. Another occasion which was not taken advantage of was the Central American crisis, which was eventually dealt with only by the sub-regional countries which make up Contadora. We should not waste the new impetus to solidarity generated by the tensions of the foreign debt. The blindness of the international banking system is causing serious injury to Latin America's economies. We need to take advantage of this to create this mechanism which will, through concertation, give us a greater bargaining capacity, strengthen the region as a whole, as well as our capacity to take a common position when needed in the OAS, the Group of 77, the Non-Aligned Movement, the UN General Assembly and in international forums generally. Furthermore, we are the only region which lacks a mechanism of co-ordination. Africa, the Arab League, South East Asia, the Islamic countries — each has a mechanism of this nature. We Latin Americans have an obligation to forge our own destiny.

Specific Forms Taken by Frontier Disputes

At present in Latin America there exist a series of different conflicts: territorial conflicts, the product of the ways in which we achieved our independence after European rule; conflicts between democracies and dictatorships, liberal and totalitarian political organizations, civilian and military governments; conflicts over resources; and conflicts which arise fundamentally from the struggle for hegemony. If we wanted to simplify, we could point out that in Latin America there are two types of conflict: structural conflicts, deriving from antagonistic interests, which can lead to military confrontations; and circumstantial conflicts, arising from differences in ideological and political system, and often from struggles for hegemony, which only in exceptional circumstances lead to military confrontations.

We will turn now to analyse specific conflicts in the South American Caribbean Basin, the Southern Cone, and the frontier disputes between Argentina and Brazil.

South American Conflicts in the Caribbean Basin

In the last decade Venezuela has become a geopolitically besieged country owing to its location with respect to Central America and the Caribbean Basin which makes it participate in its tensions as well as its own conflicts with Colombia and Guyana.

When the tensions with Guyana increased in 1970, a document called the Protocol of Port of Spain was signed which froze negotiations for twelve years. When the Protocol expired, it was denounced by the Government of Venezuela. The most critical moment came when the then President of Venezuela, Herrera Campins, declared that Venezuelan aspirations over Guyana's Ezequibo region were irrevocable. At the same time, the Prime Minister of Guyana, Forbes Burnham, stated publicly that the Venezuelan claims were without foundation.

The denunciation of the Protocol of Port of Spain coincided with the Falklands crisis, and it is possible that Venezuelan public opinion thought that a successful Argentinian military action to recover the Falklands would create a precedent for what could happen if there was a Venezuelan offensive against Guyana.

The problem of the Ezequibo is basically one of resources. Guyana is the richest zone in South America. In the territories in dispute there exist unknown amounts of oil, diamonds and gold, hydroelectric possibilities, and above all huge forest resources. If we also take into account that it is located on the Caribbean Basin, we have a clear notion of why the conflict is a serious one.

It is important to point out that from the very moment the possibility of conflict arose, the policy of Guyana has been based on winning time and international support. It became a key Latin American country in the Non-Aligned Movement, and even tried unsuccessfully to block Venezuelan entry to the movement. Guyana's relations with Cuba and Brazil also make up part of its game of political chess.

In accordance with the Geneva Agreement, the case has been put in the hands of the UN Secretary-General so that he may suggest one of the methods which the Charter prescribes for the peaceful solution of the controversy. The situation clearly favours negotiation.

Another conflict of a structural nature is that between Venezuela and Colombia in the Lake Maracaibo region. It is a territorial conflict for resources, control over a great oil basin and access to the Lake which is Venezuela's principal source of hydrocarbon resources. The area in contention covers 500 square miles across Guajira Peninsula between the Gulf of Venezuela and the Caribbean. For thirteen years conversations have taken place in Rome, and eventually have arrived at a formula. This formula establishes the median line of Lake Maracaibo as the frontier between the two countries. Former President Caldera at that point argued that it would be imprudent to expose the country to two sets of boundary negotiations, and so proceeded to freeze negotiations with Guyana.

President Herrera, facing an overwhelmingly hostile public opinion, consulted the armed forces in the Military Academy in Caracas where officers unanimously voted against the formula. Consequently, the Venezuelan Government rejected it and the situation has become even more tense. The Colombian government has announced its decision to take the matter to arbitration.

It is worth recalling that Colombia is probably the Latin American country which spends the lowest percentage of its GNP on the purchase of armaments. Colombia and Brazil each spend perhaps 1.5% of their GNP on arms although that situation seems to be changing now. Colombia has started to strengthen its naval forces. It has purchased German 209-type submarines, is buying missile frigates, and for the first time we are witnessing an arms race between Venezuela and Colombia because of this conflict.

Now Dr Jaime Lusinchi is the President of Venezuela. He has announced his intention to renew conversations with President Betancur, pointing out that 'the difference should never be the difference which separate the two countries'.

For the Reagan Administration, since the two countries are situated in the Caribbean Basin, the most important and conflict-prone region in Latin America, this conflict between Colombia and Venezuela is seen as much more important than those which could occur in the Southern Cone. Since each time there is a military conflict in the underdeveloped world, it becomes a confrontation between the Super Powers, the United States will use its 'silent diplomacy' to avoid these disagreements becoming a new threat to its peace and security requirements in the area. Moreover, the idea that the aggravation of the crisis could bring about the regionalization of the conflicts in the Caribbean Basin, and its contradiction with the fact that Venezuela and Colombia are acting in agreement to bring peace to Central America, makes for the moment militarization of these conflicts remote. In other words, for the two countries there is no alternative but peace.

The specific form, therefore, by which the disputes between Venezuela and

Guyana and Venezuela and Colombia will be settled is through diplomatic channels, relying on international law and negotiation.

Political Changes in the Southern Cone and the Specific Forms Acquired by Frontier Disputes
It seems that 1985 looked like being a year with geopolitical changes in the alignment of the forces of the Southern Cone countries which could be interpreted as the eventual emergence of antagonistic pressures in relations between Peru, Chile and Bolivia, and Peru and Ecuador.

Chile and Argentina entered a new phase in their relations when they at last ended the Beagle Channel dispute as a result of the mediation of the Pope. Paradoxically, the signing of the Peace Treaty, through which the islands became a part of Chile, was one consequence of the War of the Falklands (Malvinas). This was a paradox because the strategic value of the southern channel is directly related to the importance given to them by those who are vitally interested in them, in this case, Great Britain, since now it is settled in the Falklands (Malvinas). Historically, the British interest in Chile has been of a geopolitical nature: to assure its flank in the Straits of Magellan. That explains why in this case Britain has applied a policy which is known nowadays as a sphere of interest policy. Given this strategic Falklands (Malvinas)/Southern Passages nexus, British naval power in the Southern Atlantic will increase and *pari passu* weaken the Argentinian military position.

The areas of ocean in dispute (Beagle and Cape Horn) are particularly important for Argentina after the British occupation of the Falklands (Malvinas) eventually ends. Strategically, losing the exterior circumscribing line — Falklands (Malvinas), the Georgias, Sandwich Island, through which the Drake Pass, the Straits of Magellan and the Beagle Channel are controlled — would, as a consequence of the Treaty, add to the loss of the interior line — made up of the three island hammer, the Pineton, Nueva and Lenox, and other islands close to Cape Horn which close off access to the Beagle Channel. This would neutralize the Argentinian military base at Ushuaia. There are, of course, other considerations — natural resources and the relevance of the area to future, more extensive claims to Antarctica.

The fall of the Chilean military government, as a result of opposition pressure, has to be because the armed forces decide to retire from the political scene. Therefore the solution of the Beagle Channel dispute became a new unifying factor for the armed forces and Pinochet, and worked to the disadvantage of political sectors seeking an end to the military regime.

The Treaty cannot be seen as consequence of the world crisis; but of Argentina's geopolitical position in its conflict with Great Britain. The fact that Argentina has technically not put an end to hostilities over the Malvinas obliges Brazil and Uruguay to keep their doors closed to supplies destined for the British fleet in the Falklands. This lengthens the British line of military communications and distorts British participation in NATO. Since Argentina has now liberated itself from its conflict with Chile, it will be able to broaden its strategy in the political, economic and military fields to force Great Britain to sit down at the negotiating table. Besides, it will let it extend *sine die* its position not to declare a ceasefire, which will keep alive the Latin American solidarity which began as a result of the conflict over the Falklands.

The specific results of the Treaty, for both Chileans and Argentinians, are peace, friendship and integration. Peace is being moulded and friendship is its immediate consequence. Peace is much more than the absence of belligerency. Without a doubt, integration will be the tangible consequence of the Treaty and will soon be evident in numerous joint programmes which will encourage bilateral relations between the two countries bound together by 4,500 kilometres of common frontiers.

As for the realignment of forces, the end of this long-lasting conflict will help Chile come out of its international isolation. Its recently increased military potential will begin to be free of worries about its Peruvian–Bolivian rear; its diplomacy will be left with greater room for manoeuvre to handle the problem of Bolivia, without hurting its security interests elsewhere. As for Argentina, having resolved its problem with Chile, it will return to its traditional Atlantic orientation, stimulated by its dispute with Great Britain. Relations with Peru and Bolivia will stop having the importance they have had in recent years. And it will not be difficult, in spite of the recent Peruvian support during the Falkland Crisis, for it to choose the same alternative as in the War of the Pacific in the last century.

Within this international context, the President of Colombia, Belisario Betancur, echoing a recommendation of the OAS, proposed promoting a reconciliation between the governments of Chile and Bolivia in order to find a feasible and definite solution to the problem of Bolivia's landlocked position. It is pertinent to point out the fact that for the first time in Chilean diplomacy it has accepted the OAS intervention; previously, it has always held to a position of an exclusively bilateral solution to the conflict. The strengthening of its geopolitical position, which until recently had been preoccupied by Beagle Channel conflicts, has permitted this gesture and opened the way to others.

After the Chilean–Bolivian conversations which took place in 1975, Bolivia, Chile and Peru revealed, for the first time since the Treaty of 1929, their real strategic intentions on the problem of Bolivia's mediterraneaty. These are:

* Bolivia aspires to an outlet to the sea through territories which once were Peruvian, without any territorial compensation.

* Chile is willing to cede a passage north of Arica on condition that it receives territorial compensation. In terms of the previous agreement prescribed by the Treaty of 1929, Peru, according to Chile, only has the right to say simply yes or no.

* Peru accepts Bolivia's maritime access north of Arica on the condition of a real presence in Arica. For Peru, the previous agreement presupposes a much broader participation for it than mere acceptance or rejection.

The strategic interests of the three countries are evidently counterposed: Bolivia continues to seek possible formulae which would resolve its problem and its relations with the two countries concerned oscillate from the Peruvian side to the Chilean in pursuit of its objective of an outlet to sea.

Turning to yet another conflict, the differences between Peru and Ecuador, Peru bases itself on the Protocol of Rio de Janeiro and its application by the guarantors, while the Ecuadorian position is unilateral and not enough to invalidate the Treaty of Limits.

The Chilean–Argentinian settlement and the beginning of negotiations between Chile and Bolivia could have direct consequences for Ecuadorian strategy towards Peru. Ecuador continues to challenge the 1942 Protocol of Rio, which is accepted by the international community, and is carrying out an offensive policy of unilaterally disregarding the Treaty.

Due to the particular forms taken by frontier disputes in recent years, the possibility of international conflicts arises out of the antagonistic interests of Peru, Bolivia and Chile, and Peru and Ecuador. Meanwhile Colombia continues to promote an agreement between Chile and Bolivia different from that which is stipulated in the Chilean–Peruvian Treaty of 1929. But this proposal should not be discarded prematurely.

In any case, it is necessary to keep the dangers of an armed conflict at a distance, preventing the formation of an international focus of tension. Since the days of independence, Peru has been the centre of American unity. Many new initiatives can be taken to this end, such as taking up once again the proposal of the Declaration of Ayacucho to re-initiate Latin American meetings on the reduction of arms spending. It would be also good to take advantage of President Betancur's peaceable spirit and, just as he was able to get Chile and Bolivia to sit down at the negotiating table, he could try to do the same thing with Ecuador, encouraging it to talk with Peru so that new machinery be formulated within the Terms of the Protocol to allow the placing of those boundary posts which are still lacking. Peru could make the concessions in Article 6 and facilitate the free navigation of the Amazon rivers. Finally, a negotiated solution between the three countries over Bolivia's desire for a port is more feasible now than 30 years ago.

Changes in Relations between Argentina and Brazil

In the past, relations between Argentina and Brazil have been upset by competition for pre-eminence in the Southern Atlantic, and the struggle for control over certain natural resources rather than by frontier disputes *per se*. The need for an agreed position over payment of the foreign debt, which so affects these countries, ought to put an end to these conflicts and pave the way to closer ties between the two countries. The old struggle for hegemony in the Southern Atlantic derived from the different positions which the two countries adopted over the possibility of organizing a military alliance similar to NATO for its defence. The projected South Atlantic Treaty Organisation, SATO, would be constituted by Argentina, Brazil, Uruguay and South Africa. Brazil was not, and is not, interested in this alliance because its Northeast projection puts it in a better position to close the great funnel between itself and Dakar in Senegal and which opens up to form the immense stretch of ocean between Cape Horn and the Cape of Good Hope. Also, geopolitically, Brazil's economic frontiers are in Africa and it is not good for its interests to work hand in glove with a country like South Africa where Africans consider the only way to put an end to white domination is armed struggle. On the other hand, Argentina looked on the idea of SATO favourably because it considered that the defence of its own seas was inseparable from the defence of the Southern Atlantic as a whole.

When the British occupation of the Falklands originally occurred, the Ascension–Falkland Islands axis became the geopolitical backbone of British domination of the South Atlantic. The ocean became a new Anglo-Saxon Mare Nostrum, and therefore temporarily put an end to any hegemonic pretensions and possible conflict between Argentina and Brazil over this vast area of water.

As for conflicts over natural resources, these have focused on the struggle for Bolivian resources (tin, gas, petroleum, etc.), and Paraguay's Paraná Basin with its hydroelectric potential. This was the scene of historical competition between Argentina and Brazil. Mario Travasos, in his book *Brazil's Continental Projection*, considered the Cochabamba–Sucre–Santa Cruz de la Sierra triangle as the fundamental area, with the latter city attracted towards Brazil. Santa Cruz, therefore, if controlled by Argentina, could constitute a geopolitical spearhead reaching towards Western Amazonia, far removed from the centre of Brazil and potentially seriously endangering Brazilian development. Therefore, in order to counteract this, highways, railroads and pipelines were built into that remote zone and a great port constructed on the Río Grande river. In the same way on the Brazilian Atlantic coast, Asunción was connected with Paraguana, displacing the traditional Argentinian influence in this region.

Another point of friction has been the use of the Paraná Basin of the La Plata river for the generation of hydroelectric power. This can be considered one of the world's richest regions and has every possibility of becoming the Ruhr of Latin America and at the same time a gigantic Tennessee Valley. Brazil occupies the key position in the Basin. The majority of rivers are born in its territory, and as far as hydroelectric power is concerned, Argentina is a poor relation and Bolivia and Paraguay its geopolitical prisoners.

Nevertheless conflicts over resources between Argentina and Brazil are not likely owing to the need for concerted action over the foreign debt and the Falklands crisis. The air and sea battle for the Falklands did not resolve the conflict between Argentina and Great Britain. Recently Argentina has received the support of the United Nations, including the United States, for the resumption of negotiations on the future status of the islands. Brazil is an important piece in this diplomatic battle being undertaken by the 'Republic of La Plata'. A new military conflict for control of the islands cannot be ruled out. Considering that the British success was basically due to its nuclear submarines which tied down the Argentinian fleet in its ports and blockaded the flow of supplies from the continent to the islands, a future Argentinian strategy will rely on equipping its fleet with nuclear submarines — not necessarily armed with atomic devices. This demands a close collaboration with Brazil, since these two countries are the most advanced in Latin America in the nuclear field.

Analysis of the underlying geopolitical conflicts between Argentina and Brazil makes it possible to foresee what will follow after the Falklands problem is finally disposed of. It is very probable that the conflict of interests between the two countries will decrease, as was seen recently with Argentinian co-operation over Brazil's settlement of the Antarctic. Old controversies and differences will give way to a foreign policy free from the ties of the past, and this will rebound in a favourable way on Latin American unity and solidarity which at present is so weak.

The Central American Conflict and Possible Great Power Confrontation

The Reagan Administration, more than with any previous US government in peacetime, places great emphasis in its foreign policy on national power and security, which for the US has deep military roots. Owing to the strategic parity achieved by the Soviet Union, Reagan has believed it to be of vital importance to achieve a much bigger margin of security than was maintained under Carter. Once Reagan was elected a second time, and having obtained that margin, his second Administration took a more moderate stance at a global level. However, moderation towards the Soviet Union does not signify moderation in Central America.

In examining peace and security in Latin America, it is therefore essential to analyse Reagan's new global conflict strategy, his policy in Central America, the direct military option, the Contadora process and the consequences of Summit talks for the Central American crisis.

Reagan's New Global Strategy and Its Significance for the Central American Conflict

Reagan's policy in Central America reflects his tendency to reduce all international problems to a power equation between the Super Powers. This makes part of his world strategy aimed at giving the rest of the world the image of the US as willing to combat 'Soviet expansionism'. So it is that, for geopolitical reasons, Central America has become the battlefield for this policy. Similarly, Reagan's Caribbean Basin policy is allegedly directed at preventing the consolidation of any new Soviet base, as he claimed occurred in Grenada, and at strengthening the US presence in the area.

The new strategic orientation of the Reagan Administration is based on the following assumptions. An aggressive Soviet policy constitutes the main and most dangerous threat to US security. This is made worse by the decline in US military power and the strengthening of Soviet military power. The consequent military threat has global dimensions since the USSR now has global interests and enough strength to defend or increase them aggressively throughout the world. Moreover its fleets are present in all the seas. US security and world peace depend on its capacity — i.e. its national power — to reverse this tendency, stop Soviet aggression, and surpass its military development.

US national strength requires the US armed forces once again to reach the parity which they supposedly lost and which is essential in order to be able to negotiate with the Soviet Union. Secondly, they must be able to contain Soviet expansion and make it recede. This second requirement means that the USSR, or communism, must be restrained and rejected throughout the world by means of a greater potential or actual US presence in every region where there is conflict. Such is the case of Central America.

In order to understand the significance of the conflict in Central America in terms of a possible indirect confrontation between the Super Powers, it is necessary to understand the US's renewed security interests in the area and its rearmament programme. No army reorganizes itself, prepares and equips itself, without having specific strategic tasks in mind. Armies prepare themselves for a specific type of war, according to strategic conceptions derived from an analysis of the international situation, the opportunities that exist, the probable opponent, technological developments and the available national resources.

The great North American military expansion which is occurring now, including the so-called Star Wars, is due basically to three strategic objectives: (a) to be able to give a military response to liberation movements in the Third World countries; (b) to strengthen its capacity to intervene in a tactical nuclear war; and (c) to develop the capacity to intervene in a limited nuclear war. These objectives give a new dimension to the geopolitical value of Central America and the Caribbean Basin.

In relation to intervening in the Third World, there was a conviction in the United States, after Vietnam and until Grenada, that it was no longer in a state to neutralize the military power of Third World liberation struggles. In 1975, for example, the US avoided facing the political, economic and military risks of a direct intervention in Angola; they understood that once a guerrilla liberation movement has developed an efficient popular base, it is difficult to stop it. This was further exemplified in the cases of El Salvador and Nicaragua.

The strategic goal is to intervene in a quick, unexpected and decisive way before the leftist liberation movements gain popular support, acquire a strong enough military force and control important liberated zones from which to operate. For this reason the Rapid Deployment Force (RDF) was developed; it was designed to deploy combat forces of at least 20,000 men in any part of the world. This strategy required maintaining an adequate stock of materiel, ammunition and oil in North American bases abroad, as well as an efficient naval support at the moment of intervention.

The Grenada invasion was proof of this new strategic conception and added the most important ingredient to the North American threat to use its armed force: credibility. The only way that North American military power could have an effective political impact in the Third World was the belief that the US was ready to use its military force. The reaction to this new strategic conception after Grenada was not long delayed, and the countries which feel threatened have organized their 'peoples in arms' and are willing to resist in combat to the last man. Nicaragua has organized a militia of 400,000 men and Cuba has more than 2,000,000 armed reservists besides its regular forces.

With respect to the second US strategic objective, tactical nuclear war, it became a more realistic scenario after the USSR occupied Afghanistan and was apparently in a position to take over the oil deposits of the Persian Gulf in 48 hours with just a clap of the hands. In spite of its Rapid Deployment Forces, the United States could not successfully face such a Soviet military intervention by means of conventional war owing to the great distance. The alternative of sabotaging the oil installations and wells in advance was also not feasible because it would deprive the US's allies of this critical source of supply (Japan alone imports 60% of its crude from this region).

The only thing the US could do to neutralize a Soviet military action would be, the moment it crossed the Iranian frontier, to turn the area into a nuclear wasteland across which no army could travel. This could be done through the use of tactical nuclear weapons — missiles directed from planes stationed at their bases or by naval artillery. This requires holding large supplies of materiel and equipment in US overseas bases.

The third strategic objective of the US armed forces is to be able to unleash a limited nuclear war. This requires a qualitative modernization of the North American nuclear arsenal, abandoning the principle of Mutually Assured Destruction (MAD), and adopting a doctrine which the specialists in the subject call counterforce. New types of nuclear submarines armed with intercontinental missiles (Tridents) are therefore being built, as are a new generation of missile systems — Cruise, Pershing II and MX (with ten nuclear warheads). These constitute the central and most visible element of the ambitious rearmament programme.

The new strategic context which asserts that the best means of obtaining peace is through the strengthening of military power and changes in nuclear doctrine lead us to formulate the following questions: Are Reagan or his successors now contemplating the alternative of being able to administer a pre-emptive nuclear knock-out blow against the Soviet Union and win this kind of a war? Is persuasion and negotiation being left aside as the fundamental objective of US nuclear doctrine, substituting for it an offensive attitude?

It would seem that the main point of the so-called new conflict strategy is the adoption of a first-strike capability against Soviet military installations, as well as the ability to wage a conventional war and a long-term nuclear war. The latter is seen by North American strategists as a new type of conventional conflict — a nuclear conflict which could last for several months.

The installation of Pershing II and Cruise missiles radically changed the basis of the MAD strategy. In the first place, the Soviet time for response has been reduced. In the second place, the great precision of the new missiles considerably reduces the possibility that Soviet missiles will survive a first attack. The combination of these two circumstances forces the USSR towards a strategy of launch on warning instead of launching once the attack has been confirmed. The new missiles make more feasible a first-strike posture and the possibility of a limited nuclear war which would turn Western Europe into a nuclear operational arena. At the same time, the possibility of unchaining a nuclear war at only 10 to 15 minutes notice obliges both Super Powers to sit down once again at the negotiating table.

The new North American strategy upgrades the strategic role of Central America and the Caribbean Basin, and of Latin America in general, since its success demands three new components, all of them having a close bearing on the sub-region: the deployment of North American military forces; maintaining maritime communication lines to the Caribbean Basin; and the supply of strategic resources from the region.

The end of the Vietnam War had resulted in a substantial decrease in the North American presence in the world. The Reagan Administration, however, felt that, along with the modernization of its strategic nuclear weapons, it had also to project US forces abroad. Conventional forces should be deployed beyond the traditional areas of contention, wherever a threat occurs. For this reason, the airborne divisions, Nos. 101 and 82, are being reorganized and C-5A transports bought to deploy quickly a force of 20,000 men. In Florida a rapid deployment force of 100,000 men is also being organized. In addition, steps have been taken to expand existing US bases in East Africa, the Eastern Mediterranean and the Far East.

Central America, more precisely Honduras, also constitutes a new area for the deployment of North American forces, which are tending to be stationed there permanently. Indeed Honduras, with 17 recently built airfields has become a gigantic aircraft carrier for the United States. This not only facilitates its intervention in any country in the region — be it Nicaragua, Guatemala or Cuba — but also provides a link in the chain of bases being used by the US to project its military forces on a world-wide basis.

The Caribbean Basin is the most important and dangerous strategic area at the present moment. It has military resources like the Panama Canal, which is still essential for the defence of Europe during a prolonged war and provides the maritime route through which 12% of US maritime trade goes from the Atlantic to the Pacific. There are also the new military installations which the United States is building in Puerto Rico and those geared to anti-submarine activities in the Bahamas. Admiral Lehman, Secretary of the Navy, argues the United States is an insular nation which depends vitally on maritime communication routes both for its commerce in times of peace and to support its allies and protect access to vital supplies in time of war. Consequently, the Caribbean Basin, where fourteen of the world's routes of communications converge, becomes strategically more important today.

As for strategic supplies, Venezuela and Mexico, with their oil and mineral reserves, and Central America with its natural resources and geographical position astride key maritime communication routes, now play a role in the US's new strategy for a prolonged nuclear war. This involves the need for the US to be able to 'survive' and 'recover' from this kind of conflict, drawing its raw material requirements from an easily accessible source like Central

America. Today it is no longer possible to repeat Kissinger's remark: 'where Brazil goes, Latin America goes'; in spite of having a smaller economy Mexico plays a more important strategic role than Brazil in the eyes of the US. Unlike what occurred during World War II, the greater presence of Soviet fleets makes Latin America, and in particular Central America and the Caribbean Basin, an almost uniquely vital source of strategic resources for the US in any new confrontation, due to its proximity to the continental United States.

Reagan's Central American Strategy

Nevertheless, in terms of the US's new conflict strategy, Nicaragua, a small country devastated by an internal war, does not constitute in military terms a threat to North American security. Here the background is political in nature. In accordance with the task of containing the USSR, and making it draw back, the Central American conflict implies stopping the emergence of regimes like the Sandinistas which may constitute the germ of a new 'epidemic' in Latin America which could cause them finally to drop out of the system controlled by the US and fall into the communist orbit. After World War II, the world became divided into spheres of influence. What happens in Poland concerns Moscow and what happens in Central America concerns Washington. The areas designated by each Super Power must be respected. Exceptions like South Korea and Cuba are accepted now that they are firmly established, but when the boundaries of their spheres of influence begin to shift, the risk of confrontation between the Super Powers becomes inevitable. This is confirmed by the Kissinger Report when it says that 'the US cannot accept any Soviet military participation in Latin America or the Caribbean besides that which is already being tolerated in Cuba.'

How is Central America visualized in terms of the new conflict strategy? As we have already seen, the Reagan Administration holds that the greatest US vulnerability comes from the Soviets' military and strategic advantage, and it sees in Latin America the political opportunity to put an end to Soviet hegemonic ambitions. Central America is therefore all the more important and the conservative discourse in the US is stated in the following terms:

* President Carter neglected the Central American situation.

* Central America is going through a deep crisis.

* Central America is subject to a permanent process of infiltration from both Cuba and the USSR; and therefore the present regional situation affects US national security.

* Nicaragua is arming itself more than it needs to. It is becoming a great interventionist platform for all of Central America, as well as a focus from which to project subversion to the whole region. This platform is supported by and promotes Soviet penetration through Cuba, which makes it a very dangerous zone.

★ El Salvador is the crucial strategic area for the moment. Here the decisive battle for Central America is being fought. If after what has occurred in Nicaragua, the insurgents triumph in El Salvador, the immediate question is: what will happen in the other countries? Will there be a regionalization of the conflict and will the other countries follow as predicted by the domino theory?

This line of thought is supported by the Kissinger Report. It points out that what gives the present situation its particular urgency is the external threat of the Sandinista regime in Nicaragua which is being kept in power by massive Cuban military assistance, integrated into its intelligence and subversive orbit with the support of the Soviet Union and the Eastern bloc in the terms of armament, assistance and diplomacy.

If Nicaragua is the centre from where subversion radiates, which should North American strategic and military dispositions in the area be?

In the first place, it is necessary to contain this great raft for projecting subversion. This should be done in a way that permits the total and simultaneous vanquishing of all possible foci of subversion. The point of support must be Honduras.

Honduras permits easy access from the Gulf of Fonseca in the Pacific and from the Caribbean Basin; in the southwest it shares a common border with the rebel zone of El Salvador; and to the south with Nicaragua and to the north unstable Guatemala. Honduras has become the key centre for the US in its battle against the expansion of Soviet influence. It is the principal base for anti-subversive schemes in the region and the headquarters from where military activities are directed in order to prevent the revolutionary processes which are going on in the rest of the area.

However, its geographical position is not the only reason why Honduras is chosen. It is evident that the US has made a fundamental distinction between the Honduran military regime and other military regimes in the area. The successive military governments of Honduras have had certain peculiar characteristics which have made them relatively different from the other regimes in Central America and which offer a certain prospect of stability. A military action cannot be efficiently undertaken from an unstable area. It is necessary to undertake it from a zone which is both strategically and geopolitically possible and politically favourable. Therefore Honduras has become a fundamental launching pad from where counter-revolutionary actions are undertaken by the US.

The United States, as a result, has drawn up an integrated plan to control this zone comprehensively. Secretary of State Schultz has already defined four objectives: to support democracy, reforms and human rights; to support economic development; to support dialogue and negotiations between the countries of the region and internally; and to support regional security. The Kissinger Report conforms to this conception when it enunciates three principles which should govern relations in Central America: democratic self-determination, the promotion of economic and social development, and co-operation in confronting the dangers which threaten regional security.

In the military field, the United States militarized the conflicts through direct support for the Contras' northern and southern fronts against the Sandinista government. In order to pursue its political goals, it has also displayed its military capacity to dissuade opponents by engaging in joint manoeuvres, involving naval, air and ground units. These exercises with Honduran forces were initially for six-month periods, but may be extended successively, coinciding in some cases with offensives against Salvadorean guerrillas. The declared objective is to 'improve the training and rapid deployment of our own forces and those of Honduras'. But the real counter-revolutionary purpose is clearly to blockade Nicaragua both on the Pacific and the Atlantic, and to prevent the flow of arms to Nicaragua, and from it to El Salvador. The manoeuvres also keep open the possibility of direct intervention by US forces and hide the logistical support being given to the Contras in the north.

In the economic field, an initiative to help the Central American countries has been conceived for the first time. It consists of three types of measures: trade opportunities, incentives and assistance. There is no previous case in Latin American history where US experts have worked so diligently. It is not only a matter of financial resources. But, going further than the Alliance for Progress, the new US package eliminates North American tax barriers for a number of products from the countries of the Basin for a period of 12 years and extends investment facilities to private capital and North American capital in the region. This initiative, complemented by the economic prescriptions of the Kissinger Commission, has been implemented by the Jackson Plan with its projected investment of eight billion dollars. Many of its disbursements, however, are still pending in the Congress owing to Democratic opposition. In truth, from a power point of view, the Jackson Plan can be interpreted as foisting an even greater North American presence on the region.

On the political front, the Kissinger Commission was named in order to provide a democratic gloss on the future of Central America. Peace appeared to be its primary objective. However, when analysed in depth, it is clear that the Report was directed at guaranteeing US security in the area since it mentions sending arms, emphasizes the Cuban threat as the most dangerous and important aspect, and defines its objective as being the overthrow of communism.

The Kissinger Report did not perceive, nor point out, that the real enemy in Central America is hunger, misery, unemployment, and not communism. It also did not show a marked inclination towards a negotiated solution to the conflict. When it requested more military funds, it threw more oil on the flames of militarization and confirmed that Central America is of concern to the United States only in terms of its strategic and security interests in the region. The US is not interested in fostering peace in the region on a lasting and just basis. This bias in the Kissinger Report must cast a shadow on the important development postulates of many of its chapters.

Ronald Reagan's second Administration, whose political and strategic conduct has been framed in terms of the Kissinger Report, encourages even more the positions of its first term — namely, to stop the growth of Soviet military power in Nicaragua, with its associated premise that the Central American revolution is a Soviet aggression.

Two alternatives look possible in the Central American conflicts: either direct military intervention, where the US as the hegemonic power would supply the arms and Central Americans would provide their blood; or a continuation of the current indirect deterioration strategy, the theory of the '20 arrows', in which an economic and diplomatic blockade and intensification of the militarization of the conflicts would proceed. Of these two alternatives, the second seems to be more probable, although the first could occur if the Salvadorean guerrillas defeat the armed forces of that country or if Nicaragua were to receive sophisticated Soviet arms.

Direct military intervention, the first alternative mentioned, is not feasible for the moment, given the high dividends of the US's indirect strategy of blockading and choking the region. In fact, it would also meet with great opposition from North American public opinion, in the Pentagon itself and in Congress. A survey by the Chicago Council on Foreign Relations showed 80% of North Americans against sending troops, even in the case of an insurgent victory in El Salvador. The Pentagon itself considers the results of such an operation would not compensate for the high military costs involved, judging by its experience in Grenada. The US Congress, facing Reagan's warlike position, has also increasingly become a moderating force which would be against an eventual invasion. The House of Representatives on at least one occasion voted to stop North American aid to the Nicaraguan Contras. And in spite of Reagan's re-election, the Congressional elections have not upset the correlation of forces within the House of Representatives where the Democrats continue to be in a majority. One last factor is that Latin American reaction to a US invasion might extend throughout Central America, which is precisely what the US is trying to avoid.

Reagan will continue to promote the militarization of the conflicts without resorting to the direct intervention option. He will try to convince North American public opinion that the alternative, 'showing strength without using it', is capable of solving the situation. Moreover, it will make the Sandinistas feel under constant threat of invasion; their economic and financial crisis will continue to get worse; and the government of Napoleón Duarte in El Salvador will remain capable of preventing new offensives by the Salvadorean insurgents.

Ortega's decision to renounce the presence of 100 Cuban advisors and his willingness to accept an indefinite moratorium on the purchase of new armaments, including fighters needed by his country's air defence system, will be interpreted by the Reagan Administration as proof that its indirect strategy is beginning to show results and will remove any incentive on its part to promote reconciliation and peace.

The indirect strategy to wear down the Sandinista Revolution is being applied without any let-up. The facts are obvious. The United States suspended unilaterally (by simply not being present) the discussions to seek a negotiated solution which were taking place in Manzanillo, Mexico. Previously, it had disregarded the decision of the International Court of Justice. It has constantly prevented the development of the Contadora peace process. Documents of the US National Security Council reveal many strategems to this end: special inducements to the governments of Honduras, El Salvador and Costa Rica to oppose systematically the Contadora process and intentions to do the same thing with Guatemala and Mexico (which would violate the latter's policy that every country has a right to its own self-determination). The US blocked the Contadora meeting scheduled for February 1985 by preventing the Foreign Ministers of Honduras and Costa Rica from attending on a point of diplomatic protocol.

The Reagan Administration also constantly tries to get the US Congress to support the undercover activities of the Central Intelligence Agency which have been going for over five years against the Sandinista Revolution. With funding amounting to approximately 150 million dollars, the ports of Nicaragua have been mined, Somoza's former guards are being trained, as are the Salvadorean and Honduran armies, and joint military manoeuvres take place between the armies of the US, El Salvador and Honduras. With funds authorized by Congress, an offensive from both the north and the south against Nicaragua is being financed. This has prevented the harvesting of coffee, cotton and sugar, which constitute more than 60% of Nicaragua's exports. It has also destroyed schools, hospitals, co-operatives, warehouses and transport routes. More than 17,000 Nicaraguans have lost their lives. Billions of dollars of material damage have been wrought; in 1984 alone, 25% of the coffee harvest was lost, half the fish and gold exports — in all, some 40% of exports amounting to 150 million dollars.

The political objective of the second Reagan Administration is the unconditional surrender of its opponents and the imposition of a limited sovereignty on the Central American countries. Only during the run-up to his re-election was a conciliatory position adopted. And the moves to negotiate with the Soviet Union over arms in Geneva does not imply the same thing for Contadora; moderation in Geneva does not necessarily mean moderation in Central America.

Whatever option the second Reagan Administration chooses in future, North Americans must ask the question: what is the purpose of more US intervention? The Reagan answer will be to prevent the consolidation of a new Soviet base in Central America. However, from our side as Latin Americans, all our history tells us that the real purpose is to prevent progressive political forces from building a new truly democratic society, based on a pluralist consensus of the people, and divorced from the traditional model of dependent capitalism promoted by authoritarian dictatorships at the behest of the United States.

The Contadora Process
Right from the start Washington put up serious obstacles to the Contadora negotiations with its objections about security and control, objections which

were automatically echoed by the governments of Honduras and El Salvador. The Reagan Administration said that the control provisions were too weak. They argued that they did not make it possible to determine with any precision whether a country was abiding by the minimum norms of democracy; nor did they establish any sanctions. The same objection was made over the commission in charge of verifying compliance with the disarmament provisions.

The success of the Contadora Treaty will depend on the political will of each government to comply with the required commitments, since it would be difficult to impose a system of sanctions if faced with flagrant violation of its provisions. In the same way it would be difficult to establish a ceiling for each country's armaments. To do this, it would be necessary to establish inventories of existing arms and equipment, as well as of military installations, numbers of troops and real expenditures in arms purchases. But the situation of tension, mutual distrust, counter-intelligence activities and fear that the adversary will initiate an armed aggression, will prevent the Central American countries from showing their cards before they sign the Treaty. But if this step is not taken, the Treaty cannot get very far. The Contadora countries cannot go further than the Central American governments. That is why Washington's objections seemed to be more directed to obstructing its implementation than to guaranteeing peace.

The Reagan Administration's view is that Central America's problems and instability come fundamentally from communist subversion and not from underdevelopment. What is occurring there is nothing else but a communist threat. Naturally it is easy to adopt this posture, since it is easier to convince Congress to authorize funds to protect US security. On the other hand, North American administrations only last four or eight years, and Central America's problems are more than 100 years old. Why therefore start, some North Americans may think, the never-ending task of solving the problems of underdevelopment since in the short term that will not pay political dividends for the United States?

This situation leads us to point out the very different perspectives of the Reagan Administration and the Contadora countries concerning the solution of the Central American crisis. For Reagan the problem is the existence of a communist threat sponsored from abroad and affecting US security. The solution, therefore, is to eliminate it and substitute for the Sandinista government a regime which would abide by US interests. And this can be done only by applying coercion by means of police, military and ideological measures, not through negotiation. The Contadora countries view the matter very differently. They see the Central American situation as the result of underdevelopment and repressive military dictatorships, reluctant to change, and in power with the compliance of the United States. The solution to the crisis, therefore, is peace, which must be sought by dialogue and negotiation, stressing economic and social development, securing real democracy and human rights, and abiding by the principles of sovereignty, non-intervention and self-determination.

These enormous differences in approach and objectives lead us to doubt the success of Contadora. Washington has never taken Contadora seriously. Now it seems to be using the tactic of raising frivolous objections and ignoring Nicaragua's inalienable right to defend its sovereignty through whatever defensive means it considers necessary. But Contadora must be supported. It is necessary to defend its objectives and to be wary in case the Reagan Administration tries to use it, contrary to the spirit in which it was conceived, as an instrument at the service of North American interests.

Consequences of the Summit Meeting Talks on the Central American Crisis
The renewed conversations between Washington and Moscow in January 1985 may reflect a more moderate tendency during Reagan's second Administration and could have decisive effects on Central American events even though it is possible that, in order to improve East–West relations, they will not be felt for at least a couple of years.

Despite all the difficulties, we believe that, finally, both Super Powers will be committed to a serious effort to improve the ties between East and West. Such a development could eventually bring about the following consequences for the Central American crisis:

★ As a result of the new stage in detente, the world division into spheres of influence will reassert itself: what happens in Poland is of interest to Moscow and what happens in Central America to Washington. In future, without necessarily reaching an explicit agreement on the matter, the Super Powers will be more respectful of their respective spheres of influence.

★ Moderation and pragmatism in Geneva, however, does not mean moderation in Central America.

★ The United States will gain a greater autonomy and will have less external interference in its handling of the Central American crisis. Already, even before the restarting of talks on intermediate nuclear weapons in Europe, Moscow had shown a cautious attitude in Central American affairs; it had refused to sell the most modern MIGs to Nicaragua, although that country had requested it to do so.

★ There will be a drastic reduction in logistical support to the Central American revolutionary movements. Moscow's principal commitment in the region is to the Cuban Revolution. That is the message behind the recent presence of a Soviet fleet in Cuban waters. South Korea and Cuba are accepted by both powers as being within their respective spheres of influence; but in the future both Moscow and Washington will avoid changes in the boundaries of these spheres since then the risk of confrontation becomes inevitable. Consequently, both the Nicaraguan Revolution and the Salvadorean insurgency will suffer a substantial decrease in their support from abroad.

* In El Salvador there could be a decisive shift in the present strategic balance away from the insurgency and in favour of the armed forces, since there will be both an increase in North American military assistance for the latter and the insurgency will see their support decrease. As the Salvadorian armed forces see a greater possiblility of triumphing over the insurgents, their military chiefs will be opposed to new peace negotiations because these would deprive them of an imminent victory. And the insurgents, for their part, will avoid a decisive battle and will patriotically seek dialogue and negotiations. Their acceptance of negotiations in 1984 and President Duarte's tough response are already signs of the weaker logistic support from abroad which the insurgency is getting.

In Nicaragua, the Sandinistas are engaged in a sanguinary struggle to prevent a return to the past, but are likely to see themselves more and more hemmed in on the economic, political, diplomatic and military fronts. In order to defend the survival of their revolutionary ideals, they may be prepared to accept a process of 'Finlandization', affirming Nicaragua's neutrality in external affairs, with a non-aligned foreign policy, and normalizing relations with the US. Internally there might be a mixed economy, neither neo-liberal nor Marxist. President Ortega's recent acceptance of the withdrawal of 100 Cuban advisors is an indication of this.

In response to this scenario, the United States may use its greater freedom to manage the Central American crisis in accordance with its security interests, and free from external interference, to discard direct intervention as an alternative in Central America. As the hegemonic power, it will not need to resort to an invasion and will instead intensify its indirect strategy to grind down its opponents.

Under such circumstances, President Duarte's La Palma negotiations, the North American–Nicaraguan Manzanillo discussions and the process of Contadora itself will no longer be of interest to the Reagan Administration. Such could be the prospects for Central America in the next few years if, as foreseen, the US and USSR enter a new period of detente. Latin America should take note of this and not be caught unawares.

Economic Crisis, Political Vulnerability, Military Dependency And Geostrategic Projections

The economic crisis is affecting Latin American countries' political vulnerability, introducing changes to their military dependency and having an impact geostrategically. The Latin American countries will have to redouble their efforts if they are to recover the margin of political and economic manoeuvre which was lost in the early 1980s when the international financial system produced the debt crisis and the Super Powers tried to recover their hegemony in their traditional spheres of influence.

In the 1980s, freely elected democracies were established in Ecuador, Peru,

Bolivia, Argentina, Uruguay and Brazil, and for the first time since 1973 the opposition even in Chile exerts some pressure on the Pinochet regime. In the Caribbean Basin, countries like Jamaica, the Dominican Republic and Nicaragua have recently held elections. The new governments face the fundamental problem of their lack of financial solvency. In order to honour their debts, they are forced to sign 'letters of intent' with the IMF, stipulating measures of adjustment to be applied to their domestic economies. The adjustments directly affect the common man: increases in the price of petrol, which release a chain reaction of price increases for food, housing, medicine and clothing; elimination of government subsidies on basic services, which results in a real fall in standards of living. The great majority do not accept these deflationary impositions by the IMF and the governments which do become politically vulnerable — which endangers the consolidation of democracy. The democratic governments are obliged to take these drastic measures at the same time as they try to service the loan, although export possibilities are limited and the prices of their principal exports practically frozen. The democratic governments do not have enough economic space to manoeuvre in and there is an atmosphere of overwhelming frustration, disappointment in democracy, and a loss of hope and trust in its leaders. The crisis has made these governments politically more vulnerable.

Latin America is unity within diversity. In truth, there are several Latin American societies. There are people of European, Indo-American and African origin, which has resulted in each society having its own particular mix of values and structures. There are great differences in the degree of industrialization and the size of GNP. At the same time, we do have many things in common: language, religion, the same experience of colonial submission (which had a strong impact on our social values, economic structures and political institutions), and we share a common culture which makes us constitute and inhabit our own and different world.

There is another common element — all Latin American people have a democratic vocation. Unfortunately, we have not been able to create our own instruments corresponding to the Latin American reality. Perhaps for this reason, the process of consolidating democracy has been harmed by the lack of participation of the great majority of people in decisions; there is an absence of a culture of democratic participation.

The growing process of consolidation of the Latin American democracies makes it possible to solve the region's first economic prolem: to break the current economic blockade. In order to do this, it is necessary to act in concert with other Third World countries. It is also necessary to seek a dialogue between the industrialized countries and Latin America, and to begin negotiations with the principal creditor countries. Co-ordination is each day more urgent due to the absence of joint positions and the lack of any mechanism for regional co-ordination.

Owing to the intense crisis which Latin America is going through, there will in future be greater pressure to distribute income more fairly, relieve social penury, mitigate misery, improve health and end social violence. The demand to increase employment will also increase. The language of change and liberation will become each day more unequivocal. In spite of the IMF, there will be successful pressure to use foreign resources primarily to satisfy the basic needs of the citizens and to make the economy grow rather than to pay the debt and purchase naval vessels, tanks and other arms. The crisis has made the poor people's option a priority.

The present economic crisis, the processes of democratization which are under way and the integration mechanisms — the Andean Pact, Amazon Agreement, the La Plata Basin Agreement, the Caribbean Community, ALADI, SELA, etc. — will contribute to eliminating conflicts over systems, hegemony and resources. The structural conflicts will not disappear yet, nor will border disputes of a territorial nature. But in the search for a solution there will be a growing tendency to prefer the use of peaceful means. If the disagreements between the countries of the region are not put aside, the future will continue to be uncertain.

However, our analysis of what is occurring in Central America proves that, for Washington, the Central American crisis is a threat to its security, a political and strategic problem which has nothing to do with the real social and economic problems. So long as the Reagan Administration continues to exaggerate the strategic value of the Caribbean Basin and believes that it is possible to destroy the threat ostensibly posed by the Nicaraguan Revolution, its solution will continue to be the militarization of the conflict. If, on the other hand, the Reagan Administration were to identify the concept of security with that of development with social justice, change and regional transformation, then the road to peace in Central America would be open.

In the near future it will be difficult to maintain the same rate of arms expenditure, which in the past decade has reached 20% of exports. Sheer shortage of foreign exchange will lead to an inevitable but noticeable decrease in government military expenditure. This will assure greater confidence among the countries of the region and reduce the potential threat of local conflicts. Latin America will stop being such an attractive market for armaments.

The region will have to increase substantially its exports in the next decade. One of the characteristics of this new expansion will be manufactured goods. If these exports include arms exports, as is the case with Brazil, Argentina and Chile, there will result a decrease in the military logistical dependence — the worst form of coercion — and a greater autonomy with respect to the extra-continental Powers.

In future, with the stalemate between the two dominant worlds of the Super Powers and the gradual decline of North American influence, Latin America's political influence will increase. Its geostrategic role will require a more autonomous and agreed set of positions, in which nation states will carry out their foreign policy based on their interaction with other members of the region and not as a result of pressure from the dominant external powers to act in accordance with their interests.

Since the confrontation of the Super Powers will revolve around maintaining a strategic balance and keeping open the sea lanes, the strategic maritime areas of the Caribbean Basin, the Southern Atlantic and the straits around Cape Horn will take on a new strategic value. This will place a premium, in the interests of security, on decreasing conflicts in those areas and avoiding possible local wars. After all, the US does not want any of these countries to escape from its control. Of these areas, that which has taken on the greatest geostrategic value is Central America and the Caribbean Basin.

The Central American crisis, like the problems of the Middle East, Cambodia, Southern Africa and the Iran–Iraq War, show that the Super Powers alone cannot any longer decide the solution of local conflicts which, to a great degree, escape their control. Direct military intervention by the Super Powers has become dangerous owing to the possibility of their regional or global escalation. Afghanistan and Grenada will no longer be typical. In line with this new reality, the US will have to intervene in conflicts only through an indirect strategy — disguised intervention. However, where there are revolutionary processes counting on strong popular support, it will not be easy to use the indirect destabilization strategy in local conflicts as a warning to possible revolutions in other areas. Proof of this are Nicaragua, Indochina, Libya and Iran, which have not been significantly affected in their internal behaviour by US pressure.

The Falklands and the military conflicts of Central America put inter-American relations in a permanent crisis. These conflicts and the problem of the debt have shown that Latin American interests and objectives are not similar to those of Anglo-Saxon America; in fact, they are opposed. The Falklands showed Latin America it had to adjust its 1940 view of the world which identified its security interests with those of the US as the hegemonic power in the region. Despite this, however, in the field of joint regional defence, the Latin American countries have absolutely no strategic conception, and, on the contrary, continue to be subordinated to a Super Power which maintains them in a subordinate position. This makes much more difficult, but still necessary, a long-term plan of thought and action.

I think the risks of military conflict in Latin America are smaller than ever before. This is because of the difficult economic situation, the debt problem and the fact that interest payments take more than 30% of export income. All this makes logistical military provision more difficult. Also, Latin American countries know each other better nowadays; there is an integrationist institutional system under way, and a growing process of forming a regional identity. For the moment there are no structural conflicts (excepting Central America) which could grow into a local war, nor are there governments which feel strong enough to assume the historic responsibilities of going to war, at least in the next few years.

8. Conflict and Compromise in Latin America

Aníbal Quijano

The Current Predominance of Social Democracy in Latin America

My purpose here is to make a first preliminary exploration of one of the outstanding features of the Latin American political scene, which seems to be one of the products of the present crisis in these countries. I will start with the fact that the present governments of the Dominican Republic, Mexico, Costa Rica, Venezuela, Argentina and Bolivia are all kinds of social democracy. In Brazil and Peru, the main political oppositions are also part of the same tendency and have a real prospect of achieving office. In the other countries of South America, social democracy is also in practice the most important opposition force. Even in the convulsed Central American scene it has an important position. And it is possible to argue that the government of Betancur in Colombia, in spite of the conservative affiliation of his party, contains certain social democratic elements which contribute to its legitimacy and singularity.

Even more, a major part of the socialist left, which formerly used to be an adversary of social democracy, is now adopting its language, style of political activity and policies, in countries as diverse as Venezuela, Peru, Bolivia, Chile and Brazil.

It is obvious, therefore, to conclude that social democracy has become the dominant Latin American political tendency and the central ideological point of reference for practically the whole region.

In order to investigate the significance of these facts, we must recall the novelty of this situation. It is the first time in the political history of Latin America that this kind of ideological homogeneity has been recorded. In previous periods, such situations had only been characteristic of a small group of countries; indeed heterogeneity had been precisely the dominant characteristic of the prevailing regional ideological movements.

In order to avoid any misinterpretations from the outset, it is necessary to say that I am not trying to gloss over the political heterogeneity existing in Latin American countries. In spite of their limitations, some middle-class democratic regimes have been able to survive during the present crisis. In others, there still exist bloody and repressive military dictatorships, as in Chile and, until recently, Guatemala. In Brazil and Uruguay the military dictatorships have retreated, opening the way to democratic recovery. In Haiti and Paraguay, repressive dictatorial regimes continue to survive. A generalized civil war affects El Salvador and there is the threat of another in Peru, while Colombia shows signs of only a very temporary pacification. Honduras is militarily occupied by the United States, with the consequent threat of a military intervention against the Sandinista Revolution of Nicaragua, where the character of its revolutionary regime is not yet clearly defined. Democracy in Bolivia walks a tightrope. In truth, a very heterogenous panorama.

Nor is it the case that there have not been other ideological currents existing at the same time in several countries, and even on occasion holding power. That was the case, for example, with the so-called Aprista and Christian Democratic parties and, in another way, the so-called populist parties. And certainly, since the 1930s, there has always existed some expression of the communist movement in almost all the countries of the region.

Nevertheless, it is the first time in the political history of Latin America that the same political tendency has acquired a simultaneous presence in almost all of these countries. Moreover, it is the first time that the same political current has presided over the majority of governments, more than any political current before, and has become the ideological tendency common to almost all the political forces seeking to face up to the present crisis, establish middle-class democracy and, at the same time, change and develop society.

In my judgement, the questions which are involved here are decisive for any debate on the scientific representation of the present power structure in Latin America, as well as for its concrete choices in the near future.

Two Levels of Question

From the point of view of the complex problematic which this phenomenon opens up in Latin American, it is useful to formulate two levels of question.

First, what is there in common among the different political processes of these countries? And what does this general tendency count for in the Latin American scene?

On a second level, there are two questions: What is the significance of the fact that it is precisely social democracy which has emerged as the expression of that general tendency? And what perspectives does the ideological predominance of social democracy open up for shifts in political power in Latin America?

It is probably premature, and especially in relation to the second level of questions, to go further than some hypothetical propositions.

From Oligarchical Power to Middle-Class Power

The following hypothesis can be suggested with respect to the first level of questions. In the first place, the fact that, in spite of the particularities of each country, it has been possible that the same political and ideological tendency has established its predominance in practically all of Latin America probably signifies that the whole region is at present experiencing the same general power pattern. Politically, that power leads to entrenching the middle-class character of the State. If this is so, it means that the problematic of the oligarchical State has been at last left behind in our political history. This is fundamental, since it means the demise of a phenomenon which kept Latin American social scientific investigation and debate busy for such a long time. In other words, the conflicts around redefining the social basis of the State have ended, establishing in all countries the same middle-class orientation. This is regardless of the particular roads and processes which were followed in each case, or the differences in the specific forms of State institutions that resulted.

This implies that the economic and social arenas are being reorganized in line with the now generalized functioning of the capitalist mode of exploitation and domination. That mode is not only, as in previous stages, the dominant relation over others, but the central matrix within which the others form merely a part of the historical specifications of capitalism in this particular space — i.e. Latin America — of the international order.

From Populism to Social Democracy

As for the second level of question, it is relevant to begin by verifying that, in Latin America today, the social democratic perspective has been adopted by ideological currents and movements of quite diverse character and origin:

(1) Practically all the currents and groups which were previously called populist (an example is Brazil).
(2) The democratic rationalism originating in the 1930s, in particular the so-called Apristas in Venezuela, Costa Rica, the Dominican Republic, Peru and Bolivia.
(3) The democratic liberal currents which originated in the Nineteenth Century, such as the Radicals in Chile and Argentina and their equivalents in Uruguay.
(4) The nationalist and socialist left emerging mostly after the Cuban revolution, in Peru, Venezuela, Brazil and Bolivia.
(5) The diverse tendencies constituted by nationalist regimes like Velasquismo in Peru.
(6) And finally, political movements which had always been social democratic ever since their origin, such as in Ecuador.

It is therefore inevitable to pose the question: what is there in common among all of them, even in the political tendencies like Peronism or some sectors of Christian Democracy? Probably part of the answer can be found in the fact that, following World War II, and above all in the past two decades, all these ideological currents and political groups have had, even though in different degrees, populist elements.

In Latin America, the question of populism has been basically debated around issues such as mass manipulation, the redistribution of income and property, and the social and ideological changes brought about by the processes of industrialization and urbanization. The debate on populism has not really focused on the nature of conflict, of power relations, and the structural composition of political movements and regimes. For these reasons, very heterogeneous regimes and movements, amidst conflicts of a very diverse nature, were viewed as populist.

Even though this is not the place for an extended discussion, it is necessary to point out that populism did characterize intermediate or transitional movements and regimes between the oligarchical power structures (influential in the State even if already in an advanced state of decline) on the one hand, and the middle-class structures, on the other, with their growing power but unwillingness to face the mounting popular revolt or expel the previous oligarchs from their place in the State through violence. The various regimes which were established in these conflict-prone circumstances were made up of middle-class urban industrial groups and middle-class bureaucratic and professional strata, with the support of large dominated sectors. All these movements or regimes were characterized by their democratic, reformist, modernizing discourse. They all put into effect income redistribution measures, resorted to various symbolic actions and to some extent increased the participation of the middle and dominated classes within the State.

As can be seen, the central question of this type of movement and political regime, and consequently for the character of the conflict which produced them, was the consolidation of social and political democracy. But the issue of democracy was not always resolved, as is shown by those instances where middle-class democracy had a longer history (for example, Chile or Uruguay), or where the economy and society were already middle class (for example, Argentina and Mexico).

Populism as a political phenomenon in Latin America can, therefore, to a great measure be acknowledged as a compromise in the conflict between oligarchical power and middle-class democracy.

Nevertheless, the commitment to democracy did not always prove feasible. In those countries where it had been carried out, owing to their pluralist character, by movements of the dominated classes which had come into power, populist democracy seemed to jeopardize the middle-class character of the State. These populist regimes were then overthrown by military regimes. Each of the rather different forms of military regime proceeded with the work of resolving the conflict between the oligarchical State and the middle-class State; but none led to the consolidation of middle-class democracy.

As a result, by the end of the 1970s, repressive military regimes prevailed in the majority of countries of the region, while in the rest of them middle-class democracy was on the defensive. The question of democracy not only remained, however, on the agenda but took on first-class importance, even though the oligarchic state was becoming exhausted as a regime type in the whole region. The social bases of the State were finally being shifted in a middle-class direction, even if middle-class democracy was not the inevitable result.

Both the defeat of the populist compromise by the military and of its radical and violent extremes, such as the defeat of the Allende compromise, served to maintain power within the limits of its middle-class character, but at the expense of middle-class democracy. Consequently, the Latin American political scene now contains a new conflict between authoritarian regimes (military and non-military) and democratic regimes, in a context of the general supremacy in society of the middle class itself.

Is that what explains the prevailing presence of social democracy? But if that is the character of the principal axis of conflict, why are other middle-class democratic forces in a minority or feel the need to wrap themselves in the colours of social democracy? Is social democracy the point of compromise in this conflict?

To find answers to these questions, it is necessary to go back to the late 1970s. We see that the defeat of the previous compromises and the predominance of authoritarian regimes in Latin America coincided with the generalization of the effects of the international capitalist crisis in those countries. And as the military dictatorships imposed crisis policies, they were met by movements of popular resistance. These movements of popular resistance, particularly in Brazil, Peru, Bolivia, Ecuador and Colombia, had real social support and consequently an unusually strong force. Even though they did not get as far as formulating definite revolutionary alternatives, they had that potential and created a crisis as to which social forces should constitute the basis of power in the State. This was because in those movements organized labour was in the ascendant and took the lead in motivating the vast and diverse social warp of the dominated classes, as well as many in the middle layers of society affected by the violence of the crisis. At the same time, there was the Central American civil war which led eventually to the Sandinista popular insurgency taking power in Nicaragua; as well as the El Salvador civil war and a revitalized Guatemalan insurgency.

With the violent effects of the economic crisis on the dominated and the middle layers of society, the conflict between authoritarianism and democracy (still a conflict taking place within the middle class) tended to combine with the greater conflict between capital and labour which heralded the possibility of revolutionary conflict.

It is true that all these great potentially revolutionary movements were contained everywhere and their revolutionary development potential blocked and defeated. But it is impossible to explain without them the decomposition and retreat of the military regimes in Peru, Bolivia and Ecuador, which were forced to hand over the government to elected regimes. Nor did the retreat of the dictatorships of Brazil or Uruguay take place without massive popular pressure. Even President Betancur's rather singular regime in Colombia was subject to these pressures. And the Malvinas adventure of the Argentinian dictatorship also led to the masses occupying the streets to demonstrate against it.

In other words, the pattern of revolutionary conflict which tended to emerge was contained and reduced to one of its elements: the conflict between authoritarianism and democracy within the limits of ongoing overall middle-class power. But because of this popular pressure and with the economic and social crisis getting worse, the situation could not be resolved without treating the underlying conflict between capital and labour.

The social bases of populism had been exhausted (in their structural sense) and, for the moment, the bases of the Allendist compromise also no longer existed. The popular movements with revolutionary potential had been contained. So although elections produced new political forces demanding a direct understanding with the middle-class State, the conflict between authoritarianism and democracy began to dissipate without any revolutionary risks, but needing democratic mediation between capital and labour. This is perhaps one way of beginning to explain the reason for the present predominance of social democracy as the main political tendency emerging from the resolution of that conflict.

However, this explanation does not seem to be enough to explain a phenomenon which to some extent is contradictory. At the same time that the social and economic crisis has advanced, most of the revolutionary socialist political currents have also ended up taking on a social democratic hue in their language, styles of action, and proposals to face the crisis. These revolutionary currents seem to be becoming one of the political bases of middle-class democracy itself, provided it is redeemed by allowing direct political interventions by the dominated classes and their allies among sectors of the middle class closest to them. These groups have clearly broken with their previous strategy when the crisis was just beginning and they were trying to obtain a violent rupture with the powers that be.

The defeat of the popular movements in the second half of the 1970s may be part of the explanation. But another part lies in the disillusion felt with existing socialist paradigms, especially as a result of Solidarity's confrontation with the Polish regime. In addition, there has been a collapse of confidence in Marxism as a model for the scientific representation of society and its explanatory and predictive power. This can certainly be seen in the present state of debate of the Latin American social sciences.

Under these conditions social democracy seems to be the best option, even for the formerly revolutionary socialist groups and currents in these countries, if the democratization of society and the State is to be consolidated and further explored.

The Problem of Perspective

In any deep crisis, above all if it is a prolonged one, there not only exist disarticulation and disruptive mechanisms, but also change and reorganization tendencies, and no one has any doubts that the present crisis is the longest and most severe in half a century.

Therefore to admit that, under the present circumstances, the conflict between capital and labour appears subordinated to that between authoritarianism and middle-class democracy should not lead one to minimize the conditioning role which the former is exerting on the latter. Nor does it avoid the many problems and questions produced by the crisis within the system of power itself, and on which the immediate future depends.

The fact that the first level conflict has in practice taken on the form of an opposition between authoritarianism and *social democracy* makes it necessary to consider the eventual direction in which political power will be used. It will not be able to break away from the basic economic and social behaviour of people, even if the revolutionary movements have been defeated. The influence of these interests will be particularly great, as seldom before in our history. The growing ideological predominance of social democracy indicates the pressure of these factors on the consciousness of very well-defined social classes and groups.

Much of today's debate is preoccupied by what is occurring economically and the immediate social effects of the crisis. There is not yet efficient analysis of changes in the social bases and tendencies of power which the crisis could be producing. Therefore it is premature to try anything more than a first approximation of how any social democratic regime will treat the conflicts it has to face.

The National Question and its Dimensions

The first thing that I think it is pertinent to point out is the re-emergence of the national question.

In the first place, there has been an intensification of the tendency towards greater inequality between the countries of the region. Without a doubt the principal example of this tendency is the emergence of what has come to be known as ABRAMEX — that is, Argentina, Brazil and Mexico.

Brazil and Mexico now conentrate 64% of the direct foreign investment in the whole region. They account for 61% of total regional GNP, 43.5% of exports and 45% of imports. Industrial ABRAMEX production is 78% of the Latin American total, while Colombia, Chile, Peru and Venezuela together contribute only 16% and the remaining countries only 5.5% of the total. The three ABRAMEX countries also concentrate the largest amount of the Latin American foreign debt.

It becomes more and more arbitrary to speak of Latin America. Competition for resources, markets, and areas of influence are implied by the emergence of ABRAMEX, as are questions relating to the autonomy of Latin American countries, especially if there are moves towards their integration.

It is not a mere coincidence, therefore, that the frontier disputes, which seemed to have ended in the last century, are once again a leading issue in Latin America. And the question of arms is not just a problem of the export of military materiel with the object of contributing to the balance of payments. These changes in relative power relations among Latin American countries will probably affect the national problematic of those countries and regional peace and security.

The second dimension of the national question today relates to the effects of the far-reaching reorganization of Latin America's economies as a whole, and within each country to the social system on which the nation is built. One of the consequences of the violent interruption of the democratization process, especially in the past decade, seems to have been the dissolution of a great part of the social bases of the national process. The nation itself seems to have been put in doubt together with democracy.

There has been the dismantling of many of the previous state controls over production. There has also been a dismantling of productive structures themselves. This cannot be seen only as a problem of conventional recession and unemployment. It also implies, it seems, a decisive change in the process whereby people, and particularly the proletariat, are exploited. In several countries, large numbers of people have been forced out of the ranks of the working class into what is called the informal sector of the economy, which, in countries like Peru, is said to produce more than 70% of the country's industrial output and more than 60% of GNP.

This is not just a case of unemployment or underemployment. A more significant and lasting reorganization has taken place, whose consequences for classes and the class structure cannot yet be identified. The decrease almost everywhere of the numbers of workers organized in trade unions — from 18–20% to less than 10% of the labour force — was at first just a problem of unemployment. A decade later the recession has been superceded by the wholesale reorganization of the productive apparatus. The consequent reorganization of wide sectors of exploited workers does not seem to be only an effect of the recession, which, if so, could be reversed if the economy expanded again under better conditions. It seems to be the consequence in large measure of the new and not yet clearly consolidated structures of transnational power.

We are mentioning only some of the most obvious questions even though they have yet not been investigated. What power patterns are they leading to? What is the social system which will result? Or, put another way, how national can that new system be? Is it only the national middle class which is taking on a new consistency?

Finally, the possible (and/or desired) relations between what is national and what is transnational are contained in the national question. They arise in the structure of capital accumulation and its corresponding productive structure; and the place of the nation state in the international system characterized by transnational power. The question is particularly acute when there is a breach between the social interest and the national identity of the dominant fractions of the middle class. And of course, it arises in cultural questions, which are again the subject of debate in several Latin American countries where there exist several counterposed cultural currents.

In each area of this confusing problematic, what answer can a social democratic position come up with? Is it, to use a metaphor, a case of restoring an old building which is in ruins (as the resurrection of populist nationalist proposals disguised in social democratic ones would suggest)? Or does it demand the complete removal of the old ruins and the construction of new patterns of power? And is it possible to expect that these conflicts will have peaceful solutions or are the necessary changes so important that they cannot be imposed by compromise?

This summary of some of the major questions does not really venture to give their answers. It is simply a call to take the initiative, to discover the problems and to take steps to investigate them.

In any case, it is good to remember that the original populist compromises were pushed aside by repressive military dictatorships everywhere. Those conflicts did not have peaceful solutions. But the new conflict emerging today is not simply a struggle between middle-class dictatorship or middle-class democracy. It is something more fundamental and it seems difficult that the central elements of this crisis will be resolved through peaceful means.

9. The Pax Americana in Central America and the International Economic Crisis

Armando Córdova

Introduction

At the present time, the Central American region constitutes one of the most divided and tense areas in the world. The United States has co-ordinated a programme of growing political and military intervention as a response to the victory of the Sandinista revolution over the pro-North American dictatorship of Somoza. And the national liberation struggles of El Salvador and, for a time, Guatemala, also expanded. The rationale for this aggressive policy by the US is clearly stated in the report of the Central American Bipartite Committee presided over by Henry Kissinger:[1]

> The Central American crisis constitutes an immense and acute preoccupation for the United States of America because Central America is our neighbor and a strategic crossing of worldwide significance; since Cuba and the Soviet Union invest massive efforts to extend their influence and therefore carry out in the Hemisphere plans which are particularly hostile to the interests of the United States; and because the people of Central America are troubled and in urgent need of our help.[2]

However the whole development of the Central American political crisis confirms that the United States is not interested in a peaceful solution to the problem because its real objectives are very different from what they pretend.

My purpose here is to prove that North American policy in Central America is directed towards destabilizing and defeating the popular government of Nicaragua and the annihilation of the national liberation movements of the other countries in the region. This is the starting point for imposing a *Pax Americana* in line with the general strategy of the government of Ronald Reagan. This strategy aims at constructing world-wide the political conditions they consider necessary to achieve their fundamental objective, which is to overcome the severe economic crisis which the capitalist system is undergoing and to restore the weakened hegemonic position of the United States as the world system's dominant power. Overcoming the world crisis is clearly a necessary condition for restoring the balance of power between the two great world systems — capitalism and socialism.

I will start by describing the present crisis of the world capitalist system and the strategies which its leading powers, headed by the United States, have been following in order to confront it. I will go on to discuss the objectives of North American policy in Central America as stated in the Kissinger Report on the economic, social and political situation in the region, and will show how it corresponds with the Reagan version of global North American policy.

The World Capitalist Crisis and North American Responses

There is a wide and growing consensus among analysts of the present world economic situation on some of its important aspects.

First, it is a 'great crisis' or 'great depression'. This suggests the exhaustion of the present accumulation model on a world scale and the necessary emergence of a new one.

Second, the radical structural transformation of the world capitalist order which the emergence of a new model of accumulation implies raises problems of singular importance economically as well as politically and socially. In the economic sphere, the consolidation of a third industrial revolution and new forms for the management of workers have not yet been completely and clearly defined. In the meantime, there exists the latent danger of a financial collapse like 1929. In the political sphere — besides the presence of the socialist system which may limit the alternatives available for overcoming the crisis, there also exist other factors — the internal opposition to the capitalist system within the developed countries themselves, and the contradictions between these countries and their underdeveloped periphery (which are possible foci for insurgency or at least latent conflict against the status quo).

In the third place, the international order seems to reflect a virtual paralysis of the mode of articulation of the different national formations in the system, i.e. the international division of labour. Other problems include the traditional mechanisms for extracting surplus from the Third World and, above all, the growing ineffectiveness of the ideological, political and military legitimation apparatus of the world capitalist order. This aspect is of special relevance here because it is the main reason for capitalism's weakness in general and the decline in North American power in particular. The US can no longer easily use the language of force in the Third World to create the conditions demanded by the emergence of a new model of accumulation.

The repeated humiliations of the US in Iran and Lebanon are clear examples of that weakness. There are many others — the crisis in bourgeois economic theory; the changing relations between Centre and Periphery; the efforts to deepen the South–South dialogue; and the crisis of the OAS as the organ of Pan Americanism and the search for new forms of Latin Americanism. Added to all this are the destabilizing effects of the national liberation movements in Asia, Africa and Latin America.

When at the end of the 1970s the first symptoms of the present economic crisis began to appear, it was also evident that there would emerge a leadership crisis within the world capitalist system. The Vietnam defeat and the collapse of the Bretton Woods monetary system had put in doubt US hegemony over the system.

When Nixon and Ford were Presidents, Secretary of State Henry Kissinger attempted to reconquer the US's lost hegemony with his policy of detente. This sought to build a more inter-dependent world which would embrace the USSR and put a limit on the expansion of its military power.[3] Within that strategic vision, the Third World constituted an important preoccupation, owing to its political instability and the opportunities this gave to revolutionary movements.[4] Kissinger's solution to the problem was to support authoritarian regimes in the underdeveloped periphery as a guarantee of political stability. In Central America, this meant, as everywhere else, a support for the already existing dictatorships.

As the world economic crisis spread, however, it became obvious that the Achilles heel of that policy was not the Third World but the allies of the US — Western Europe and Japan. They carried out, in their own way, a poly-centrist alternative to the irresolute North American mono-centrism. Eventually important sectors in the US itself got together with their European and Japanese partners to revitalize the leadership of the system. This was the so-called Trilateral Commission which had its heyday during the period of President Carter.[5]

The promoters of the Trilateral Commission wanted to create a political consensus among the dominant groups of the large capitalist countries so that they could proceed to construct a new international economic order which would progressively replace the accumulation regime which was in crisis. In general terms, that economic programme wanted, in the centre, to build new sectors based on the most advanced technologies[6] and new ways of organizing production and relations with the labour force. Simultaneously, this involved a new division of labour between Centre and Periphery.

To achieve those objectives, a fundamental economic instrument was promoted, so-called industrial relocation. This meant transferring to some Third World countries the exhausted industries with three objectives in mind: (a) to create the necessary economic space in the centre for the development of new sectors; (b) to increase unemployment so as to discipline the labour force as a necessary condition for that development; and (c) to avoid, by transferring them to the periphery, the growing economic, social and political costs generated by the pollution caused by some of the industries relocated.

With Reagan's rise to power, the fundamental economic objective remained overcoming the world crisis. But there was a fundamental change in the political goals. The US government decided to try to recover its world hegemony. This meant giving priority to solving its own country's economic crisis, even at the risk of undermining the recovery of the other developed capitalist countries. The Reagan Administration also sought the self-interested support of the international financial elite which, frightened by the insolvency of Third World debtor countries, came to support the Reagan policy because it implied a harsher treatment of those countries.

Another important change introduced by the Reagan Administration was the imposition of the liberal monetarist model as best suited to its general strategic objectives,[7] since it legitimized maximum freedom of action for international capital and the imposition on both its major allies and the periphery of the conditions required by the new model of accumulation. This freedom for the forces of the market gravely reduced the role hitherto played by national states in the Third World and redounded to the benefit of international capital.

The unilateral imposition of US strategic designs on the rest of the capitalist world demanded that it have a wide variety of political instruments at its disposal, backed by force. But this was difficult as a result of the crisis itself. The old political and ideological mechanisms based on the former unquestioned leadership of the US did not always work. North American weakness could be seen in the Middle East, and also in some areas where it used to command the greatest influence, such as Central America and the Caribbean. Until a short time ago, North American marines went in and out of there without having to give explanations to anyone.

The Reagan Administration understood from the very first that one of the preconditions of recovering its credibility as a hegemonic power was to overcome these weaknesses. It is not by chance that the Santa Fe Document, Reagan's original electoral platform on international relations, began with these words: 'War, not peace, is the norm in international affairs'.[8] This implied a threat directed both to the Soviet Union and its allies of the socialist bloc, as well as to the capitalist periphery.

The Reagan Administration's Consolidation of its Latin American Strategy

In accordance with its global strategy, the basic objective of the Reagan policy in Latin America is to impose in the whole region the necessary conditions for the emergence and consolidation of a new international model of accumulation headed by the United States. In political terms, this means an attempt to revive the old and unquestioned North American hegemony in the region based on the Monroe Doctrine. This implied abandoning the multilateral approach to world affairs — the North–South dialogue — in favour of a divide and rule strategy based on bilateralism and the imposition of neo-liberal economic doctrine. It also meant a denial of ideological pluralism since one of the principal arguments of Reagan's advisors was that 'it does not allow a serious discussion of what corresponds or not to a legitimate North American security interest'.[9]

The policy established two areas of priority interest. On the one hand, the so-called growth pole countries (Brazil, Mexico, Argentina and Venezuela), and on the other, Central America and the Caribbean. Each area would receive its own specific treatment within a global strategy. In the large Latin American countries, where the use of force would cause unmanageable problems, a policy of economic pressure via the IMF and using their high foreign debts as a lever was used. In Central America there was a mixture of bilateral economic assistance and the strengthening of the military apparatus of friendly governments so that they could repel the national liberation movements. These efforts soon proved ineffective, particularly in El Salvador. The result was a growing inflexibility on the part of the US, resulting in an escalation leading to possible direct intervention by its military forces.

One of the most active interpreters of the new strategy towards Latin America has been Henry Kissinger, co-author of the Vail Report[10] on how to handle the foreign debt of countries in the region and the previously mentioned report on Central America.

The Vail–Kissinger Report, which was meant to pull Brazil, Mexico, Argentina and Venezuela into line, establishes two basic conditions for the payment of the Latin American debt, directed towards depriving the debtors of the weapon of repudiation.[11] The first sought to establish the jurisdiction of North American tribunals over the new negotiations; the second established non-fulfilment clauses which authorize the creditors to impose their own policies. This would be done not only through pressure from the IMF but also through more direct actions such as a seizure of State assets belonging to the debtor countries. These measures would have given big capital and the United States a real capacity to manipulate the Latin American economies in whatever manner desired by the new imperialist strategy and completely contravening Latin American sovereignty.

The Kissinger Report Strategy for Latin America

The Kissinger Report is a clear example of the adaptation of general US strategy to a concrete regional situation characterized by political instability. It began, surprisingly, by renouncing use of the 'big stick' of the foreign debt, which was a fundamental weapon in the rest of Latin America.[12]

In the political sphere it clearly intends to maintain the US role as the main party responsible for the maintenance of internal order within the area of its Caribbean *mare nostrum*. The US invasion of Grenada was significant as a successful first step in recovering its lost prestige as global policeman.

In the economic sphere, the Kissinger Report tries to impose on Central America a new development scheme fitting with its world strategy to overcome the crisis. The subordinate economic role envisaged for the region involves not only the old economic methods of unequal exchange but also creating a regional political superstructure dominated directly by the North American government and transnational capital, in collaboration with the most servile sectors of local capital.

The Kissinger Report put forward three fundamental proposals:

(1) The reorganization of the economies of the Central American countries, and particularly their export sectors, based on the experiences of South East Asia. The document points out that the Central American countries are in a position to become, in the long term, important centres in the production of

middle and low technology goods which can be exported to the United States of America, the rest of Latin America and Europe. The leaders of Panama, the document emphasizes, are presently studying the experiences of countries such as Hong Kong and others, in an effort to imitate their success as leading countries in export production.[13]

2) The imposition of neo-liberal policies on the region.

> The Central American countries must improve the atmosphere for both internal and foreign investment . . . These countries need to begin to change their economic policies which at present discourage investment . . . The taxes on exports should be reduced and each country should maintain a realistic exchange rate policy.[14]

The whole document emphasizes the role of private capital (national and foreign). Its whole thrust is to impose the neo-liberal scheme as the most convenient way of achieving industrial relocation, thereby transforming Central America into an export platform for the large transnational corporations which would exploit the region's cheap manual labour, its rich natural resources and exchange rate policies designed to reduce still further the remuneration paid by capital to the workers, the national states and the owners of the land and mineral rights.

(3) The imposition of a sophisticated scheme of integrated colonialism on the region. This is the boldest and most innovative aspect of the Kissinger Plan. It involves an integrated regional development plan to revitalize the Central American Common Market via private national and transnational capital, and the direct participation of the government of the United States in a Central American Economic Integration Bank. This would make the US the controller of the Central American Common Market. It would also be able to use bilateral assistance as a means of putting pressure on the different countries of the area. Thirdly, an Emergency Action Committee for Private Capital would be created 'with the purpose of advising on the development of new mixed initiatives which may promote regional growth and employment'. This committee would be formed by representatives of private capital. Fourthly, a Company of private capitalists for Central America would be set up by experienced businessmen with the support of the United States.

The cornerstone of this whole new imperialist scheme for the region was 'the long-term commitment of the United States of America as well as of the Central American countries to coordinate economic, social and political development', for which purpose a new Organization for the Development of Central America was proposed. This would be open to the participation of all the countries of the region and the United States. However, 'the Director of the Organization must be a citizen of the United States of America with a Central American Executive Secretary.'[15]

To sum up, the commission presided over by Mr Kissinger invites the Central American peoples to accept voluntarily a new integrated colonial scheme.

The United States would not only participate but dominate. The region's nation states would have to renounce all possibility of making their own economic development decisions. Instead these would be made by private national and transnational capital. Not only that, but the commitment to 'Coordinate economic, political and social development' with the US government implies renouncing the exercise of national sovereignty. Economic power would lie with the US and its great corporations, with the explicit support of local economic groups. The support of the latter for the Kissinger proposals shows the unrooted character of capital and its real fear of the advance of the popular revolution.

The Kissinger Report clearly shows us North American designs for the Central American periphery in the new international order which President Reagan is constructing.

Implications for Peace in Central America

Several passages of the Report show, in a very precise manner, that the Sandinista revolution in Nicaragua represents the fundamental obstacle to establishing in the whole region this scheme which would subordinate Central American interests to North American ones. The Report presents Nicaragua with an explicit ultimatum. It is given two choices. The first the revolutionary process to surrender:

> Nicaragua would be invited to participate in CADO [the organization for Central American development directed by a North American viceroy] with a view to promoting an authentic political pluralism and the economic and social development of that country in harmony with the rest of the region.

> The participation and access to the assistance within the framework of CADO by Nicaragua — or any other country — would be conditioned by a continuous process towards defined political and social objectives.[16]

The second alternative is direct military intervention as a preliminary to imposing the *Pax Americana* on the region. The Report expresses this direct threat like this:

> Finally, Nicaragua should know that force is always the last resort. The United States and the countries of the region retain that option. Of course, there are additional non-military measures which have not been used yet, as for example economic restrictions and the decrease of diplomatic contact. Respecting the military option, the precise instant which may be considered essential for US security is not the concern of this Commission.[17]

As can be observed from this, Kissinger and his colleagues assume a total coincidence of interest between the United States and the countries of the region. This would seem to imply that the scheme for integrated colonialism which the report proposes is already considered as being in place. The truth is that the situation is exactly that, at least in the political sphere.

After 1983, there was an intensive increase in North American aggression in Central America, with direct attacks on Nicaragua by armies — for the time being, irregulars — financed, equipped and trained by the United States, based in Honduras (the northern front) and Costa Rica (the southern front).

So far, the heroic Sandinista army has been able to ward off this aggression on all fronts, while the national liberation front of El Salvador has continued to strengthen its positions.

The Contadora group — made up of Colombia, Mexico, Panama and Venezuela — has also had a certain degree of success in discouraging the aggressive North American policy in the region. This has obliged the counter-revolutionary forces to retreat.

To end, it is necessary to say that both the intolerable proposals of the Kissinger Report as well as Reagan's war policy aimed at turning back US relations with Latin America to the days of Theodore Roosevelt's 'big stick' constitute a clear expression of the exasperation felt in ruling US circles at the decline of its position in world politics.

The Feasibility of the Reagan Policy in Central America

To affirm that those are the objectives of the present US Administration in Central America does not imply accepting that those objectives will be achieved. That will depend on a variety of factors in the international situation and United States and Central America.

On the international level, the international economic crisis and the East–West confrontation may influence North American policy in any particular region in the world. The more optimistic view points to a prompt international recovery. This view is not shared, however, by many analysts who do not see any immediate resolution to the crisis since the technological, financial, economic and social problems to be solved before a new model of global accumulation can be constructed may persist for a long time. In addition, the price which the United States economy has had to pay for its present recovery must throw doubt on its permanence. I refer, of course, to the huge increase of the US trade deficit which rose from 43 billion dollars in 1982 to 100 billion dollars in 1984. The Federal Government's fiscal deficit is also soaring. In fact, the whole economic system of the US rests to a degree never before seen on deficits and the creation of credit. This 'onerous recovery'[18] is based on spending far beyond the available means, relying on credit, and basically foreign credit, as W. W. Rostow has emphasized:

Americans (. . .) answer to their short-term needs, contracting debts to a level never seen before. This is called living over and above one's means. The day will come when we will have to render accounts. (*International Herald Tribune*, 28.11.84).

The questions which arise in this respect are: How long can this policy last? And what effects could a sharp fall in the economy of the imperialist Centre have on the situation of Central America?

As for the development of the East–West confrontation, the chess game has not yet got far enough so as to define a winner, nor — what is more important in our case — to define its effects on each piece on the board. Certainly, Nicaragua continues to receive support from important sectors of public opinion in Western Europe, as well as support from the socialist countries, which have always up to now been openly supportive of the struggles for national liberation of the Central American peoples.

Turning to the possible course of events inside the United States, it is necessary to point out that Reagan and his advisors are not the only actors able to decide on international policy in that country. The North American people, shaken by what has been called the Vietnam syndrome are resisting, even though not always effectively, the warlike designs of the US administration.

However it is necessary to make a wider and stronger effort on behalf of everyone who defends peace in order to stop the criminal escapades of the US in Central America. They constitute an intolerable intervention against its peoples which augurs badly for the future of world peace. If successful, it will strengthen, without a doubt, the position of the hawks of the developed capitalist world, and increase the possibilities of military interventions in other parts of the world. Alternatively, if defeated, the dominant circles of the United States might become desperate and make a bid to win or lose all in a holocaustic direct confrontation with the socialist world.

Notes

1. The Kissinger Report was not the first expression of the marked interest of the Reagan Administration in Central America and the Caribbean. At his first press conference as Secretary of State, Alexander Haig, in April 1981, talked the interventionist language of the theory of the domino. The United States also tried to commit Mexico, Canada and Venezuela to its Central American policy at Nassau, in July 1981. Once those efforts failed, Reagan proceeded to elaborate his Caribbean Basin Initiative, which he made public in February 1982 in a meeting of the Organization of American States. That Programme, directed at strengthening the private sector of the Central American and Caribbean countries, afterwards proved ineffective, and gave way to the establishment of the Bipartisan Committee presided over by Kissinger to design a more efficient policy.

2. For this and all the other direct quotes from the Kissinger Report, we have used the reproduction of it which appeared in the review, *DOSSIER*, Vol. 1, No. 3, April 1984.

3. See Carlo Portales: 'Consensual Problems in North American foreign policy', in *Latin America in the New International Economic Order*, edited by Carlos Portales, Editora Fondo de Cultura Económica, México, 1983.

4. In this respect Kissinger wrote: 'The problem of political legitimacy is the key to political stability in regions where two-thirds of the world's population lives. A stable internal system in the new countries will not bring about a new international order in an automatic way, but a new international order is impossible without a stable internal system. US assistance should include some conception of what we understand by political legitimacy.' H. Kissinger, *American Foreign Policy*, Plaza & Jones, Barcelona, 1971, p. 94.

5. Even though it was constituted in 1973 on the initiative of the great transnationals. the Trilateral Commission kept discreetly in the shadows until President Carter took over power.

6. Portales summarizes the position of the Carter Administration in the following terms: 'The scientific and technological development of the United States is producing the change from an advanced industrial society to a *technotronic* society. characterized by the development of technology and electronics which. according to Brzezinski is not occurring in the socialist countries. The United States, Western Europe, and Japan could "stop the world's tendency to chaos"', C. Portales, op. cit., p. 37.

7. The marked monetarist character of the so-called Reaganomics. and in particular the manipulation of the rates of interest. are a clear expression of the 'me first' policy. This seeks to obtain a flow of the greatest possible liquid funds from other countries to finance its own recovery and accelerate the launching of new sectors through what is beginning to be known as the Third Industrial Revolution.

8. Santa Fe Report. cited by Carlos Bujanda. *DOSSIER*. op. cit. p. 2.

9. R. Fontaine, et al., 'Castro's Ghost'. *The Washington Quarterly*. 28 January 1981. p. 26.

10. See 'Operación Juarez'. Special Report of the Executive Intelligence Review. New York. 1984. p. II.

11. Ibid.. p. III.

12. The Kissinger Report reads as follows:

'the United States of America and the governments of other debtor countries should encourage private money lenders. especially the commercial banks. to renegotiate the existing debts at the lowest rate possible'. and further on. hurrying to discourage any effort by other countries to take advantage of the Central American example. makes clear the specific case: 'The representation of creditor governments constitutes an *important deviation* with relation to the present point of view. We don't pretend that this affects the negotiations over the debt of other countries outside Central America. but we believe that the burden of the debt should be treated as part of the effort of emergency stabilization.'

13. For those who may fall into the temptation of considering that such forms of industrialization signify an advance for Central America. I will quote the French investigator Alain Lipietz, referring to this form of industrialization in South East Asia: 'It could be described as sanguinary Taylorization. Taylorization because it relies on intensive manual labour industries (clothing. electronics) which exploit female labour. submitted to the necessary type of discipline. Sanguinary because its advantages of ferocious competitivity come from the exploitation of labour based on force.' 'Le fordisme périférique etranglé par le monetarisme central', mimeo, Paris, 1968.

14. *Kissinger Report*. op. cit.. p. 31.

15. Ibid. p. 33.

16. Ibid. p. 34.

17. Ibid. p. 54.

18. See Marie France Toinet, 'Expensive Recovery, Persistent Decline', *Le Monde Diplomatique*. January 1985.

10. The Malvinas War: Implications of an Authoritarian State

Atilio A. Borón

In this case study we wish to sketch a frame of reference for the study of the international consequences of state authoritarianism. We try to suggest some hypotheses about the mechanisms and the dialectic through which authoritarian regimes can unleash situations which put world peace in danger.

For the purpose of the present discussion we have left aside the analysis of the domestic aspects of state authoritarianism. This, however, is not to say that the internal processes of dictatorships lack a decisive importance in understanding their international conduct; merely that we will not make an exhaustive analysis of them. We will content ourselves with emphasizing the overall elements which constitute the complex and at times underlying political process of authoritarian regimes and give preference to the study of their international projections.

The specific case we use is the Malvinas (or Falklands) War. It is difficult to exaggerate its importance both in relation to the collapse of military authoritarianism in Argentina as well as in consolidating the Conservative government of Mrs Margaret Thatcher, whose political difficulties were becoming acute and which, had it not been for the absurd decision of the Argentinian armed forces, would probably have lost the subsequent general election. In addition to these domestic repercussions, the Malvinas War had considerate consequences on the international level since it finally demolished the long held premise that our Latin American continent was immune to international wars. When we add to this the *coup de grace* the War dealt ITRA, the rebirth of a generalized anti-imperialist and anti-North American feeling and the coincidence of the War with the explosion of the continent's foreign debt, it is easy to see that the adventure of the Argentinian military will leave a deep mark on the history of our countries.[1]

The Problem

The Malvinas War presents almost all the components of the misery of authoritarianism: the terror, the myth, the madness, the grotesque, the absurd and death itself appear inextricably combined in what constitutes the apogee of the so-called National Reorganization Process which was initiated by the armed forces on 24 March 1976. Its result was military defeat, the effective occupation of the islands in dispute by Great Britain and the indefinite postponement of any negotiation over their sovereignty; domestically, the War led to the death throes of the military regime and the return to political democracy. Let us see how we arrived at this situation.

It is a fact which has been well established, that in the decade of the 1970s, several Latin American democratic regimes were devoured by the social contradictions which stirred within them. The result was the emergence, above all in the Southern Cone, of a new type of authoritarian state characterized by a systematic and unlimited resort to all forms of violence to a point where, according to various authors, the common denominator of this new modality of domination was precisely terror. These authoritarian states, new forms of the so-called 'states of exception', expressed the interests of what Fernando H. Cardozo called a complex 'pact of domination' in which the most concentrated sectors of the national middle classes as well as the representatives of imperialist capital acquiesced, while the armed forces reserved for themselves the functions of direct political domination. This task fell upon them not because of some kind of personalist intervention by an individual military *caudillo*, as for example has been suggested by Octavio Paz,[2] but because the armed forces, facing a situation of generalized crisis, were the only branch of the state apparatus capable of successfully acting in order to assure a violent recomposition of middle-class order.

The excuse used by the military to justify their interruption of the fragile Argentinian democratic process of the Peronist restoration (1973–76), was that the attendant chaos and social anarchy not only militated against the progress of the economy but also threatened the very conditions for national survival. The proponents of authoritarian intervention argued that the recomposition of social order could only be obtained by drastic and violent means, purging the agents who carried the seed of destruction within the body politic. In this way the typical, multiple contradictions of dependent capitalism, above all in its periods of crisis, were brutally and temporarily abolished.

Besides the structural violence of poverty, there now existed the institutional violence of a terrorist state: sequestration and theft of property, torture and other violations of the person. The ostensible high moral purpose of these new leviathans left in reality a deplorable legacy of mutilated human lives, of suffering and horror which, at least in the case of Argentina, severely injured the cultural and moral foundations of social life.

Today it is possible to affirm without doubt that these new kinds of authoritarian regime failed to fulfil their self-imposed historic mission. Far from resolving the structural problems of Latin American capitalism, these dictatorships made things worse. The economies of Argentina, Chile and Uruguay lie in ruins and even the economic miracle created by the military in Brazil is today judged with highly critical eyes. As for the so often proclaimed social peace created by the authoritarianism, this is now seen to be completely artificial: in truth, it was not peace but a sort of paralysis produced by generalized terror. Once beyond a certain critical threshold, the increase in violence no longer produced a proportional increase in obedience. And history is full of cases like these where the increase in repression generated not the quietism of those which have been dominated but their unrestrainable mobilization. Politically, Argentinian military authoritarianism was unable to create a minimum consensus, except initially during the phase when the regime was first installed. But that was not sufficient to process and contain the demands which were originated by a complex and multidimensional society. Therefore, *pari passu* with the failure of the authoritarians, there emerged a powerful democratic aspiration throughout the Southern Cone. If it proves possible to consolidate and institutionalize the democratic state, the plague of political despotism may have come to an end.

In Argentina, the adoption of repressive measures to control severe social confrontations produced the most acute economic, social and political crisis to have occurred in the last one hundred years, and the disastrous finale to military authoritarianism put the country on the verge of collapse. Now it is imperative to reconstruct the national community on the basis of the essential values of a humanistic tradition (equality, justice, peace, democracy). It is also necessary to reconstruct an economy which was ruined by the monetarist experiments promoted by financial capital and the perverse combination of a free market and a despotic state. Political democracy has to be re-established, too, and with sufficient institutional and psycho-cultural solidarity to prevent any regression to authoritarianism in periods of crisis. For all these reasons, we believe that the Argentinian state constitutes an important example due to its extreme characteristics: in few places has violence gone so far in order to fail so pitifully. And as far as its international relations are concerned, the country was on the verge of going to war with Chile in 1978 and actually precipitated it with Great Britain in 1982.

In what follows we will concentrate our attention on the interaction which existed between domestic and international factors in the genesis of the Malvinas War. More specifically, we will try to explore to what extent the contradictions and internal dynamics of authoritarian states are, in themselves, principal determinants of international violence. Naturally, this does not imply denying the existence of other causes of war. But we want to stress that authoritarian domination should not simply be considered as a national affair or a disgrace for the particular political communities which fall under the yoke of these regimes. True as these things may be, what we want to point out here is that the authoritarian state is a permanent threat to world peace. Since Latin America has been structurally oriented towards political authoritarianism, owing to the peculiarities of its capitalist development as well as the weight of its cultural legacy of intolerance (dating back to a time before the pre-eminence of the middle classes), it would seem clear that new wars could occur as a result of present or future authoritarian regimes in the region. This is especially so if they are in a position to control the necessary resources for the production and use of nuclear weapons.[3]

The Bankruptcy of the Authoritarian State in the War

As it has been continuously emphasized by political philosophy since its beginnings, the search for an external enemy and going to war have been traditional strategies used by all sorts of different regimes when threatened by popular discontent and the consequences of their own failure. In even broader terms, not only war, but also diplomacy is conditioned decisively by the internal contradictions and antagonisms within states. That is why an external conflict permits a search for new ways to reconstruct domestic consensus which can again mobilize large sectors of the population who, although disillusioned with the regime, are still sensitive to chauvinist appeals from their dominators. It bears mentioning, of course, that resort to this ploy is not the exclusive preserve of dictatorships; it is possible to find more or less similar examples in democratic states. The present argument for Star Wars put forward by the Reagan Administration in the US is, at least in part, a tactic to strengthen, through militarism, a political consensus whose material base has been eroded as a result of an uncertain economic recovery and high rates of unemployment.

In any case, in both democratic as well as authoritarian states, internal problems and tensions are suddenly relegated to a secondary position and the social struggles and contradictions which the regime had been unable to control momentarily disappear from the political scene.

This was, indeed, the case with Argentina where, towards the end of 1981, the regime had plunged the country into its worst crisis. The economy was in ruins, the victim of unrestrained speculation promoted by international financial capital and its loyal national allies. Civil society was beginning to revive and to defy the military's more and more inefficient mechanisms of coercion and control, and threatening to overwhelm the regime's fragile negotiation mechanisms. The political system was in a state of suspension or at least disarticulation, incapable of fulfilling its essential role of guaranteeing the State, the government of civil society and the running of the economy. If we add the awakening of a moral and cultural criticism which was destroying whatever slight legitimacy the governing groups retained, and the massive repudiation of the military junta internationally, it is easy to see that the prospects for the regime were not very promising. Faced with an extraordinary mix of three digit inflation and deep recession, great sectors of the population tried to articulate their demands in a wide opposition front. This gave a great impetus to the delayed resurrection of political parties and other groups which had been frozen by the dictatorship. Besides this, the international acknowledgement of human rights activists, particularly the Mothers and Grandmothers of the Plaza de Mayo, and above all after Adolfo Pérez Esquivel won the Nobel Peace Prize, emphasized even more the international isolation of the regime. In short, the situation which preceded the outbreak of the War showed all the signs of a deep economic crisis which was combined with the loss of almost all legitimacy on the part of the authoritarian state and the rapid mobilization of vast segments of civil society demanding the displacement of the military and the return of a democratic regime. As a result, the military, which had subjugated the society by means of terror, became paralysed and lost its capacity to take initiatives which might have led to a negotiated solution to the crisis. The despotic Supreme Disciplinarian, the State against which no appeal lay, was humiliated by civil society — which once again shows how difficult it is to control.

Facing this unfavourable correlation of forces, the government decided to play its last card and ordered the military occupation of the Malvinas (Falklands). This action was not a sudden ploy or the product of some general's ill temper. It was a decision which had been carefully analysed and studied by the military; the only thing that had not been decided was the concrete date on which it would be carried out. The event that transformed what for years had been a remote possibility into a sudden actuality was a series of street demonstrations against the regime's economic policy. So it was that in the early hours of 2 April, the Argentinian armed forces informed the country that the military government had recovered the Malvinas for the national patrimony.

Since the connection between domestic conflict and external military adventures has received so much attention down the ages, we can omit any extensive argument about what is so well known and of which the Malvinas War is such a magnificent example. It is important, however, to keep two things in mind.

In the first place, we need to remember that the internal dynamic of the authoritarian state contains mechanisms and generates initiatives which in themselves tend to the extension of their use of violence into the international arena. This is why the traditional argument is correct that, even where authoritarian regimes do not find themselves threatened by a growing internal opposition, they often seek to unify the internal front by escapades abroad. Hence authoritarian regimes are characterized by a strong tendency towards the generation of international conflicts and, eventually, war. The cases of Nazi Germany and Fascist Italy are quite clear in this respect. Therefore any authoritarian state, whether stable or encountering opposition, is in itself a potential threat to peace. The Argentinian military dictatorship brought the country to the verge of war with Chile at the end of 1978, even though the regime at that time enjoyed a certain legitimacy derived both from the conditions which preceded it (the social class which characterized the last year of the government of Isabel Perón) and from its chauvinist manipulation of the 1978 World Cup finals and the consumerist illusions encouraged by the artificial over-valuation of the peso. In spite of these conditions, which meant that there was no threat of the opposition mobilizing, the military regime was on the point of declaring war with Chile.

The second proviso which it is necessary to add, by way of qualification to the classical tradition, is as follows: whatever structural determinants exist require the presence of precipitating conditions. We must take into account what Gramsci called the nexus between that which is organic and that which is circumstantial, i.e. even though there may exist an objective tendency towards the search for an 'external solution', its internal dynamic can only operate under certain circumstantial conditions, both domestic and international. It is not enough, in order to explain the Malvinas War, to point to the contradictions of dependent capitalism because these are a permanent feature of this kind of society in the present historical period and they do not automatically lead to war. Only under certain internal and international circumstances is resort to war perceived by a despotic and threatened dominant class as an efficient way out of their political control problems. An important role is played by a large number of different types of variables: the economic, of course, but also others of psychological, cultural, ideological and political character, and others linked to the short-term instance of the international system. To take another well-known example: it is clear that German monopoly capital was particularly interested in promoting the imperialist expansion of its country into Europe and North Africa. The rationality of its development as a bourgeois class within German society and as a 'late arrival' in the imperialist carve-up of the world, pushed it in that direction. But it would be an error of interpretation to suppose that, besides this objective, it necessarily needed the leadership of Adolf Hitler or the extermination of six million Jews.

It is therefore necessary to seek a non-determinist, non-lineal, non-reductionist and multi-causal explanation, if the objective is to reconstruct the complex and dialectic articulation of the many levels of reality which come together in particular historical phenomena. The 'hard' and 'soft' variables always combine to produce unique events and the Malvinas War is no exception to this rule. The logic of the reproduction of finance capital in Argentina did not necessarily need to end in war; however, since its domination demanded the mediation of the military apparatus in order to help it impose its 'order' on the different classes and strata of the population, the probability that an internal crisis could become an external adventure increased extraordinarily. The War now depended on a series of other highly changeable conditions and was much less connected with the rationality of the economic calculations of the capitalist classes. In this way two logics became mixed, that of capitalist accumulation and that of politico-military domination. And even though the latter was at the service of the former, the chain of mediations which were interposed between the beneficiaries and the usufructuaries of the policies of the despotic state, and the armed bureaucracy which administer it, guaranteed for the latter a degree of autonomy which in situations of crisis could be very high. In this way, a regime which had committed all sorts of atrocities for the purpose of facilitating the economic reorganization of those middle-class structures which were most closely linked to the United States and Great Britain, launched itself into an undeclared war against these two nations in the Southern Atlantic.[4]

Implications of Domestic Conflict Resolution for the International Scene

Authoritarian states, I suggest, show a strong tendency to extend their practices to the international sphere. The case of Argentina clearly shows that the military dictatorship imposed 'peace' at home through the indiscriminate and unrestricted use of violence against the population. The excuse for this was the overriding need to end the local insurgency. Contrary to what had occurred earlier in the struggle against political terrorism in Germany, Italy and Spain, the South American military supposed that the citizenry would renounce all their human, social, civil and political rights indefinitely. This extreme Hobbesian view held by the Argentinian armed forces evolved into a model of state political control which rested on two pillars: the arbitrary application of violence which the state legalized and legitimized, and the absolute manipulation of social communications. Power arose as a messianic entity, not responsible for its acts (the 'natural errors and excesses' recognized publicly by General J. Videla as something normal) and unquestionable. The political parties, trade unions and voluntary organizations were either proscribed or coerced into blindly obeying the new masters while the press and other mass media were corrupted or, in a few cases, silenced.

On the other hand, the military junta, as well as the officers and functionaries in charge of the so-called dirty war, enjoyed an impunity which had been explicitly granted them by the junta, its ideologues, the dominant economic groups, and the Church's hierarchy which fervently blessed the new crusade. Sequestration of people's property, torture and murder could not be challeged in any court of justice, and in the triumphant euphoria of the moment no one remembered the Nuremberg Trials. Absolute power corrupts absolutely, said Acton, and the recent history of Argentina confirms the validity of that maxim. Under these circumstances it is easy to understand that the governing circle, almost completely separated and isolated from public opinion, was unable to listen to its demands and see the disastrous results of its own conduct. No wonder it considered that the same methods of dirty war could be used in the international arena.[5]

This perception was reinforced by the view the Argentinian military took of international affairs. They saw the weakness of international law, the feebleness of the agencies charged with enforcing it, and the difficulties of applying sanctions. All this made the armed forces feel it possible to repeat their outrages in the international sphere with total impunity.

But the extension of violent political methods to the 'solution' of international disputes could not have occurred if there had not existed a much more profound condition, one which we will merely point out here, namely the deep-seated militarization of Argentinian civil society. This phenomenon, whose incubation began even before the cycle of military coups inaugurated on 6 September 1930, reached its climax in the crisis of the Malvinas. The militarization of civil society should not be thought of as a simple imbalance in 'civil–military relations' nor as something which has to do with the more or less abundant presence of military officers in the high levels of the state apparatus. In truth, it has to do with much deeper and more extensive processes, which relate to the creation of a political culture with strong, authoritarian and military components. This process had begun in the 1920s and by the 1970s had lent a warlike tone to the social discourse of the most diverse groups and institutions of civil society.

This military colouration, which reached its culmination during the years of the 'Process', saturated both successive governments as well as opposition forces; it deeply penetrated the communication media, public opinion, the educational system at all levels, the Church and even daily social life. It is natural that the predominance of these intolerant and violent elements in the system of beliefs, values, and loyalties which constitute the political culture of Argentinians predisposed them to accept not only the new course of events, but also the improbable official explanations put out to account for what led up to the outbreak of hostilities.

In fact, the militarization of civil society implied the classic reduction of politics to war and Argentina became a battlefield where different armed institutions fought for supremacy in the name of the people. According to the apologists of the military regime, this need to put an end to politics had its origins in the severe economic, political and social problems of the country. The monetarist panacea advocated by finance capital, backed by the despotic state, demanded the complete suppression of dissent and the end of what they called sterile social antagonisms. But this prohibition on 'making politics' that they so ardently desired only culminated in an irresistible politicization of all expressions of social life, which invariably became carriers of some kind of message which the regime's ideologists were striving to impart. From the top levels of the regime, however, there was only one answer: exclusion, repression, unlearning and the primacy of senseless rules and norms. Force, not reason, prevailed and the few voices which dared to resist were drastically silenced by the new 'commonsense' orchestrated by the militarized state face to face with an astonished and frightened population.[6]

Consequently, the military regime prohibited politics because it was supposedly synonymous with war, disorder and anarchy. Owing to this simplistic military attitude, any expression of disagreement was prevented, even in trivial matters, under the suspicion of being politics and, therefore, a carrier of violence. The official answer was repression, and consequently, the signals emitted by civil society were misinterpreted as being subversive and pitilessly repressed. In this way, the 'negative feed-back' (to use Karl W. Deutsch's cybernetic idiom), which is essential in enabling government's learning capacity and hence society's governability, was suppressed and the authoritarian regime embarked on a mad logic. Having been literally deprived of eyes to see and ears to hear, its actions followed a catastrophic course which ultimately ended up on the shores of the Malvinas.

It follows that, if these 'solutions' of force were regarded not only as efficient but as morally acceptable in the domestic field, little was needed for the leading circles of the regime to decide to use the same method of violence to settle an international question like the recovery of the Malvinas. The ruling military saw such a process as serving not only to repair the critical internal front, but also to consolidate the regime by means of the glory of a certain victory against the United Kingdom. Since brute force and absolute impunity were considered by these modern barbarians as legal procedures which were ethically acceptable, the militarization of domestic policy was followed by the militarization of international strategy. Direct action took the place of long and tedious negotiations and discreet diplomatic compromises; only the weak could doubt that force was the most efficient means of intervening in international affairs.

A final point should be noted. The congruence between the rules of the domestic game and those applied to the international scene should not be taken too far. It is true that authoritarian regimes tend to reproduce their domestic practices in the international arena, but the converse is not necessarily true. Democratic states, for example, can also be intolerant and brutal in managing their foreign policies: the cases of Britain and the decolonization of Asia and Africa, or France and the war with Algeria and the United States in Vietnam are highly eloquent in this respect. However, the possibility which democratic regimes open up of conflict, which is inherent in the civil society, being expressed peacefully, do make it possible for their foreign policies to be flexible and tolerant, and the governing groups may 'read' the signs and messages coming in from the international arena.

The Argentinian military launched the country on an absurd war which was lost before it ever started. No corrupt government can win a war, and even though Argentina showed it had legitimate rights over the Malvinas, it was evident to any national observer that the outcome of the adventure could not be anything else than a humiliating defeat. The explanation of this gross error would not be complete if only the aggressive course of Argentinian capitalism and the militarization of the civil society are taken into account. It is also necessary to pay regard to the amazing incapacity of the military leaders and their civil advisers to decipher the complex but not totally impenetrable labyrinth of international affairs.

The Declining Capacity to Learn of the Authoritarian State

The military occupation of the Malvinas cannot be fully understood without taking into account the complete restructuring of Inter-American policy promoted by the Reagan Administration. The crucial element of this conservative strategy has been euphemistically called the stabilization of the Central American situation. This means defeating the insurgency in El Salvador and the Sandinistas in Nicaragua and reinforcing those dictatorships in the region friendly to the United States.[7] Central America is the centrepiece in this new strategy to contain communism, the latter being a label which denotes any type of movement which doesn't yield to the leadership of a Super Power which regards it as its mission to face the enemy in every corner of the planet. Compared with the old conceptions which were popular in the early days of the Cold War, where the emphasis was on Europe and certain key positions in Asia, now the scene of the confrontation is worldwide and a military defeat will always, according to this strategy, have serious consequences for US internal security. If such a defeat happened within what this new North American geopolitical line of thought calls its third frontier —

that is. Central America and the Caribbean Basin — it would have catastrophic consequences.[8]

According to this strategic vision. the new members of Reagan's Administration should have taken advantage of his electoral victory and proceeded to a rapid revaluation of the Argentinian military. After Carter's electoral downfall. and with him his ambiguous human rights rhetoric. it had been evident that a wide field of common interests had potentially opened up. with an outright conservative administration in Washington humming a very expensive tune in the ears of the Argentinian military. It is not surprising that Argentina began to play a role of growing importance in Central America. supplying arms. military technology and training. and even contributing regional combat troops. The military government quickly reversed what traditionally had been a relation of incomprehension. when not of open antagonism. between the United States and Argentina. This tendency was reinforced even more when General Leopoldo F. Galtieri assumed the Presidency in December 1981. becoming the most pro-North American President in the history of Argentina.

In this way. Argentina became a convenient proxy. once more executing a 'dirty war' that the North American government was not willing to approve publicly but which President Reagan wanted to implement at any price. The new military gang and its civilian allies thought that. in exchange. the North American government would back any initiative that the regime undertook. The change in the State Department's orientation. its jettisoning of the human rights policy. and the reappearance of the Cold War rhetoric were more than enough signals for the regime that they would have their hands free to manage how they liked the complaints and protests of the opposition and would gain tacit support for their efforts at national reaffirmation in the Inter-American sphere.

Since the world was irretrievably fractured because of the East–West confrontation. as Reagan's advisers had made so abundantly clear. and taking into account that Central America was a key *locus* in that conflict. the Argentinian strategists merrily concluded that the United States would never abandon to its fate a government which was collaborating intensively with it in one of the world's hottest spots in the total confrontation with so-called communist subversion. With the recovery of the Malvinas. the military dictatorship expected to repair the internal consensus for a long period. It also expected that the United States. which had been informed of the projected military occupation of the islands. might be temporarily uncomfortable at this potential confrontation of its two closest allies in the Americas and Europe. but would finally incline to the side of Argentina and persuade the British to desist from any retaliatory action. This incredible logic. a sad mixture of caricature and omnipotence. was not only strongly accepted by the military establishment but also by its many civilian advisers. as well as most of the press and large sectors of the population who were trapped by the chauvinist rhetoric of the Galtieri Government.

It is clear that this peculiar reading of international alliances and conflicts was irredeemably erroneous. But it must be remembered that one of the effects of the prolonged authoritarian domination was the isolation of the country from the international system, at least in terms of the flow of information. This therefore constitutes a fascinating example of the wayward effects of what, in cybernetic models of political behaviour, is called positive feedback and which pushes a political actor to repeat his initiatives compulsively, persisting in a course of action and closing his eyes and ears to any information which could call into question the prevailing options. In this way the learning capacity, which is essential in adjusting the behaviour of an actor to a complex and changing environment, is completely blocked, as are the possibilities of change as a consequence. In the Argentinian case, any information or restatement of the problem in terms inconsistent with the official version was discounted as enemy propaganda, while some old truths about the international system were intentionally ignored by the regime's strategists.[9]

It is evident that this disconnection from the real world, the high price for which had to be paid in terms of the horrors and deaths of a war, was possibly due to certain particular features of the dictatorial regime in Argentina. In effect, the authoritarian regime had projected to the summit of the state apparatus a social class, a corporation, the armed forces, structurally ill equipped to treat with the complexities and subtleties of modern societies and the international system. Without entering into a complex argument, let us simply say that the armed forces were incapable of deciphering the puzzle of international relations because their professional training and socialization led them to perceive reality in Manichaean terms; besides which, all their strategic thought was based on the arbitrary reduction of the complexity of really existing systems. It is a cruel irony that, faced with a situation of political crisis, when democratic struggles were increasing and a certain sensation of disorder was being created (which the eternal apologists of the *status quo* simply defined as anarchy and subversion), the military replaced the politicians and intellectuals precisely at the moment when the complexity of the system demanded the maximum flexibility. The application of 'hard' policy did nothing but worsen things, because what were needed in those circumstances were innovative and creative proposals. The pseudo-authoritarian solution simply ended up making things worse. In international terms, the example of the Malvinas could not be a greater lesson: the islands are now farther removed from Argentina than before.

It would be worthwhile pointing out another thing: even though the incapacity of the military *establishment* to decipher the complexities of the modern world can be understood, this ineptitude was shared, less explicably, by the great majority of its political and literary representatives and by its own ideologues. The adhesion to rigid ideological schemas actually provoked a paradoxical support from important sectors of society for the Argentinian military's adventure. What are the reasons why a big majority of the population accepted this clearly irrational, bellicose message? This phenomenon has also been observed in other totalitarian experiences: Hitler's discourse in Nazi Germany awoke an intense and massive echo in great sectors of the population although that same message had been rejected as insane only ten years before. It is difficult to explain this politico-cultural pathology. But the impact that this kind of chauvinist and warlike appeal can have on wide layers of the population should not be underestimated. for it can become an important ingredient in the stabilization of an authoritarian regime. Without pretending to give a conclusive answer, it would seem reasonable to maintain that the success of such an appeal has to do with the previous existence of some sort of authoritarian syndrome, to a large degree unconscious, which makes possible the favourable reception of clearly irrational and senseless discourses. This is an aspect which we think is closely related to what we have said before about the militarization of the Argentinian civil society and should. we think. be systematically explored in the future. Too many analysts have discarded it because they have assigned a practically exclusive explanatory power to economic factors.

However, a comparative analysis of Latin America capitalist states would easily show that transnational and dependent accumulation exists everywhere, but doesn't always appear associated with a highly authoritarian psycho-cultural constellation. It would seem more adequate to think that the anti-democratic spirit of peripheral capitalism has been combined, at least in the case of Argentina, with a strong authoritarian, historical legacy which made possible the surprising popularity of Galtieri's regime during the Malvinas War.[10]

Authoritarianism, War and Democracy

A last reflection before passing on to our conclusions: authoritarian states tend to produce international crises and, in this sense, they are a serious threat to peace. However, if the dictatorships are defeated in their military adventures abroad, the doors to democracy may eventually open at home. Consequently, it would be reasonable to reverse the traditional argument and think of the possible implications of international conflicts for the domestic transformation processes of the authoritarian regimes. If autocrats, for example, are glorified as a result of a great military victory abroad, the consolidation of the dictatorship is practically certain, at least in the short term. Equally, if they are defeated, the regime will become weaker and eventually fall, opening a space where the opposition will try to reconstruct political democracy.

This, to us, constitutes a topic of the utmost importance. especially if one remembers that a large number of modern democracies, such as Germany, Italy, Japan and more recently Greece and Portugal, were established only after their despotic regimes suffered serious military defeats. It could be said that of the many routes to democracy, one of them has been rightly called by Goran Therborn 'democratization by defeat'.[11] This means that it is not only necessary to examine the impact of the authoritarian state on international peace but also the feedback consequences of the different 'ways out' of the international crisis on those regimes. In the case of Argentina, it is totally clear that the disintegration of the military regime, which had begun *before* the Malvinas War, acquired an accelerated rhythm and irreversible character after the defeat at the hands of the British forces. This made possible a profound redemocratization of public life. The defeat weakened and disorganized the military autocrats. They were no longer capable of containing the democratic impulse coming from civil society which suddenly, facing the unexpected triumph of the British, became aware of the deceit and manipulation to which it had been subject during the long years of the Process.

In this way Argentina began once again its long march towards democracy. But the transition should not be confused with what constitutes only an initial step: the ousting of the military rulers. Important as this is, it is very far from assuring by itself a full-scale and successful transition to a democratic state. The consolidation of this process will take years and requires many things. In his famous reflections on political life, Machiavelli spoke of 'fortune' and 'virtue', and through these terms constructed a metaphor of two complex constellations of factors. On the one hand, the whim of political elements which, however, cannot hide certain deep tendencies which make predictable and eventually controllable the impact of the changing winds of fortune. In effect, beneath the instability and unpredictable nature of events, Machiavelli pointed to the presence of social structures and the more permanent, objective factors of social life. On the other hand, there was virtue which entailed a much more subjective component, an attribute of the spirit, which made it possible for men to create and maintain cities, that is, live in a civilized manner. It is, therefore, a case of the quality of civic spirit, and the great question which Machiavelli put to himself was whether or not it existed among the inhabitants of a nation. Or, what amounts to the same thing, one must find out if there are citizens and statesmen; without them, he said, there could be no democracy.

The question posed by the great Florentine political philosopher could not be more urgent in present-day Argentina. Without disregarding for an instant the importance of objective conditions, it would seem clear that the prolonged institutionalization of an authoritarian and intolerant political culture constitutes a ballast whose weight has been much felt during the long political crisis which the country has suffered. In order for Argentina happily to complete its democratic transition, it must therefore know whether, as a society, it has enough reserves of 'virtue' to face the challenges of this complex and risky process. More than the rejection of the structures of dependent capitalism, more than the chastisement of an openly authoritarian, formerly dominant class, the key to the successful transition lies in the progressive dissolution of a predominantly authoritarian political culture. We know that there also exist in Argentina deep cultural reserves of a democratic, tolerant and humanist nature which, even if they were eclipsed by the long years of military domination, were able to survive the winter of despotism. Now their day has come and the idea of a relatively quick recomposition of the political culture should not be discarded although it is a process which will demand the efforts of a whole generation before it is fully completed. In this connection, it should be kept in mind that Machiavelli's 'virtue' not only referred to a civic spirit which is characteristic of both the social leaders as well as the masses; it also demanded courage, strength, boldness, and the skill to be a political leader. Wisdom, prudence and courage — essential virtues of democratic politics — are urgently required to overcome the heavy ballast of authoritarianism.

Conclusions

I think that the external consequences of the Malvinas War have been dealt with in sufficient detail: initiated to promote the reconstruction of a front to support the military regime, the defeat ended up precipitating the democratic transition in Argentina. Even more, in the elections that followed, the victorious majority party was that party which put the greatest distance between itself and the discredited military establishment. As for Great Britain, there were two main domestic consequences: in the first place, a reversal in the declining popularity of the Conservative government; in the second place, a new military commitment to defend the Malvinas which will be a burden on the state's finances.

If the international consequences of the War are examined, it seems obvious that it was not only Argentina which lost the war. The United States came off badly since one after another of the fundamental premises of its collective security doctrine and the harmony of interests supposed to exist between all the Americas collapsed. The War proved that Latin America was not immune to external aggression. Secondly, and contrary to what one would expect from the doctrine of national security and the US's prevailing strategic conceptions, the aggression did not come from the Soviet Union; it was the US's principal European partner which sent its expeditionary forces to Latin American soil. In the third place, the Malvinas War laid bare the true character of the Inter-American Treaty of Reciprocal Assistance (TIAR), revealing it as an ideological instrument with which the US subordinated Latin American armies to its Super Power designs. Fourthly, Washington's alignment with London deprived President Reagan of one of his most important regional allies in the 'stabilization' of Central America. Today, several years after the Malvinas War, the Central American crisis remains largely unresolved and the Reagan Administration has not found other partners to wage the 'dirty war' on its behalf in the region. Lastly, the conduct of the USA stimulated an anti-imperialist wave throughout Latin America and dissolved the myth of the Inter-American 'community', which will take a long time to rebuild. Even though the solidarity of the countries of Latin America did not in many cases transcend the plane of rhetoric, it was valuable in clearing the ground for new forms of regional confrontation with imperialist policies. Reagan's quick trip to Latin America after the War must be seen as a reckless and not very profitable effort aimed at reconquering the alliances which had deteriorated as a result of the North American position during the conflict.

In another train of thought, the War of the South Atlantic precipitated the further militarization of this area of the planet. The US now has a permanent presence in Trinidad and Great Britain in the Malvinas. It also showed the tenuousness of European support for the anti-imperialist demands of the Latin Americans, including their call for a New International Economic Order. The bottom line is that the close inter-penetration of the capitalist systems of the Centre establishes longer lasting and stronger solidarities than mere ideological sympathies with respect to the Latin American demands. In any event, the North American hegemonic crisis is serious enough for there to be new room for negotiations which our continent must not waste. There are better conditions under which to exercise national autonomy. In this way the decline of US leadership over the Inter-American system could be intelligently used to consolidate the achievement of our peoples' age-old aspirations and Europe could perhaps decide to play an important role in this new stage.

Notes

1. The literature on the crisis of the Malvinas is very extensive. See among others, Juan Carlos Moneta, 'Fuerzas Armadas y Gobierno Constitucional después de las Malvinas: hacia una nueva relación Civil–Militar', December 1984; Alejandro Dabat and Luis Lorenzano. *Conflicto Maviniense y Crisis Nacional*, Mexico D.F., 1982; Kaufman Purcell, 'War and Debt in South America' in *Foreign Affairs*, Vol. 61, No. 3, 1982, pp. 660–74; Viron P. Vaky, 'The Interamerican System in the Falklands Aftermath', Washington D.C., mimeo, 1982; Guillermo Barclay Arce, 'La reivindicación de la Soberanía en las Islas Malvinas. Georgias y Sandwich del Sur durante el Gobierno Militar Argentino, 1976–1983', tesis licenciatura, Facultad de Ciencias Políticas y Sociales, UNAM, Mexico, 1984; Maritza Arienza, 'La Guerra de las Malvinas y el pasaje de las Fuerzas Armadas del "brazo armado de la oligarquía" a clase "dominante autoritaria"', Bariloche, mimeo, 1984; also the *Journal of International Studies* (London) Vol. 12, No. 1, Spring 1983; and the Peruvian review, *Quehacer*, DESCO, Lima, June 1982.
2. On this subject, see the collection of articles published in the *Revista Mexicana Sociología*, 1977, 1 and 2. The articles by Octavio Paz are found principally in *El Ogro Filantrópico* and *Tiempo Nublado*.
3. Cf. Atilio A. Borón, 'Democratización y dictadura: el manejo del legado autoritario en el desarrollo latinoamericano'. EURAL, Buenos Aires, mimeo, 1984.
4. Cf. Oscar Landi, 'Conjeturas políticas sobre la Argentina post-Malvinas', Río de Janeiro, mimeo, 1982. See also Juan Carlos Moneta, op. cit.; Guillermo Barclay Arce, op. cit.; and Alejandro Dabat and Luis Lorenzano, op. cit.
5. A more generalized reflection on this topic can be found in the interview with Guillermo O'Donnell by Andrés Fontana. See *El Porteño*, Buenos Aires, Vol. 1, No. 12, December 1982.
6. There is a study of this topic in the book by Pablo Guissani, *Montoneros: La Soberbia Armada*, Buenos Aires, Planeta, 1984.
7. Cf. Jean Kirkpatrick, 'The Hobbesian dilemma in Central America', Washington D.C., mimeo, 1982; Luis Maira, 'La política latinoamericana de la Administración Reagan: del diseño armonioso a las primeras dificultades', Mexico, Siglo XXI, 1982; Mirta Botzman, José Miguel Insulza and Patricia Sosa, 'El conflicto de las Malvinas: Estados Unidos y America Latina', *Quehacer*, op. cit. pp. 57–65.
8. See Norman Podhoretz, *The Present Danger*, New York, Basic Books, 1979.
9. Cf. Karl Deutsch, *Los nervios del Gobierno*, Buenos Aires, Paidos, 1976.
10. Surveys made by the Gallup organization in Buenos Aires in May 1982 showed that 93% of the persons interviewed belonging to the lower middle and working classes backed the initiative of occupying the Malvinas militarily.

11. See 'Dominación del capital y aparición de la democracia', *Cuadernos Políticos*, Mexico, No. 23, January–March 1980. A reflection on the Latin American case can be found in 'Latin America between Hobbes and Friedman'. *Cuadernos Políticos*. No. 23. op. cit.

Part III
The Institutional Framework and the Management of Conflicts

11. The Institutional System and the Management of the Crisis

Clovis Brigagao

Latin America — 22 different countries, unequal and each with its own dynamic — is a cauldron where social forms and forces, cultural patrons and technologies collide and coexist. New orders of priority emerge and the old ones seem to be living out their last days. Internal and external patterns play their roles, trying to define what the future of our region will be. In this chapter we have the temerity to try and reveal these aspects and their tendencies.

What we want to do is treat a certain order of problems which have been forgotten by Latin American social scientists but which, little by little, have assumed a destructive character in our values, economies and hemispherical political relations. Militarism and the arms race have invaded the whole Latin American region. It is obvious that the relations of militarism and the arms race with other dimensions of Latin American development are not lineal. If we think that by eliminating militarism from the regional context, leaving the other socio-economic factors intact, we will be promoting continental peace, we will simply be accomplices in a false ethic and political irresponsibility.

Let us look at what occurred with the Malvinas (Falklands) War as an example to illustrate what we are proposing. The War helps us to understand the region's vulnerability, what the National Security Doctrine really means, the institutional Inter-American structure, the role of the armed forces and the dilemma of our so badly treated democracy. The War opened our eyes and showed us how hemispheric affairs have been managed and what interests they have served.

From a geostrategic point of view, our regional instrument for hemispherical security and collective defence has depended since World War Two on the Inter-American Treaty of Reciprocal Asistance (TIAR). This was supposed to serve as a protection for the Hemisphere against foreign threats or aggression, a crucial point during the Cold War. And it became the pattern for other transnational military organizations (NATO, 1948; ANZUS, 1951; SEATO, 1954; CENTO, 1959). But it ended as an instrument for the defence of the strategic and military interests of the US, as well as of the military structures and anti-democratic governments of Latin America.

TIAR and the OAS: Weak Pillars

Until the outbreak of the Malvinas conflict, at least three things were clear about the TIAR. First, it showed its irrevelance to the current collective security requirements of the Hemisphere. Second, it showed its inability to uphold regional defence against external aggression, whatever the origin of the latter. And last, the TIAR ended up being used as an instrument for the consolidation of the United States and its atomic umbrella, under which the Latin American countries would ostensibly remain protected.

From a strategic point of view, the TIAR showed the real role of the Latin American governments: the region had to produce and continuously supply the United States with strategic raw materials; it also had to protect those military and economic installations which were essential to the interests of the United States. Individually, each Latin American country had to sign a bilateral military agreement with the United States and support the latter's military operations where its national interests were in danger.

With the Malvinas War, the TIAR was revealed in all its weakness. The War was evidence of new international tensions, now transferred to the Periphery and provoked by supposed allies. It became clear that the Malvinas conflict also had an element of North–South conflict. The TIAR, which was originally organized as a collective security instrument of the Inter-American community, suddenly confronted another much more powerful defence system — NATO, the Atlantic Alliance, which prevailed over regional Latin American interests, and served as a more important instrument in the strategic context of East–West confrontation.

It is also clear that, if the Argentinian government had been victorious, it wouldn't have been peace and democracy which would have come out stronger. On the contrary, it would have led to the advance of militarism, with an increase in military expenditures, and a greater autonomy for the armed forces in relation to civil society.

As for that other pillar of the Inter-American system, the Organization of American States (OAS), it simply remained paralysed, unable to provide any effective demonstration of its power to impose a solution or protect the sovereignty of the Latin American States. A successor to the old Pan-American Union, the OAS was intended as an institution created to represent the new pattern of political hemispherical relations. In truth, both the TIAR and the OAS reflected a situation characterized, fundamentally, by the economic, technological and military superiority of the United States (and of the Atlantic Alliance) over the Latin American countries, individually and as a whole.

Changes in Relations in the Hemisphere

Consequently, at least two risks appeared. First, contrary to what was believed, the military intervention against Argentina did not come from the supposedly traditional enemy, the Soviet Union or the Warsaw Pact; it came from a traditional ally, England. Second, the War showed that even a military government can call for the re-establishment of its sovereignty over an island and obtain the support of almost the whole society. Military authoritarianism knew how to manipulate the nation and light the flame of 'national salvation' against the forces of colonialism, even where the regime had itself obtained economic and military assistance from the United States and Britain during its most dictatorial period. Having kept up close relations with them during its anti-democratic crusade in Central America that same regime suddenly appeals to the solidarity of almost all of Latin America, including some governments which had hitherto been traditional enemies of the Argentinian military.

In the same way that some European countries came to disagree with the North American strategy towards the Soviet Union, the Latin American countries now regard with suspicion North American policy on economic, energy and nuclear co-operation issues, after years of co-operation and 'reciprocal assistance'. There is a resentment, a wall of distrust, which has been raised in hemispherical relations. Even though there does not exist any natural inclination towards the Soviet Union, the Latin American countries no longer hold to the old 'implicit alliance' with the United States. Without a doubt there already exists a potential neutrality. The structure of hemispheric security, in the form that it was devised in the days of the Cold War, now seems to be on the point of being redefined. It is already clear that Latin American interests have been relegated to a subordinate position in relation to other more powerful actors under the protection of multinational institutions such as NATO, the EEC and the OECD. These highly efficient supranational structures protect their interests through the agency of concerted economic pressure, military force and arms exports throughout the whole Latin American continent.

New Actors in the Arms Race

Another effect of the Malvinas War was that it provided a justification for entering into the local production of arms. Until then, only Argentina and Brazil had the industrial capacity to manufacture their own armaments and maintain a significant presence in the Latin American arms market. Now it seems that some other countries in the continent are also initiating an industrial effort to produce arms locally as well as a mutual association of economic interests and political prestige between State and private, national and international companies. A new hierarchy of regional power could arise as a consequence from the ashes of the Malvinas, thereby increasing even more the militarization tendencies of our societies and economies.

In this way the arms race contributes to what has become known as a security market, in other words, a defence-oriented economic policy in which a new economic role is assumed by the armed forces. The security market represents the institutional, financial, industrial, and research and development complex of the Latin American armed forces and their interests in the continent. The political and economic power concentrated at the highest levels of the State also means a relatively autonomous power of decision without social control over the budget or fiscal and investment resources, in a situation of poverty for broad sectors of society.

A third effect of the militarist tendency could be the danger of nuclear proliferation. Until a very short while ago, and this makes Latin America different from Europe and other regions close to potential nuclear conflict zones, the Latin American region had not been threatened by the atomic rivalry of the Super Powers. Admittedly, in 1962, there had been the Cuban missile crisis. But in 1967 the Treaty of Tlatelolco was signed which denuclearized the region. Nevertheless, as a result of the development of nuclear power programmes, increases in the transfer of technology and links with transnational companies (which ignored the formal denuclearization policies of sovereign Latin American States) the international nuclear industry has stimulated regional competition by offering advantages to this or that country and taking advantage of differences between them. The result has been to unleash a chain of nuclear proliferation.

It is now necessary for the potential nuclear-capable countries of the region to find a real programme to maintain regional denuclearization. If one country perceives that another country's nuclear programme could lead on to nuclear arms production, it will find the necessary arguments and justifications to accelerate the development of its own nuclear capability, albeit at an extremely high cost to the nation.

The questions of regional and international prestige and the debate arising from nuclear non-proliferation arrangements which freeze the current dichotomy between nuclear and non-nuclear powers, have a great significance for the nuclear technology purchasing policies of Latin American countries. Any competition between the United States, Germany, France, Japan, Britain and even the Soviet Union may increase the danger of nuclear proliferation in Latin America.

The result is, therefore, that the resources which might be available for social purposes are destined to be spent on functions which generate militarism and an arms race with the object of guaranteeing the supremacy and increasing the structures of the security market. At the same time, any elimination of democratic rights and guarantees in their broadest and deepest sense — that of consecrating goods and services to the community in the political, economic, cultural and environmental spheres — opens the way to the security market becoming more important than other processes of social interchange. Militarism acquires an overriding priority. Moreover, even when democracy begins to become a more dynamic process and re-establishes the citizens' primacy over the sovereignty of the State, it has not been possible to control the new dynamic which the military economy has been assuming. Violence, uncertainty and the existence of armed conflicts are expressions of the present form of existing social organization in Latin America.

The Central American Context

The great powers project their strategic interests geographically when they seek territorial bases outside their own national frontiers. The object may be to provide themselves with intermediate links to serve their desires for alliances, appropriation of resources, or even wars of conquest.

Central America has been one of those intermediate links where those interests external to the region have extended their policy of confrontation. The situation reveals the dangers of the growing world military escalation which is impinging on the Central American region and risking hemispheric security and the self-determination of its peoples. The interference is based on the massive presence of foreign armaments which are all the time becoming more sophisticated.

The local causes of the situation in Central America are well enough known: the alliance of the old oligarchies with military dictatorships; the brutalities and violation of the most elementary human rights; the non-existence of solid democratic institutions and the long chronicle of social injustice. The situation is permanently explosive. As more and more arms are brought in, the region runs the risk of a veritable profusion of civil wars.

The external factors are also very obvious in this long history of struggle. The United States plays a central role to the extent that it transfers to the regional scene its global disputes. Since the end of the last century, the United States has considered the Caribbean Basin as an extension of its national political and military frontiers. Ironically, by its very support for oligarchical and dictatorial regimes, the US actually serves the cause of Soviet power rather than of Central American democracy. With this Manichaeist and imperialist policy, the necessary space for the growth and consolidation of authentically national and democratic movements and regimes is denied. On the other hand, even though the Soviet Union doesn't get any immediate advantage in this situation, it tries to obtain recognition of its policy of support and solidarity with the liberation movements as well as parties which have reached power, taking advantage of its allies involved in the armed struggle. In this way, the Soviet Union also injects new and disturbing elements which transform the regional context to a wider East–West conflict.

The regional initiatives to get negotiations going which would lead to the re-establishment of legitimate governments tend to reflect the varying correlation of political forces in the region, which hitherto have been polarized around radical right- and left-wing positions. There still exists a whole context which prevents real, negotiated solutions being arrived at — both internal political forces as well as the external factor of the Reagan Administration's aggressive policy. In the midst of this impasse, a billion dollars of US military aid and 'economic assistance' is channelled to chosen countries, leading to even more regional discrimination and injustice.

No To External Intervention and Militarization

The Contadora Group, through the Declaration of Cancun and its subsequent initiatives, has a policy which is more conducive to peace. Its objectives are clear:

* End all types of external aggression, including those which involve the indirect backing of particular countries of the region;
* Stop the flow of arms to all sides in the conflict so that the population gradually develops a feeling of trust which will allow it to constitute its own democratic institutions and choose its own legitimate, representative governments;
* End all military assistance in the region — arms and troops — and ban the use of military bases in the region;
* Sign a compromise which will assure the Central American peoples' right to self-determination so that they can seek their own political, economic, social and cultural models; and
* Demand that no foreign power intervene in the internal affairs of any country in the region.

The proposals of the Contadora Group involve a new element. For the first time in the history of hemispherical negotiations, there is a desire to free the negotiating process from the formal and bureaucratic forum represented by the OAS and from the operational inactivity of the TIAR. This new resolve commands the support of the majority of Latin American countries. And it expresses itself in the Contadora Group's opposition to external intervention and the militarization of Central America. This position provides a genuine support for democracy and social transformation in the region. The Contadora Group also counts on the support of political forces in Europe, non-governmental organizations, and US public opinion as well as a widespread international recognition. The Plan has been useful in showing how political imperatives must prevail over military imperatives if the latter are not to transform the region into another arena of international confrontation between the Super Powers.

This regional initiative is a political instrument which can lead to an effective negotiated way out of the present conflict. It has the advantage of opening the autonomous space needed for a negotiation which will demilitarize the present *status quo*, open up opportunities for the re-establishment of an effective democratization process and bring peace to the countries and their peoples who are the principal victims of the present situation.

Foreign forces, of course, are still trying to prevent the internal political forces from finding common ground for negotiations to resolve the differences. Arms supplies are still a powerful instrument in the hands of the Super Powers, which can be used to stall the negotiating process and divert resources that the majority of the population could use to tackle their present situation of desperation and injustice.

Disarmament: A Priority Question

In view of the present regional situation, the military tendencies and arms race reveal the uncertainty in which we live. The question of disarmament must be acknowledged as a priority in the calendar of negotiations. If we don't stop these tendencies, which sprout like ivy in the regional scenery, Latin America will become even more vulnerable and compromise its own course in civilization.

It would be a significant contribution to peace if the United States as well as the Soviet Union would come to an agreement involving a complete disarmament programme. After so many years of rivalry, mutual retaliation, and conversations on disarmament, we are however sceptical about the prospects of a lasting agreement between the two Super Powers. As for the initiatives of the world community of States in general, there exist many contradictions which prevent the formulation and implementation of policies to secure regional conventional and nuclear disarmament. National interests are a real impediment. While in certain situations, governments act resolutely, in others they show themselves passive and imbued with inertia. In some cases they are even outright adversaries. There does not exist a consistent and coherent policy on these issues which all States subscribe to.

It would therefore be very opportune were proposals like that of the Contadora Group to gain more support and become political decisions which could reverse the present tendencies in the region. Their proposals constitute effective steps towards a collective security system. They would involve more democracy, with greater participation and responsibility which are indispensable for the articulation of governmental and non-governmental networks if they are to guarantee new forms of development and peace. The greater and wider this bond against militarization, the arms race and the continuation of degrading social circumstances, the more quickly we will reach a greater state of democratization, social justice and liberty, and stimulate constructive development at a national, regional and global level.

12.   The United Nations Model: Could it be a Road to Peace in Latin America?

Felipe MacGregor

Little by little, the vision of peace as security born of and preserved by justice is taking its place in the world. This vision, a common aspiration of humanity, is today more than just a Utopian aspiration. It is a social force in those parts of the world which have no peace because they have no cultural, judicial, economic or political security. Latin America is a part of this world.

Lack of security does not come from incapacity, but from unjust interactions between countries. The United Nations has led the search for peace along the difficult paths of security and justice. What, it may be asked, are the characteristics of the United Nations dynamic of social transformation? And can this United Nations model inspire Latin America in its search for peace?

The reflections that follow in order to try to answer these questions are presented in two parts. The first explores the strength of the United Nations model; the second, its weaknesses.

The Strength of the United Nations Model

The formal model of the United Nations is its Charter. The real model is formed by what the United Nations actually does, which on occasion has been so compelling as to add riders to the Charter.

My first reflections are centred on the members of the United Nations themselves, Articles 3 and 4 of the Charter; on the promotion of Human Rights, Articles 1.3 and 13.1.b of the Charter; and on some consideration of the possibility of transforming the international order and even reforming the United Nations Charter (Articles 108 and 109).

Articles 3 and 4 of the Charter define two kinds of members: the 'originating members' and those which may subsequently become members.

The status of being an originating member is related to particular facts of history: having signed the United Nations Declaration on 1 January 1942, or having participated in the United Nations founding conference in San Francisco on 25 April 1945. The Declaration of 1 January 1942, was only signed by the 'Allies', which were those states — 26 in all — that were fighting the Axis Powers during World War Two. In their Declaration, the Allies chose the name of the United Nations. At the San Francisco Conference

46 countries were present. What had happened was that, between January 1942 and April 1945, 20 more States had signed the Declaration of the United Nations. At the San Francisco Conference itself, four more States were admitted — as was Poland a little later. Thus the number of 'originating members' rose to 51, which, according to the Preamble to the Charter 'have convened in the present Charter of the United Nations and through this act establish an international organization which will be named the United Nations'.

In order to become a member of the United Nations, any other State must fulfil the conditions fixed by Article 4 of the Charter: 'to care for peace'; 'accept the obligations assigned in the Charter'; 'be qualified, according to the Organization, to fulfil those obligations' and 'be willing to do so'.

The incorporation of a new member depends on the opinion which the Organization has of it: the Organization must judge the capacity and the will of a State to fulfil a series of moral obligations. The extreme difficulty of deciding this had led the Security Council 'to consider all formal petitions of a State to be member of the Organization as proof that it "fulfills the requisites of Article 4.1"'.[1] The result is that the number of members has now risen to 160.

Between the Declaration of 1942 and the Conference of 1945, in addition to the recruitment of new members, there was another less visible but more important process carried out by the representatives of China, the United States, the United Kingdom and the Soviet Union, first in Dumbarton Oaks, then in Yalta. The purpose of this was to construct the political outlines of the future organization.

One comment is called for at this point. The difference between 'originating members' and 'members' has become relatively insignificant over the years and has eliminated the danger that the organization would be manipulated in favour of its founders. True, there still remain the exceptional powers of those States which are 'permanent members' of the Security Council,[2] but even these have been modified, or at least attenuated, because the sphere in which they may be exercised in practice is becoming smaller and there is the more extensive presence in the Security Council of non-permanent members.

The increase in the number of member States and the creation of what the Charter calls regional organs have helped establish today a different hermeneutic in the interpretation of Articles 3 and 4. To be a member now signifies also being a part of one of the regional organs mentioned in Articles 52 and 53.

In his September 1984 Report to the General Assembly, the United Nations Secretary-General, Ambassador Javier Pérez de Cuellar, spoke of 'multilateralism which is practically incarnate in the United Nations, and one of its basic premises'.[3] To be a member of the UN signifies not only depositing along with other States part of one's interests and trust in the Organization but also assuming a responsibility for the totality of nations and the whole human race.

This new significance of membership leads me to the second topic of reflection — Articles 1.3 and 13.1.b of the Charter. In the Preamble, the United Nations reaffirms 'faith in the fundamental rights of men, in the dignity and value of the human person, in the equal rights of men and women'. And Article 1.3 expressly points out as one of the UN's purposes 'the development and promotion of respect for human rights and the fundamental liberties of all without distinctions of race, sex, language or religion'. In almost the same terms, the Charter suggests (Article 13.1.b) that the General Assembly 'make recommendations' to 'help and make effective the human rights and the fundamental liberties of all human beings'.

Let us examine some of the tensions between Articles 2.7 and 13.1.b; and Articles 51 and 1.4 so that we can search for ways to resolve that tension in favour of the rights of persons as against States.

The United Nations has defined the fundamental rights and liberties which all persons have. The Universal Declaration of 1948 has also been followed by two agreements, one on civil and political rights and the other on economic and social rights. In terms of UN jurisprudence, the rights of nations to their wealth and national resources belong to the *general context of the rights of man.*[4]

Part of the mandate assumed by the United Nations in defence of human rights is contained in other declarations and instruments — those referring to the Independence of colonized peoples (1960); the 1963 Declaration on the elimination of all forms of racial discrimination; and the 1967 Declaration on the elimination of all forms of discrimination against women. The protection of refugees has also been part of the United Nations functions since 1951 when the General Assembly set up a special organ for this purpose.

In this non-exhaustive summary of the actions of the United Nations on human rights issues can be found what I called the internal tensions of the UN Charter. Articles 3 and 4 restrict membership to States. The juridical relations between States are governed by international public law, in terms of which only States have rights. But a State is neither masculine nor feminine. It is not yellow, black or brown. A State is not a refugee nor can it be subject to torture. So when the United Nations approves declarations on racism, colonialism, and so on, it leaves their enforcement to the free decision of States in accordance with Article 4.7 of the Charter. But it is obvious that what happens in practice is much more complicated.

In practice, several of the six committees which conduct much of the work of the General Assembly, take care of human rights questions. At its first session in 1946, the Social and Economic Council constituted a Commission on Human Rights which has, as part of its mandate, to devise effective means to ensure respect for man and his fundamental liberties.

The Economic and Social Council also helped initiate General Assembly Resolution No. 32/130 of 16 December 1977, on practical ways and means of improving within the United Nations system respect for human rights and fundamental liberties. The Resolution has deeply marked the activities of the United Nations.

All these conventions, declarations and resolutions make up the moral context on which human coexistence is based, governed by norms of universal application and validity. The next step has to be a qualitative one. There must come a time when, in addition to the International Court of Justice whose competence (according to Article 34.1 of its Statutes) is only over States, there will also be an International Court of Human Rights where people can take past and present cases concerning the violation of human rights.

This qualitative step forward, however, is highly problematic and depends on what happens more generally in the struggle to reform the international order.[5]

How to construct a more appropriate international order has long been the subject of intellectual debate. Many of the great intellectuals of international political thought have participated, including such authorities as Saint Thomas Aquinas, Machiavelli, Bodin, Hobbes, Vitoria, Suarez, Grotius, Kant, Rousseau and Hegel. Closer to our own times there have been the theorists of Hans Morgenthau's Realpolitik School, which Henry Kissinger adhered to more or less cynically, and Raymond Aron. And the enormous intellectual effort at Princeton and Columbia where K. Jaspers, Richard Falk, Sol Mendlowitz and Rajni Kothari played an important part in setting up the World Order Models Project.[6] In Latin America, the Peruvian, Carlos García Bedoya, has contributed in the realpolitik tradition.[7]

By temperament and vocation I belong, in contrast, to the Utopian School. I work on the United Nations University Project on Global Transformation and Peace. I owe my initial inspiration to the classics, above all Vitoria and Suarez. The doctrine of Natural Right nourished my philosophical upbringing, as did the Church's social doctrine and reports like the Brandt Commission *North-South: A Survival Programme* and the Palme Commission's *World Security*. My participation in UNESCO activities, and above all in the General Assembly of the United Nations, confirmed my Utopian vision.

Utopianism blended with rational optimism commands a certain logic. It considers human institutions to be endowed with an inner reality which is expressed, more or less faithfully, in external manifestations. The space beween these two is the terrain of politicians, social scientists and diplomats bent on making the external manifestations of international institutions more consistent with their inner essence and the rational nature of man.

The UN Charter, for example, is an external manifestation of the United Nations whose essential reality comprises us, the men and women who are represented by the member States. The will of real people has brought about an extension of the limits of the formal order proclaimed in the Charter, expanding the space between inner essence and external manifestations, as is shown by those members of the Organization who have defended human rights.

Utopian thought is not determinist. Unlike biological changes which are written into a genetic code and inexorably succeed one another, changes in the external manifestations of human institutions have as their cause the free will of man, born not simply of past experience but also perceiving a future that is possible. To take one inspiring example of the validity of this optimistic position: the increase in the number of UN Member States (and consequently the new composition of the General Assembly) is the result of the political will, decisions and struggles of many peoples against colonialism.

The very UN Charter is an expression of Utopian intent. The first commitment of the Charter is to the future, to the coming generations: 'We, the people of the United Nations, decided to preserve the succeeding generations from the scourge of war . . .'

The optimism of Utopians stops being rational, of course, when it is simplistic in its vision of reality or ignores the dangers. In his first Report to the General Assembly as Secretary-General, Ambassador Javier Pérez de Cuellar pointed out with integrity and clarity that the international stage has two classes of actors. One is the class of 'acknowledged' actors, or States; the other, possibly more influential, is the wide-ranging category 'political ideologies, transnational corporations, military alliances, etc.' He urged us to look in clear-sighted fashion at the differences in power between these two categories of international players in order to reconstruct the international system on a realistic basis. He also reminds the Great Powers that 'the world has become a much more complex one and much less orderly than was foreseen in San Francisco'.

Kant, the great rationalist advocate of Utopian thought and author of a plan 'for perpetual peace', considers that peace, whose place in civilized life must be assured, needs to take into account adversity. The greater the adversity, he argues, the greater is the effort to overcome it, and the greater the expectation that man will responsibly seek a solution.

The Christian vision of peace is also a rational Utopian one, optimistic, and moreover, invested with the light of faith. The Second Vatican Council put it as follows:

Peace is not the mere absence of war, nor is it just the equilibrium of opposed forces, nor does it sprout from a despotic hegemony, but with complete exactness and propriety is called the 'work of justice' (Is. 32,17). It is the fruit of order planted in human society by its Divine Founder, and which men, always thirsty for a more perfect justice, must carry out. The common good of mankind is governed primarily by eternal law, but in its concrete demands, during the passage of time, is submitted to continuous changes; therefore, peace never is a thing completely done, but ever happening. Given the fragility of human will, wounded by sin, the care for peace claims of each person the constant dominion over oneself and vigilance on behalf of the legitimate authority.

This however, is not enough. This peace on earth cannot be achieved if the well-being of the people and the spontaneous communication between men of their intellectual and spiritual wealth is not assured. It is absolutely necessary to have the firm intention to respect other men and peoples, as well as their dignity, and the passionate exercise of fraternity, in order to construct peace. In this way, peace is also the fruit of peace, which surpasses everything that justice can realize.[8]

The vision which is described here takes in the real inequality between, and the complementarity of interests of, member States of the United Nations, as well as the tension between the two categories of actors mentioned.

The new concept of peace which needs to be built into the Charter, when it is possible, according to the procedures of Articles 108 and 109, may be formulated in this way: Peace is the result of security; and there is no security without justice.

The first security required is that of persons, then social communities, then the nation (which is after all the community of communities), followed by the State and finally that of the whole global community of States. This sequence does not signify an order of importance, but a complexity of institutions.

The Preamble of the Charter contains this vision of security, either expressly or at least the germ of the idea.

The Security of the community of States, which can result in peace among them, must be assured first by the mechanisms of the Economic and Social Council and then by those of the Security Council. The modifications to the Charter proposed to this end are: First, the Economic and Social Council (Articles 61 to 73) should precede the Security Council (Articles 23 to 51) not only in the text but also in terms of relative power. Second, security should be given a priority over peace in all statements like Article 1.1 which says 'maintain peace and security'; this should say, 'maintain security and peace'.

It may be argued that this, like any Utopian vision when it is laid out in all its glory, seems to ignore reality. But then so did the majestic vision contained in the opening words of the Charter approved at San Francisco.

In order to advance beyond that, the Secretary-General invites us to examine the basic premises of the United Nations' activities, and to contrast its present practices with the majestic vision of the Charter. Skilful diplomat that he is, he invites us to follow the road of what is politically possible. He poses the question:

> Why has there occurred this retreat from internationalism and multi-lateralism at a time when real events, in relation to both world peace and the world economy, would seem to demand their strengthening? We need to consider this problem carefully to enable our institutions to work better. I ardently expect that experts in political science and intellectuals everywhere, as well as the political leaders and diplomats, will consider this essential problem on the occasion of the 40th Anniversary of the United Nations.[9]

Its Weaknesses

The causes of the deficiencies of the United Nations in practice are many. Whoever wants to know the more important ones, can see them exposed with frankness and objectivity, uncommon in this type of document, in the UN Secretary-General's successive annual reports to the General Assembly in the early 1980s.

The centrepiece of our new approach is security. But it differs somewhat from the Charter's conception of security. Article 57 defines security as consisting of the 'stability and well-being necessary for friendly and peaceful relations between the Nations'. The same conception inspires the fourth objective of the Preamble to the Charter and is the third purpose proclaimed in Article 1 of the Charter.

The principal instrument to achieve this security is international co-operation, 'a mechanism to promote economic and social progress of all the peoples'. International social and economic co-operation is described is Articles 55 and 56 of the Charter:

Article 55:   With the purpose of creating the conditions of well-being which are necessary for the peaceful and friendly relations between nations, based on respect for the principle of the equality of rights and the free determination of the peoples, the Organization will promote:

a)   higher levels of living, permanent work for all, and conditions of progress and economic and social development;

b)   the solution to international economic, social and health, and other related problems; and international co-operation in the cultural and educational field; and

c)   the universal respect for human rights and the fundamental rights of man, without making distinctions for reasons of race, sex, language or religion . . .

Article 56:   All the Members commit themselves to take measures, as a whole or separately, in co-operation with the Organization, for the realization of the purposes outlined in Article 55.

The Economic and Social Council only has such authority as is delegated to it by the General Assembly. From that delegation springs 'the responsibility for the performance of the functions' of international co-operation (Article 60).

Human rights are an extension and concrete expression of the 'dignity and value of the human person (in the words of the Preamble), but their realization is conditional on 'existing or living in society', a condition which imposes the demands of society.

Article 24 has another conception of security which consists of maintaining peace among nations through the peaceful settlement of disputes. The Security Council has the power of decision in this respect and to fulfil its mission it is required to exercise continuous vigilance. Member States are obliged to accept and implement its decisions (Articles 25–49). Another instrument available to the Security Council is military force (Articles 42 to 48).

The first conception of security discussed was based on the notion of co-operation. The present one is based on coercion, the exercise of moral or physical force. There is obviously a potential and real tension between the two conceptions. Which, then, is the most important? And which should prevail? Article 26 of the Charter expresses one of the manifestations of this tension when it speaks of maintaining security 'with the least possible diversion of human and economic resources to arms'.

The two conceptions of security present in the Charter, and which have been briefly outlined here, are explicable because security, like peace, has several different meanings. One of them is protection, expected as a result of superior power or possessed by virtue of the exercise of force itself. Another is alliance, a concept in which security and peace drink from a same spring of water. Alliance signifies the joining of forces, either between equals or with dependent allies, to increase security. Another meaning of security is confidence — confidence in oneself or in others, whether rightly or wrongly grounded, and as a result being sheltered from all danger.

In our approach we associate the notion of security with force or power and we counterpose it with fragility or weakness. Security and fragility are made more specific by words such as corporal, spiritual, cultural, moral, social, economic, political, national, etc. People acting collectively as social communities defend and seek to increase their security. The social network which unites individuals is part of their security, the essential possession of a community, and is both the shelter and motor of its dynamism. The security of the person depends on their individual strength and on their exercise of rights as a member of the community. The security of a social community depends, in turn, on that of the people which integrate it and on the inter-dependent relations with other communities within or outside the national territory.

Among the different social communities, the nation — the community of communities — represented by a State has a special importance. The security of a State resides in its capacity to consolidate and maintain through time and space its fundamental identity. From this perspective the security of the State is that of its constitutive elements: the inviolability of the human rights of its citizens, the stability of its government, the integrity of its territory.

Between the security of the community and that of the person, there is a dialectical tension. This tension is particularly acute in the case of the elements which comprise the State.

These points which have been made provide us with ways to start exploring, for example, notions of cultural, judicial, economic, political and military security and fragility. The cultural fragility of persons proceeds from the lack of integration of the cognitive valuation systems which embrace them: that which is received from their ancestors, the formal educational experiences they have had, and that resulting from cultural interchange. The cultural security of a social community depends on its creativity and initiative in building up the formal education system over the ancestral and reducing, with respect to both of them, the margin of profit of cultural commerce and assuring judicial protection.

Judicial fragility is closely related to culture. In the West the basis of the judicial system is the person and their rights. When a culture has not recognized the person and their rights, their natural environment, and does not take into account how they can be exercised in practice, it constructs its judicial system on abstractions. Protection through authority, essential in all judicial systems, ceases to be a reality.

Judicial security does not consist only of constitutional, legal and administrative declarations, etc., nor even of the impartial administration of justice. It is more bound up with the cultural security on which the citizen's possibilities of demanding justice depend.

In political terms, Wolfers describes security as a value:

> Which is possessed to a smaller or greater degree and which it can aspire to have more or less of. Security has much in common with wealth and power, other important values of international interchange. Wealth measures the amount of capital goods which are possessed by a nation; power measures the capacity and ability to control the actions of others; security objectively measures the absence of threat to acquired values, and, subjectively, the absence of fear that those possessions may be attached.[10]

To measure a nation's security is a risky calculation which involves measuring these two other variables, wealth and power, and the correlation between them. For many centuries, military power was the criterion used to measure the security of a nation. From 1930 the USA, and from 1946 Latin America, searched for a different way to measure power. The extreme complexity of the modern State, but above all the confrontation with the socialist bloc, promoted the search for the new measure.

That new yardstick was called national security. In Princeton, in the 1930s, the notion of national security began to circulate in the university community. Scholars discussed the relationship between military affairs and foreign policy and put forward national security as the unifying link between the two concepts. They began to discuss whether the US should fight in a new world war which looked increasingly probable, and they arrived at the conclusion that, if it did fight, it should not be for the idealistic reasons advanced by former President Wilson to justify its participation in the First World War, but this time should be for reasons of realpolitik, in other words, national security reasons.[11]

Suddenly, national security entered the everyday vocabulary of the military, politicians and bureaucrats. They all began to invoke national security. And they didn't seem to notice that there had occurred a real revolution in thinking. In the School for Advanced Studies at Princeton, the military, politicians and officials concluded that national security must be the new bond holding the Union together, and the guiding idea in the relationship between foreign policy and the armed forces. Constant use gave a content and visibility to a notion which until then had had a merely abstract meaning as 'value' — to use Wolfers' term. In this way national security became equated with national interest in the United States.

What are the characteristics of national security? Yergin points out the following features:

* *Expansion:* that is, the tendency to extend the subjective ideas of national

security to more and more areas, not merely geographical, but to more and more problems, including internal security for example.

* *Alert:* that is, the country assumes a posture of continuous military preparation, since the country must be on permanent alert.
* *Technological development:* both the conduct of domestic policy and foreign relations, as well as the preparation of the armed forces, will not be achieved without an adequate development of technological capability; in this way, the arms race becomes inevitable.

The Charter of the United Nations was drafted at a time when the guiding idea of US internal and foreign policy was national security. In the socialist countries also, above all in the USSR, a parallel security policy, that of a state of total security, informed internal and foreign policy. Without a doubt, both doctrines influenced the general design of the Charter.

The great weakness of the United Nations model is that it has not been able to overcome these national security and total security doctrines. Even the Security Council where these opposing conceptions confronted each other, has not been able to reconcile or transcend them in the decades since its foundation.

The consequences of this weakness of the Charter have been the strengthening of two hegemonic blocs in the world, the multiplication of States inspired by the national security doctrine, and the consequent limitation of multilateralism to only those countries already sharing common interests.

To predict whether the United Nations model will become stronger or weaker is a task for fortune tellers. Our task, as investigators, is to build on what strength the model has now through the means within our reach.

Notes

1. D. Nicol (Editor), *Paths to Peace*, Pergamon Press, 1981, p. 42.
2. United Nations Charter, Article 27.3.
3. Report of the Secretary-General to the UN General Assembly, September 1984, p. 3.
4. K. Vasak, *Les dimensions internationales des droits de l'homme*, UNESCO, 1978, *passim*.
5. Jan Clark, *Reform and Resistance in the International Order*, Cambridge University Press, 1978.
6. R. B. J. Walker, *One World, Many Worlds: Struggles for a Just World Peace*, Zed Books, 1988.
7. Carlos García Bedoya, *Política Exterior Peruana, Teoría y Práctica*, Mosca Azul Editora, 1981.
8. Second Vatican Council, *Const. Gaudium et Spes*, No. 78.
9. Report of the Secretary-General, op. cit.
10. A. Wolfers, *Discord and Collaboration, Essays on International Policy*, Baltimore, 1962, p. 150.
11. D. Yergin, *Shattered Peace: The Origins of the Cold War and the National Security State*, Houghton Miffin Co., 1977, p. 194.

13. The Inter-American System: Its Framework for Conflict Resolution

Héctor Fáundez-Ledezma

The analysis of the machinery used in conflict resolution in the Inter-American system requires us first to be clear about the nature of these conflicts. What is evident is that from the birth of the American republics, relations between them have been marked by all kinds of tensions and conflicts; besides, today there is a marked inequality between them, including at one extreme a Super Power like the United States and, at the other, the recently independent Caribbean micro-states. A great part of the conflicts which have risen in the region have been frontier disputes. Others have been conflicts which reflect the tensions produced by the economic dependence of some States and the hegemonic position of certain of them with respect to others. However, it is the controversies which have emerged as a consequence of ideological or political differences that have had the greatest repercussions within the system. Frequently, these ideological differences have provoked the intervention of a third party in conflicts which are of an internal nature; and the result has been their immediate internationalization.

We intend to explore the laws and conventions which regulate international controversies in the Americas. We will examine their evolution, vicissitudes and the institutions which have been created for the purpose of contributing to the solution of conflicts. And we must not forget that these rules and institutions are a product of political struggles which are taking place in the context of international society, and once created, they develop a certain momentum of their own and evolve according to the course of historical events and the realities of international affairs.

From a legal point of view, our attention must concentrate not only on the analysis of the rules which have been adopted for the purpose of avoiding or resolving international conflicts, but also on trying to establish how far these norms have been effective in achieving their proposed goals. From an institutional point of view, our attention will centre on both the existence of formal elements such as the OAS or the situations which are contemplated in the Treaty of Bogotá or the Inter-American Treaty of Reciprocal Assistance, and also the presence of informal factors like the presence of a dominant or hegemonic power (the United States) or groups such as Contadora which have sometimes intervened in certain controversies, occasionally to greater effect than the formal institutions.

Unfortunately, there has been no lack of conflicts and controversies of various kinds in the American continent. Many of them have been resolved by peaceful means; others, however, have taken on a more dramatic character and have compelled the utilization of collective security mechanisms and the application of sanctions, or have led openly to the use of armed force.

The intervention of regional organs which have been specially created to find peaceful solutions to international conflicts has not always been a happy one. In some cases it has been anxiously sought by one of the parties to the conflict but resisted by the other. In other cases where the organization has intervened on its own initiative or as a result of a petition by only one of the parties, there have occurred conflicts of competence with international bodies such as the UN Security Council, which has been given primary responsibility for the maintenance of international peace and security.[1]

Our purpose is to explore briefly the contribution of the Inter-American system to peace, and the experience gained in the area of conflict resolution.

The Juridical–Institutional Framework

We have to situate our analysis in the juridical and institutional framework, indicating which are the rules that regulate conflict resolution in the Americas and which institutional mechanisms have been established to resolve conflicts. There have been three phases in the development of procedures for the peaceful resolution of international conflicts. The formative period goes back to the independence of the American republics and lasts until 1898; the second or Pan-American phase stretched from 1899 to 1945 approximately; and the last period, which saw the institutionalization of the Inter-American system, has extended from 1945 to the present day.

The Formative Period
Ever since their origins, the American republics have made a continuous effort to establish common principles accepted by all for the solution of international controversies. The contribution of the Congress of Panama, called together by Bolívar in 1824, constitutes the first historical antecedent worth mentioning, together with the principle of *uti possidetis*, which fixed the criteria for the resolution of territorial conflicts between the American republics. The admitted lack of enthusiasm to ratify the instruments which were elaborated by the Congress does not, however, detract from their importance. It embodied the form in which the establishment of adequate procedures and mechanisms for conflict resolution in the region has always been latent in the minds of the leaders of the American republics.

This early period did also witness other attempts to establish a structure for the management of regional crises and controversies, but they were unsuccessful.

The Pan-American Stage
The concept of Pan-Americanism began to be popularized with the first

Pan-American Conference which took place in Washington in 1889–90, the Monroe Doctrine of 1823, and the clear perception of the unequal relations existing between the United States and the rest of the American republics. Almost every one of the subsequent conferences which took place during this second stage dealt with the problem of the peaceful resolution of international disputes, leaving us an abundant legacy of international instruments, many of which are still in force.

In what is known as the First Pan-American Conference, a proposal was approved — though not ratified — for arbitration to be obligatory in certain specific areas, and optional in others. At the Second Pan-American Conference, which met in Mexico City (1901–1902), a Protocol was adopted which followed the Hague Convention of 1899, and established arbitration as an option in the solution of legal controversies.[2] This became a part of American international law.

The Fifth Pan-American Conference, which was held in Santiago, Chile, in 1923, made an important contribution to the peaceful resolution of international disputes when it approved a treaty to prevent conflicts between the American States. This became known as the Pact of Gondra.[3] It laid down a thorough investigation procedure for disputes which were unable to be resolved through negotiation or arbitration. Two permanent commissions were established — one with headquarters in Washington, and the other in Montevideo — which would consist of the three most senior diplomats in those capitals. They would convoke the commission each time it was necessary. Each party to the controversy would designate two members and the four would then choose a fifth. The intervention of these investigatory commissions would have the effect of delaying the use of force while they were fulfilling their functions and for six months after they had presented their reports. During this period the States concerned were obliged to seek a settlement of the dispute.

The International Conference on Conciliation and Arbitration, held in Washington in 1928–29, approved two treaties affecting conflict resolution. In the first place, a General Convention on Inter-American Conciliation — the Washington Convention — was agreed. This compelled the parties to submit any unresolved controversy to a conciliation procedure. It affirmed that the investigatory commissions set up by the Pact of Gondra would also have a conciliation function. In the second place, this conference adopted a General Inter-American Arbitration Treaty which required obligatory arbitration in the case of legal controversies arising between parties.[4] But it did not define any procedure for determining whether a dispute was legal or political in nature. Moreover, with respect to the procedure for designating the tribunal, a lack of co-operation between the States who were parties to the controversy might make it difficult to constitute. Little wonder that Pedro Oliveira commented 'it is not an obligatory Arbitration Treaty in practice due to serious defects in procedural aspects'.[5] Besides, in cases of disagreement, each party could name two arbitrators without guarantees of their impartiality. This in effect transformed the process of arbitration into something very different and quite similar to negotiation where States designate lawyers to defend and represent their positions and interests, and try to arrive at a practical agreement which is more political than legal.

In conducting this brief historical overview, we should not forget the 1933 Treaty on Non-Aggression and Conciliation, better known as the Saavedra Lamas Pact, which was proposed by Argentina and subscribed to in Rio de Janeiro on 10 October 1933. Unfortunately, this agreement constituted a step back from the goals achieved in the Gondra Pact and the 1929 General Convention on Inter-American Conciliation. In fact, the Saavedra Lamas Pact allows several exceptions to the conciliation procedures it provides for.

In December 1933, the Seventh Pan-American Conference adopted an Additional Protocol to the General Convention on Inter-American Conciliation in terms of which the *ad hoc* commissions of the Pact of Gondra became permanent commissions, called Investigation and Conciliation Committees. However, in spite of the progress which this Protocol might have signified, it was only ratified by 11 states, which limited considerably its possible efficacy in the resolution of regional conflicts.

Prompted by the end of the Chaco War,[6] an extraordinary conference was convened — the Inter-American Conference for the Consolidation of Peace, which took place in Buenos Aires in 1936 and whose fundamental purpose was to reinforce the Inter-American System in order to prevent another conflict of the same kind. Several very important agreements were concluded. In the first place, the Convention for the Maintenance, Preservation and Re-establishment of Peace. Secondly, the Additional Protocol relating to Non-intervention. Thirdly, the Treaty on the Prevention of Disputes which provided for the creation of permanent bilateral commissions charged with studying and proposing adequate measures to eliminate difficulties between parties. Fourthly, the Inter-American Treaty on Negotiation and Mediation, which lays down that, in case of conflict, the parties may resort to the mediation of an eminent citizen of any American country which is not involved in the dispute. And lastly, a Convention to co-ordinate, extend and ensure the fulfilment of the existing treaties. This contains provisions for consultations between the American States.

The Institutionalization of the Inter-American System

This third phase in no way represents an absolute rupture with the Pan-American principles which had been established, even though it did attempt to establish a more balanced treatment in the relations between the United States and the other American republics. This endeavour, however, remained a mere aspiration since in practice it has proved difficult to overcome the hegemony exercised by the United States due to its immense military, industrial and economic power. But during this period the institutions of the Inter-American System did begin to consolidate and take on a permanent existence with more regular meetings and conferences.

In Mexico City in February 1945, an Extraordinary Consultative Conference took place between some Latin American countries[7] and the United States which was known as the Inter-American Conference on the Problems of War and Peace. Among the topics which were examined were problems relating to an appropriate international organization for the maintenance of collective peace and security.[8] In particular, they discussed the promotion of the Inter-American System and its co-ordination with the new world organization which was being created and which would emerge from the San Francisco Conference in June of that year. A conference resolution gave its general support to the Dumbarton Oaks Proposal for World Organization, but stressed the 'convenience of resolving controversies and questions of an Inter-American character according to Inter-American methods and systems in harmony with the General International Organization'. It is interesting to note that at this moment, it was the Latin American countries which insisted on the supremacy of regional over global mechanisms for the solution of conflicts, while the United States, at that stage fully committed to the search for global and universal solutions, favoured the pre-eminence of the world organization over a regional institution. It took the Cold War and the hegemony of the United States within the Inter-American System to cause these positions soon to be reversed.

Another resolution which was approved in this Conference recommended to the Inter-American Legal Commission that it elaborate a Project for an Inter-American Peace System which would co-ordinate the regional instruments for the peaceful resolution of international conflicts with the mechanisms and procedures of the new world organization, the UN. It was suggested that the American countries should be obliged to submit disputes to the regional organs before bringing them before the UN Security Council. The Washington and Montevideo Commissions, created by the Pact of Gondra, were to be abolished and their functions transferred to the Executive Council of the Pan-American Union. But, without a doubt, the most notable idea behind the Project of the Inter-American Legal Commission was the attempt to systematize in one text the regional mechanisms for international conflict resolution, which by that time were numerous. Eventually in 1947, a definite project was elaborated. While admitting that arbitration was unquestionably an adequate means for the solution of legal disputes, it proposed extending it to other kinds of issues and making it an obligatory means for the solution of all controversies. It thus enshrined the principle that any controversy between American States should be resolved through arbitration or juridical settlement. It must be observed, however, that once again no adequate mechanisms were agreed for setting up an arbitration tribunal in cases where one of the parties rejected the procedure. In any case, the principle of compulsory arbitration generated such opposition that final approval of the project proved impossible.

At the Extraordinary Conference in Mexico, a resolution was approved which would provide the basis for the present Inter-American System. This was Resolution VII, known as the Act of Chapultepec. It established machinery for collective security and reciprocal assistance in cases of aggression or the threat of aggression. The resolution recommended the adoption of a treaty in which these principles would be set out and more adequate procedures to confront threats of aggression be given substance. At first, it was agreed that a Special

Inter-American Conference, which would meet shortly in Rio de Janeiro starting 20 October 1945, would take care of the preparation and adoption of the definitive text of the treaty. However, owing to the cool relations between Argentina and the United States at the time, the meeting had to be postponed until August 1947, when it took place in Petropolis. This conference gave birth to the Inter-American Treaty on Mutual Assistance, known as the TIAR.

The Treaty reaffirmed the intention of the parties not to resort to the threat or use of force in any way that was incompatible with the Treaty or the United Nations Charter. It proclaimed the solidarity of the continent against any aggression in which an American State was the victim at the hands of any other State, American or non-American. The parties committed themselves to resolve any dispute which might arise between them by peaceful means, resorting first to the procedures in force in the Inter-American system, failing which they would have recourse to the UN Security Council. In the case of conflicts between American States, the Contracting Parties, gathered in conference, would urge the States to suspend hostilities and restore the *status quo ante bellum*.

Where conflicts involved extra-continental forces, the Treaty stipulated that an armed attack against any one American State would be considered as an attack on all of them. In cases of aggression falling short of armed attack, the Consultative Committee would meet immediately to adopt whatever measures were necessary for the common defence and maintenance of continental peace and security. In fact, the TIAR was conceived fundamentally as an instrument of the Cold War. It concentrated on potential aggression coming from the socialist world and was quite ineffective where the aggression originated from elsewhere, as was clearly demonstrated in the case of the Malvinas (Falklands) War.

However, the TIAR has been extensively used in the case of conflicts originating within the Inter-American System. The situation has in practice only benefited the United States since it is the only country which need not fear the intervention of any other country in the region, being able at the same time to invoke the treaty to legitimize its own interventions in any of them.

In 1948, at the Ninth International American Conference, it was proposed that the Consultative Committee be able to recommend to the parties that they resolve their disputes through peaceful means chosen by the parties themselves, and where they did not reach agreement, the Consultative Committee would indicate a means for its specific solution. This proposal met with several objections.

In the end, the Chapter on Conflict Resolution which was inserted in the Charter of the Organization of American States stipulated the following principles. In the first place, all regional conflicts must be submitted to the procedures laid down in the OAS Charter before being taken before the UN Security Council. Secondly, the means of peaceful solution to which the parties must resort comprise direct negotiation, mediation, investigation and conciliation, judicial proceedings, arbitration and any other procedures which the parties agree on at any moment. Thirdly, in those cases where a controversy cannot be resolved by the usual diplomatic means, the parties are obliged to agree on some other peaceful procedure which will allow them to reach a solution. Finally, Article 23 of the OAS Charter promises that 'a special treaty will establish adequate means to resolve disputes and will determine the procedures pertinent to each particular peaceful means, in a way that no dispute arising within the American States will remain without a definite solution within a reasonable period of time.' The Conference proceeded to adopt the American Treaty for Peaceful Solutions — the Pact of Bogotá.

The Treaty deals with mediation, investigation, conciliation, judicial proceedings and arbitration. It should be pointed out that, in legal circles, there is a marked preference for recourse in the International Court of Justice (ICJ) over arbitration or regional legal solutions. This preference conflicts with the principle that disputes between American States should be submitted to regional mechanisms for solution. On the other hand, the Pact establishes that in the case of disputes which do not have a legal character and cannot be submitted to the ICJ, recourse must be had to the conciliation procedure.

Unlike previous initiatives, the Pact of Bogotá contemplates compulsory machinery for the constitution of an arbitration tribunal in cases where this is the procedure to be used and one of the parties is reluctant to co-operate.

The purpose behind the adoption of the Pact of Bogotá was, above all, to incorporate in one legal instrument all the rules relating to conflict resolution in the American continent, and so replace the numerous pre-existing agreements and impose uniform solutions to end the previous chaos. However, this intention was frustrated since the Pact stated that it would only come into effect for each of the Contracting States when they deposited their respective instruments of ratification. It would have been more logical for it to have come into force once ratified by the unanimous vote of the signatory States, or a large important majority of them.[9] Even today, of the 32 members of the OAS, only 14 have ratified the Pact. Those who have not are usually neighbouring countries. The result has been to add a new element of confusion to the numerous existing regional treaties on the matter. Relations between States who are a party to the Pact are governed by it. Those who are not abide by some other previous agreement where both the contestants have subscribed to it. As for relations between a State that is a party to the Pact and one that isn't, these have to be governed by some instrument accepted as valid by both.

Leaving aside all these problems, it should be noted that this Treaty has never actually been invoked, even by countries which ratified it.

The total picture of the legal institutional framework for the resolution of international disputes in the American continent would not be complete if it did not include a brief reference to the Treaty for the Proscription of Nuclear Arms in Latin America — the 1967 Treaty of Tlatelolco. With the sole exception of Argentina, this has been ratified by all the Latin American republics. Curiously, the only instance in which this instrument has been invoked was the Malvinas War, and that by the only country which has not ratified it — Argentina. On this occasion the United Kingdom, which had ratified the Additional Protocols I and II of the Treaty of Tlatelolco, was accused of introducing nuclear arms into the region.

The multiplicity of legal instruments for the peaceful settlement of disputes constitutes one more demonstration of the struggles and tensions which have characterized relations between the American States. As a general rule, these mechanisms have been created thinking not of hypothetical, future conflicts but of present and latent ones. On the other hand, these international treaties are intimately related to each other, mutually complementing each other and making reference to the rules and institutions established in a previous agreement, or reformulating some of those rules or institutions. Besides, there also exists a very close relation between these procedures and those contemplated by the United Nations Charter.

Of the agreements which have been created and referred to here in chronological order, the 1947 Inter-American Treaty for Reciprocal Assistance (TIAR), the OAS Charter and the Pact of Bogotá (both agreed in 1948) constitute the fundamental pillars of the Inter-American System. It is precisely the ineffectiveness of these instruments which has brought out the weaknesses of the Inter-American System, and made it necessary to convene in late 1985 an extraordinary conference of the OAS in Cartagena, Colombia. This had the purpose of revitalizing the organization and discussing possible reforms to the three conventions. However, one cannot be too optimistic since previous reforms of the OAS Charter in 1967 and of TIAR in 1975 did not succeed in taking the Inter-American System out of the paralysis in which it finds itself.

The OAS and the Solution of International Conflicts

Since the Organization of American States is the most representative institution of the Inter-American System, it is natural that we concentrate our attention on the functions that it carries out in situations of crisis and conflict.

One of the purposes of the OAS is to secure the peaceful resolution of disputes which may arise between the Member States. Besides urging the parties to a dispute to seek a peaceful solution, the Organization can itself intervene directly in the search for solutions. The General Assembly may consider any matter relevant to the American States. The Permanent Council of the Organization oversees the maintenance of friendly relations between the Member States, and is ready to help them resolve their disputes peacefully. It can mediate itself or remit the controversy to the Commission. The Permanent Council may investigate the facts, including entering the territory of either party with their prior consent. In addition, the Council may recommend procedures to the parties concerned for the peaceful resolution of the dispute. The effect of the OAS's intervention, however, may be as varied as the motives which prompt the Members of the Organization to enter into dispute in the first place.

The Resolution of Conflicts
Without a doubt, the most significant political function that the OAS may fulfil

is to help resolve regional conficts. But it is not adequately equipped to fulfil that task. The divorce which exists between the UN Charter on the one hand, and the Pact of Bogotá on the other, is perhaps one of the causes for this inability to act. But the principal deficiency is of a political kind, since it should not be forgotten that, if the Organization is to intervene in a conflict, the key to success always lies in the co-operation of the States which are involved, and it is this co-operation that is difficult to achieve. Normally, while one party may desire the intervention of the OAS, the other will resist it.

It might have been expected that the considerable authority achieved by international organizations generally in the field of conflict resolution would have contributed to the success of the OAS in this field. However, it is difficult in our continent to find a more disreputable organization than the OAS. As a result, it has been suffering for several years from a serious financial crisis, occasioned by delays in the payment of their contributions by some Members.[10]

But the main obstacle to effective OAS action in the solution of regional conflicts has been its lack of authority over its Members. This is due to the immense imbalance between the military, political and economic power of one of its Members, the United States, and that possessed by all its other Members. This has caused the OAS on numerous occasions simply to be used as an instrument of United States foreign policy.

The Legitimation of a Specific Method of Seeking a Solution

In the second place, the intervention of the OAS may at least serve to legitimize the adoption of a specific means of solving a dispute. For example, in 1957, in the dispute between Honduras and Nicaragua, the OAS was able to persuade the parties to submit their controversy to the International Court of Justice, whose decision put an end to the conflict. Similarly with conflicts involving Powers outside the region, as in the case of the Malvinas (Falklands), the OAS urged the parties to seek a negotiated settlement. However, in part owing to the same weaknesses which were pointed out above, the American States have not usually expected or welcomed OAS intervention in their conflicts. It is not surprising, therefore, that when relations between Chile and Argentina over the Beagle Channel became particularly tense in 1978 (taking both States to the verge of an armed confrontation), the suggestion that the Pope should mediate did not come from the OAS.[11]

Escalation or Reduction of Tensions

In the third place, the OAS could play a moderating role which, in situations of crisis, could at least reduce tensions and provide a forum where the parties could discuss their differences. The public character of parliamentary diplomacy tends to mitigate confrontations by allowing people to present their arguments before the bar of international public opinion, persuade the world of the justice of their cause and abandon intransigent positions. Public presentations by representatives of the parties to the conflict before the organs of the OAS may facilitate understanding and serve as a basis for a negotiated agreement, or open the door to subtle forms of pressure which make conciliation possible. In those cases where the parties do not maintain diplomatic relations with each other, the OAS (like any other international organization) has an opportunity to make informal contacts with them and discuss possible solutions through the discreet mediation of third parties and without the publicity attendant upon a formal meeting.

In such circumstances, the OAS can provide an alternative to the use of force. In situations where war already exists — as with the war between Honduras and El Salvador in 1969, or the war between Peru and Ecuador in 1981 — or in situations of extreme tension such as the Central American conflict, especially from 1983 on — the OAS may not be able to impose its own solutions, but it may be able to avoid the conflict escalating and open the road to a peaceful solution.

Endorsement of the Claims of One of the Parties

The intervention of a regional organization may undoubtedly also lead to the endorsement of the claims of one of the parties to the conflict. Thus the repeated inclusion of Bolivia's claim to an ocean port on the agenda of the OAS General Assembly constitutes at least a sign of sympathy with the Bolivian case. This subtle backing for Bolivia's claims may even little by little lead to conditions where a solution satisfactory to both Chile (the stronger military power) and Bolivia can be negotiated.

Something similar happened in 1965 when the US invaded the Dominican Republic. The US attempted to legitimize its invasion by calling on the OAS to set up a multinational 'peace-keeping' force, even though this was only symbolic since it was dominated overwhelmingly by US contingents acting under the OAS mandate.

The OAS can also be used to organize hemispherical solidarity with a Member State involved in a conflict with a power from outside the region. The United States, during the Cuban missile crisis, first announced its quarantine of the island, and then requested an urgent meeting of the OAS Consultative Committee so that it would support the action already undertaken by the US and take blockading measures of its own. Similarly in the case of the Malvinas (Falklands), Argentina resorted to the OAS not so that it could resolve the conflict (which it could not do since one of the parties to the controversy was not a member of the Organization), but in order to obtain continental support for its claims and so cloak its position in a cape of legitimacy.

The Inter-American System and the UN

The absence of co-ordination between regional organizations and those with a global responsibility (particularly the UN) has generated conflicts with both the OAS and the UN contending they have jurisdiction over Member States of the Inter-American System. It is by no means clear which body has priority, or indeed exclusive competence, to resolve regional American conflicts.

On the one hand, Article 24 of the UN Charter points out that the Security

Council will have primary responsibility in maintaining international peace and security. On the other hand, Article 52(2) of the same Charter requires UN Members who are signatories to regional agreements, to solve local disputes through those organizations before submitting them to the Security Council. These clauses have led to contradictory interpretations about appropriate procedures for resolving international conflicts. For defenders of the universalist position, peace is indivisible and the competence of the Security Council to handle a conflict which may constitute a threat to international peace and security must never be disregarded, even when it may delegate its functions to a regional organization. The followers of the regionalist position uphold the primacy of regional agreements to try and resolve local conflicts, before they are handed over to the Security Council.

In the Americas there are supporters of the regionalist position who invoke some of the treaties subscribed to in the Inter-American System, especially the Inter-American Treaty for Mutal Assistance, the OAS Charter and the Pact of Bogotá, since these contain explicit clauses requiring States to use regional procedures to solve disputes before requesting the intervention of the UN Security Council. However, this line of argument is vitiated by Article 103 of the UN Charter, which says that, in case of conflict between the obligations of UN Members by virtue of the Charter and those obligations arising from any other international agreement, the obligations imposed by the Charter shall prevail.

In general, it is accepted that the Security Council has exclusive competence with respect to the application of coercive measures. But there is by no means a consensus concerning the peaceful resolution of disputes. Article 52 of the Charter concedes that there should be regional attempts to resolve those conflicts which have not resulted in the use of armed force and which are susceptible to being resolved by peaceful means. However, we should not forget that Article 35 of the Charter authorizes all members of the UN to draw to the attention of the Security Council or the General Assembly any controversy or situation which may lead to international friction. Neither this nor any other article exempts Member States who are also parties to regional agreements. Moreover there is nothing obliging organs of the United Nations to abstain from intervening in a dispute which is already being heard by a regional organization. Indeed the UN's pre-eminence over regional organizations forces the conclusion that its organs, and especially the Security Council, may hear any conflict whose prolongation could threaten international peace and security. It is up to the UN to decide whether to remit the examination of a conflict to a regional organization or to handle it itself.

The debate on this point has been outlined in some detail because the issue arose in 1954 as a result of the denunciation, made before the UN Security Council by President Jacobo Arbenz's Government of Guatemala, of Honduran aggression and the United Fruit Company's destabilization, both prompted by the United States. During the Security Council debate, the representatives of the United States, Brazil and Colombia (all members of the Security Council) insisted that the correct forum to examine

Guatemala's complaint was the Organization of American States and not the UN Security Council. Guatemala was supported by the Soviet Union and France in the Security Council, both of which countries considered that Guatemala had been the victim of aggression and that under these circumstances the competence of the Security Council was unquestionable. When on 22 June the Arbenz Government once again resorted to the Security Council, it — without pronouncing on the question of its competence — refused to include the Guatemalan question on the agenda. As a result, the affair remained totally in the hands of the OAS and its Inter-American Peace Commission. Initially, Guatemala had refused to acknowledge the jurisdiction of the Commission. However, on 26 June 1954, it invited the Commission to send an investigation committee to Guatemala. The Commission accepted but was not able to carry out its task because on the night of 27 June, the Arbenz Government was overthrown and the Commission was immediately informed of an alleged mediation effort being undertaken by the US and El Salvador in order to reconcile the new government of Guatemala and the rebel forces which had invaded the country with foreign support. On 2 July, the three countries thanked the Commission and informed it that the controversy which had prompted the invitation to the Commission no longer existed.

The conflict over competence was repeated in July 1960 when the government of Cuba resorted to the Security Council, accusing the United States of carrying out an aggressive policy against it — intervening in its internal affairs, giving assistance to counter-revolutionary elements and helping them in their plans to invade the country and overthrow the established government. The US government once again held that the competent entity to hear this controversy was the OAS, which already knew of the tensions in the Caribbean, and not the UN. This position got some support from Argentina and Ecuador — the two Latin American countries which at that time were on the Security Council. They proposed that, since the OAS was already cognizant of the affair, the Security Council should merely take note of the circumstances and suspend any consideration of the case until it received information from the OAS. This resolution was approved on 19 July 1960, and accepted by Cuba. However, in October of the same year, after a trade embargo had been imposed by the United States, Cuba once again presented a complaint, this time before the UN General Assembly, but without success. On 31 December 1960, and 3 January 1961, Cuba again requested the Security Council to consider the threat of aggression against it by the United States together with the breaking off of diplomatic relations by the latter. Once more, the US denied the competence of the Security Council. Subsequently, after the invasion of Bay of Pigs on 21 April 1961, the UN General Assembly accepted a proposal of seven Latin American countries and approved a resolution exhorting all Member States to take the necessary steps to remove the existing tension from the region.

The problem arose once again in September 1960. At a Meeting of the Consultative Committee of Foreign Ministers which took place on 21 August in accordance with the TIAR, Venezuela denounced the Dominican Republic for having participated in a plot against the life of the Venezuelan President in an attempt to overthrow the country's government. The Meeting approved a resolution breaking off diplomatic relations with the Dominican Republic and partially cutting economic relations, beginning with the suspension of arms supplies. In this case, the Consultative Committee was not acting as a means for solving a regional conflict, but on the contrary, as an instrument to punish a Member State which was thought to have acted against international law. On 5 September 1960, the Soviet representative on the Security Council requested an urgent meeting to consider this regional decision on the grounds that, since it was a case of coercive measures which, according to Article 53 of the UN Charter, could only be taken on the authority of the Security Council, the latter ought to be asked to approve these measures. During the debate that followed, the Argentinian representative contended that the authorization of the Security Council was necessary only in cases where the measures taken implied the use of armed force. This opened up a discussion on the meaning of coercive measures. He proposed, in the name of his own government and the governments of Ecuador and the United States, that the Security Council should only note the report previously submitted by the OAS Secretary-General indicating the measures adopted against the Dominican Republic. This was finally approved by the Security Council, although not all who voted for it agreed on the interpretation which should be given to Article 53 of the Charter.

A similar situation occurred in 1962. At the Eighth Consultative Commission Meeting of Foreign Ministers in Punta del Este, it was resolved that the government of Cuba was incompatible with the principles and objectives of the Inter-American System, and that this incompatibility precluded it from participating in its affairs. The Ministers also resolved to suspend immediately any traffic in arms with Cuba. Cuba responded by requesting a meeting of the Security Council on 8 March to examine these measures and to request the International Court of Justice for a consultative opinion on their legality. However, on this occasion, the Security Council was not able to adopt any resolution on the issue.

During the Cuban missile crisis of October 1962, there arose a new occasion for the OAS machinery to come into action (in combination with the TIAR and the UN). In his speech of 22 October 1962, President Kennedy announced a strict quarantine of the island of Cuba to stop the shipment of military equipment which was on its way. He also summoned an immediate Consultative Meeting of OAS Foreign Ministers to consider, in accordance with the TIAR, the alleged threat to the security of the Hemisphere and to adopt the necessary counter-measures in terms of Articles 6 and 8 of the Treaty of Rio de Janeiro. Unlike on previous occasions, the US Government also requested an emergency meeting of the Security Council to take action 'against the latest Soviet threat to world peace'. The US proposed a resolution requiring the 'rapid dismantling and withdrawal of offensive arms from Cuba, under supervision of UN observers'. While having recourse to the UN was understandable considering the USSR was not a member of the Inter-

American System, it should not be forgotten that Cuba *was* — the resolution approved by the Consultative Meeting of Foreign Ministers in January 1962 had not expelled Cuba from the OAS; it had simply declared the present Cuban Government incompatible with the principles and objectives of the Inter-American System and that this incompatibility precluded it from participating in it. This did not mean that, once there was a conflict, it would not be possible to use the machinery contemplated in the Inter-American System to resolve it.

What actually happened was that the OAS Council resolved to 'call for the immediate dismantling and removal of the missiles and other offensive arms' from Cuba, and recommended that OAS Member States, individually or collectively, take all measures necessary, according to Articles 6 and 7 of the TIAR, including the use of armed force, to ensure that the government of Cuba stop receiving military materiel from the Soviets and Chinese which could threaten continental peace and security. As in the case of the measures which were taken against the Dominican Republic in 1960, the Security Council was informed of the resolution. This time, however, the Security Council did not take any action on it, beyond recommending to the UN Secretary-General that he offer to mediate in order to obtain a solution to the conflict.

One of the most interesting cases of UN–OAS concurrence of competence arose in the Dominican Republic in April 1965. This very obviously internal conflict became internationalized as a result of the armed intervention of the United States. The OAS Council considered the crisis and, as a first step, requested the doyen of the Diplomatic Corps in the Dominican Republic, the Papal Nuncio Monsignor Emmanuel Clarizio, to transmit to the parties the Council's fervent desire that they should cease hostilities. The Nuncio succeeded in obtaining a ceasefire, to be supervised by the OAS Commission. Meanwhile, the OAS Council called a Consultative Meeting of Foreign Ministers and instructed the OAS Secretary-General to inform the UN Security Council (in accordance with Article 54 of the Charter) of the efforts by the OAS to put an end to the conflict. Worried by the course of the events, the OAS Council also decided to send its Secretary-General to the Dominican Republic in order to evaluate the situation and report to the next Consultative Meeting. When it met, the meeting created a special five-member commission to visit the Dominican Republic and offer its assistance to the parties concerned. Thanks to their co-operation, the commission played quite an active role in resolving the conflict. As part of the OAS intervention, the meeting responded to a request from the US on 6 May 1965, to create an Inter-American Peacekeeping Force. OAS Member States were invited to contribute military or police contingents. But, before this resolution was approved, certain Latin American countries — specifically Venezuela, Mexico and Chile — tried to obtain the withdrawal of the North American forces already stationed in the Dominican Republic. Venezuela even suggested the Peacekeeping Force should only comprise Latin American contingents, but without success.

On 1 May 1965, the Soviet Union requested an emergency meeting of the UN Security Council to debate the 'question of the armed intervention of the United States in the internal affairs of the Dominican Republic'. The Security

Council, at the request of Jordan, approved a resolution in which, without mentioning the OAS, the parties were urged to cease fire and the UN Secretary-General was instructed to send his representative to the Dominican Republic to investigate and inform the Council on the situation. CEPAL's Executive Secretary, Antonio Mayobre, was appointed. During the debate in the Security Council, it was argued that the presence of the OAS Inter-American Peacekeeping Force constituted a coercive measure in violation of the United Nations Charter, since it had not been authorized by the Security Council. While the debate regarding the UN–OAS concurrent jurisdiction was certainly not new, the discussion was centred on two points: the competence of the Security Council to deal with a dispute which was already being handled by a regional organization, and the steps which a regional organization could validly take to maintain or restore peace. During the debate it was held that the primary responsibility of the Security Council could not be supplanted by the action of a regional organization. On the other hand, it could be argued that, taking into account the common purpose of the UN and the OAS in the field of conflict resolution, their functions are not mutually exclusive, but rather complementary and should reinforce one another.

The special commission of the OAS in the Dominican Republic regarded the appointment of a special envoy by the UN Secretary-General in a critical light, if not with downright hostility. It believed that his intervention could obstruct the progress of the negotiations. In similar fashion, the Pan-American Union's Legal Affairs Department went so far as to affirm that the UN intervention at a time when the regional organization was making every possible effort to reach a peaceful settlement was an 'abuse of power'.

Meanwhile, the Security Council discussed several proposals to resolve the crisis. Finally, on 22 May 1965, at the suggestion of France, it approved a final resolution on the Dominican crisis in which all reference to the OAS was omitted. It demanded that the temporary suspension of hostilities become a permanent ceasefire, and the Secretary-General was invited to submit a report on how to put the resolution into effect.

As can be appreciated in all these cases, the role of the Security Council was fairly discreet and it did not pronounce on the conflict of competence between the OAS and the UN. Nor, in practice, did it prevent the OAS from being active in the settlement of disputes. Even though it did not authorize the measures taken by it, neither did it disapprove of them.

It seems paradoxical that, while in the beginning the United States defended the UN's supremacy and the Latin American countries took a regionalist line, before long, the United States (in a new version of the Monroe Doctrine) chose to support regional solutions as a way of keeping the USSR and its allies at the margins of conflicts occurring in the American continent, while the Latin American countries themselves soon discovered that a regional system dominated by the presence of one hegemonic power could not guarantee the existence of effective mechanisms for the resolution of international disputes.

In the final analysis, what lay behind this controversy between global and regional peace-keeping machinery was not a desire to look for the most adequate way to solve regional conflicts, but rather the intention of a hegemonic power to keep these conflicts within regional organizations which they dominate versus the aspirations of the minor powers to find a more independent forum where they can air their controversies more freely.

Regional Experiences of Conflict Resolution and the Decline of the OAS

As we have been able to see, there are in theory a wide variety of institutional instruments and mechanisms in the American continent whose primary function is to help solve international disputes. However, in practice, these mechanisms have not always proved adequate and on occasion have failed lamentably to resolve a dispute, or simply been ignored by the parties. To some extent, this is because initially the OAS was only a regional alliance in the context of the Cold War, caught between the dominant presence of the United States on the one hand, and the Latin American countries' desire for leadership on the other. But the changes in power relations, especially the tense relations existing between the Super Powers, and the substantial changes in the interests of the members of the Inter-American System have slowly rendered these institutions inactive and even more ineffective.

The OAS, in particular, has been unable to adapt to circumstances and measure up to the new aspirations and demands they impose. The immediate effect has been that it is frequently ignored. New organizations, like SELA, which reflect better the wishes and hopes of the majority of Latin American countries, have moved in to fill the political vacuum that has been created. In addition, other instruments which were not set up as a means of international conflict resolution have had their purposes stretched to include this function — the Andean Pact is an example — or wholly new institutions have been created like the Contadora Group, which has completely displaced the OAS in the Central American conflict.

It is undeniable, of course, that in some cases the OAS has played a useful role. There are even some recent examples of these interventions, but they are not abundant and they seem to be declining in number all the time.

In 1969, for example, during the war between Honduras and El Salvador the OAS at first stood aside while the neighbouring countries, Costa Rica, Nicaragua and Guatemala, tried unsuccessfully to mediate. Then the OAS Secretary-General sent members of the Inter-American Human Rights Commission to both countries. Colombia and Venezuela attempted a second mediation effort which also did not bear fruit. This decided the OAS to call an emergency meeting of its Council. The appeal for a ceasefire was finally heeded by the parties and OAS observers were sent to supervise it and the evacuation of Salvadorean soldiers from Honduran territory. The evacuation was done excessively slowly and threatened to start the conflict all over again. In order to oblige El Salvador to abide by its resolutions, the OAS Council called an emergency meeting of Foreign Ministers who threatened El Salvador with diplomatic and economic sanctions. Finally, on 29 July 1969, the two countries accepted an agreement negotiated under the auspices of the OAS Secretary-General. The following year, they also agreed, as a result of prompting by the OAS, to create a demilitarized zone in the region where the fighting had originally started and entrusted Costa Rica, Guatemala and Nicaragua to supervise the Agreement.

Another recent case which occurred arose out of the rebellion against the Somoza Government in Nicaragua in 1978. On this occasion, the OAS Council called a meeting of Foreign Ministers to consider the situation in Nicaragua, followed by a visit of the Inter-American Human Rights Commission to investigate accusations of human rights violations against the Somoza regime. These efforts finally ended in the triumph of the Sandinista revolution and the fall of the Somoza regime.

In January 1981 a border conflict between Peru and Ecuador broke out which led to armed confrontations between the two countries. Once again it was necessary to convene a meeting of Foreign Ministers although only five Ministers besides those of Peru and Ecuador turned up. They urged both parties to put an end to the conflict. But Peru rejected the OAS intervention and argued that the conflict was the exclusive responsibility of the guarantor countries which had signed the Rio de Janeiro Protocol in January 1942, namely Argentina, Brazil, Chile and the United States.

The current Central American crisis is the most obvious demonstration of the ineffectiveness of the Inter-American System in resolving local conflicts. In effect, the main effort at mediation has come from a particular circle of Latin American countries, the Contadora Group. The OAS itself judged the Contadora Group to be the most appropriate framework for tackling the situation. At the same time, the participation of the United States in the conflict — including its mining of Nicaraguan ports — led Nicaragua to denounce the US before the International Court of Justice, whose jurisdiction was denied by the United States, even though the Court itself estimated that it was competent to try the case and went ahead and did so. In any case, this protracted conflict is being managed completely at the margins of the mechanisms provided by the Inter-American System.

Conclusion

There is an impression, becoming more widely accepted, that the legal machinery of the Inter-American system is irrelevant in times of crisis, and that its institutions play only a marginal role in the search for solutions to the more serious regional conflicts. In practice, the Inter-American System has proved to be inadequate to resolve the majority of disputes in the region. Its machinery may be able to solve disputes of a bilateral and non-ideological character between minor powers, but its incapacity to solve any other disputes seems to be the general rule. It need hardly be added that it cannot solve conflicts which arise between the United States and any Latin American country.

Some localized conflicts, such as that which arose between Chile and Argentina over the Beagle Channel, have been settled at the margins of the mechanisms and procedures contemplated by the Inter-American System. In this case, the machinery was ignored, and a solution found on the basis of bilateral agreements which involved extra-continental bodies. There are many other examples where a pre-existing bilateral agreement proved essential in finding a solution to a conflict. For instance, even though the OAS played a role in the 1981 war between Peru and Ecuador, it was the bilateral treaty already signed by the two states which was the key.

Even the US Government, which used to turn to the OAS in many different circumstances during the two first decades of the Organization's existence, now seems to be less willing to request its intervention in cases of vital interest to it. It seems to prefer adopting unilateral actions or bilateral diplomacy. Without a doubt, the United States no longer has the same ability to use the OAS and the Inter-American System to its advantage as it used to do.

The Malvinas (Falklands) War demonstrates that, rhetoric aside, the much vaunted Latin American solidarity is only a masquerade. There exist deep differences between the members of the Inter-American System which cannot be disguised behind flowery speeches or purely cosmetic reforms. Yet the relative ineffectiveness hitherto of the machinery for the peaceful resolution of international conflicts has not stopped the Member States of the Inter-American System from persevering once again to try and reform the three fundamental instruments: the OAS Charter, the TIAR and the Pact of Bogotá Among the new reforms now being contemplated, it has been suggested that the role of the OAS Secretary-General should be strengthened, giving him wider powers in matters of conflict resolution and allowing him more room to take initiatives himself. However, in my opinion, if the reforms to the OAS Charter of 20 years ago didn't prosper, I find it difficult to believe they will prosper today, when the OAS is more isolated and in even deeper disrepute. The real solution lies more in the political than the legal realm and requires deep changes in current attitudes to the Inter-American System.

Notes

1. Article 24 of the UN Charter.
2. In this sense, the Second Conference took a step backwards compared to the First Conference, which contemplated compulsory arbitration in all types of controversies.
3. The name is taken from Manuel Gondra, leader of the Paraguayan delegation who proposed it.
4. Not everyone regards it as really obligatory. See the opinion of Pedro Oliveira, quoted by J. J. Castilla, in *El Derecho Internacional en el Sistema Interamericano*, Cultura Hispánica editions, Madrid, 1970.
5. *Ibid.*, p. 358.
6. This war was the result of a long running frontier dispute between Bolivia and Paraguay. The armed confrontation began in 1932 (although the war was only formally declared in 1933) and it went on until July 1935, when a Protocol of Peace was signed.

7. Argentina was excluded for not having co-operated with the Allies during World War Two.

8. For the Latin American countries the Conference had an eminently informative finality. It had the purpose of informing them of the proposal for a new international organization which had been elaborated at Dumbarton Oaks by the Great Powers. This, of course, was the project to create the United Nations Organization.

9. An even more efficient procedure would have been to include the Pact of Bogotá as part of the OAS Charter itself.

10. As of Sepember 1985, OAS Members owed the Organization over $85 million.

11. In this case, the parties were persuaded to accept Papal mediation thanks to the good offices of the then President of Venezuela, Carlos Andrés Pérez.

14. The Impact of the Crisis on Human Rights

Pedro Nikken

The notion of human rights implies acknowledging that the human being is supposed to live and exist in political, social and cultural conditions which are in accordance with the dignity inherent in him. In this sense, the serious convulsions disrupting the conditions of life on the planet today, coupled with the present world crisis, affect human rights in more than one respect.

The content and ambit of human rights have been the object of a progressive evolution, both conceptually and in the recognition of what they entail and the protective devices required on the juridical level. The present chapter will consider the present situation of human rights as a legal concept, especially in international law. There is no doubt that there has been some progress in establishing the supranational status of human rights in international law. They are not only recognized in multilateral legal instruments, but have also become embedded in a universal ethical consciousness.

The first formal recognitions by constitutional law[1] of the modern concept of human rights as inviolable attributes of the person are found in the US Constitution of 1776 and the French Revolution's Declaration of the Rights of Man and the Citizenry in 1789. The US Constitution asserts that 'all men have been created equal and free, that they have been endowed by their Creator with certain inalienable rights; among which are life, liberty and the pursuit of happiness; that in order to ensure these rights for men, governments have been made which derive their legal rights from the consent of those who are governed.' And in the words of the French Revolution's Declaration, 'men are born and remain free and equal in rights. The social distinctions cannot be founded in other than the common utility.'

From these postulates, a constitutional tendency developed towards the recognition and guarantee of individual civil and political rights, whose object was the protection of liberty, security and the physical and moral integrity of the person. As a whole, it had to do with rights inspired by an individualist conception, whose purpose was to prevent the State from invading or violating certain attributes of the human being. They were, therefore, rights exercised against the State and provided those who possessed them with the means to defend themselves from the exercise of public power.

In this century there have occurred several important modifications in the conception and context of human rights. At the level of the domestic polity, the notions of economic, social and cultural rights appeared which were taken up first by the Mexican Constitution of 1917, the Weimar Constitution of 1919, the Spanish Constitution of 1931, the Soviet Constitution of 1936 and the Irish Constitution of 1937. The majority of Constitutions which came into effect after World War Two included, besides civil and political rights, a recognition of economic, social and cultural rights.

In general, this type of rights is directed towards the establishment of a regime which assures a person in society life in conditions which are in accordance with human dignity. These are rights no longer asserted against the State, but rather demanding things of the State. To a great extent, their exercise or enjoyment will depend on the economic, social and cultural policies of the State, which thus appears not only as the defender of civil order and liberty, but as the promoter of the well-being of the population. It is the State, directly or through its policies, which is charged with effectively upholding those rights.[2]

The sudden impact provoked by World War Two and the awareness of the crimes against humanity committed by Nazism and Fascism were the decisive impulse for the realization of a more remote ambition. This was that human rights which were so intrinsic to the dignity of the person should not only be guaranteed by national legal and political systems, to which the individual is subject and can have recourse, but should also have their supranational validity formally acknowledged, including international means of protection being made available to the individual.

The first instruments were declarations, which are solemn acts through which those who subscribe to them proclaim their support for certain principles of great value and which are judged to be everlasting. Even though the binding force of declarations in general is not absolute, in the case of those relating to human rights they have had great authority. They are frequently cited as providing fundamental international protection for the principles proclaimed. And there is a growing tendency to consider them as constituting a part of prevailing international law.

The first was the American Declaration of Rights and Duties of Man. This was followed a few months later by the Universal Declaration of Human Rights adopted by the United Nations General Assembly. Since then the international protection of human rights has been the object of numerous international conventions. Among them four should be mentioned which, owing to their general character, to a great extent express the progress which has been achieved in contemporary international law. Two have been sponsored by the United Nations and have a worldwide applicability: the International Convention on Civil and Political Rights and the International Convention on Economic, Social and Cultural Rights, which came into effect in 1976. The other two treaties are regional, being the European Treaty for the Protection of Human Rights and Fundamental Liberties, which came into effect in 1953, and the American Convention of Human Rights (the San José Treaty) which came into effect in 1978.

The latter two instruments, even though they establish more vigorous means of protection than has been customary,[3] limit themselves to civil and political rights.[4] However, the general system established by the Conventions of the United Nations provides for a more wide-ranging definition of human rights. Part I of each of the Conventions enshrines the so-called rights of peoples, which are basically their right to self-determination, to freely establish their political system, and to decide their own path of economic social and cultural development, and the right to freely dispose of their natural resources and wealth.[5]

Secondly, the field of individual human rights was dedicated to the acknowledgement and protection of both civil and political rights as well as economic, social and cultural ones. Leaving aside for a moment the reason why two separate conventions were signed, the Preamble to both emphasizes that the 'ideal of the free human-being, freed from fear and misery' cannot be realized 'unless the conditions be created which permit each person to enjoy their economic, social and cultural rights, as well as their civil and political rights'. And the Preamble to the Universal Declaration states clearly that 'liberty, justice and peace are based on the acknowledgement of the intrinsic dignity and equal and inalienable right of all members of the human family'.[6]

These categorical assertions reflect a new development in international law and a new consciousness around the issue of human rights. There is a growing recognition that the holder of any particular human right should be allowed, within given conditions, to request the protection of certain organs of the international community in order to protect their basic rights *vis-à-vis* the State they are subject to. Until recently this intervention by the international community between the State and its subjects was inadmissible.

A variety of legal systems are acknowledging, even though often only in theory, the priority that must be given to the protection and promotion of the fundamental rights of the person. The fact that these rights have been the object of public treaties and real negotiated agreements between States indicates that in the world today oppressive regimes are regarded as pariahs and measures which offend the intrinsic dignity of the human being are forbidden.

We can draw the following conclusions from the various treaties and declarations concerning human rights:

(1) Human rights are acknowledged as being of unquestionable value, to the point where they are now considered a matter appropriate for a 'Universal Declaration'.
(2) There are certain values which should inform world affairs, and these include liberty, dignity and the freedom of the person, the independence of peoples and the sovereignty of States.
(3) It is therefore not legal to pursue public policies which involve the violation of the network of human rights.

The contrast which it is most interesting to emphasize between the current crisis and human rights is that policies involving the violation of fundamental rights of the person have on occasion been adopted for the apparent purpose of overcoming the crisis. The question arises: to what extent have attempts to solve the crisis led to the imposition of public policies which are illegal from the point of view of international law and human rights? The question embodies, it is important to stress, both the area of civil and political rights as well as that of the economic, social and cultural rights.

Civil and political rights

The intensity of the crisis involves social convulsions which obviously affect the simple exercise of civil and political rights. These consequences range from the inauguration of authoritarian regimes by force and the establishing of a State of Exception, to the merely limited restrictions on the free exercise of public liberties and certain civil rights as a result of public disturbances arising from the privations to which a considerable proportion of the population are subject.

However, right now it is not possible to define the relationship between the crisis and the violation of civil and political rights. In the first place, this is because there have been recent political changes in several Latin American States which signify undeniable democratic progress. Secondly, it is not possible to determine, without a detailed investigation of each case, to what extent the social and political conflicts that have occurred in several countries of the continent are exclusively a product of the crisis and to what extent they depend on other ingredients. Finally, in a technical sense, not all restrictions on public liberties can be considered violations of human rights.

However, while bearing in mind these considerations, several situations can be examined in which the present crisis has clearly impaired the complete exercise of civil and political rights. It is to these that we now turn.

Authoritarianism
As far as the form and legitimacy of governments are concerned, the crisis has led to a flourishing of authoritarian tendencies. Many factors have contributed to this: the existence of a convulsed and unstable social situation; the growth of unemployment in all sectors, including among middle-class technicians and professionals; the considerable increase in the proportion of those living below the poverty line; the general awareness of governments' inability really to solve the economic situation; the limits of constitutional regimes in repressing public protest; as well as the interference of foreign interests.

This was the context in which a number of military regimes were installed in the 1970s. But these authoritarian governments failed, and the most general tendency has been to resort to the democratic–liberal model and a celebration of elections to choose leaders to lead their countries out of the crisis.

States of Emergency
Another situation which violates human rights is the declaration of states of exception or emergency. This has occurred many times in Latin America in order to face supposedly irresistible situations of public peril. And they serve as

a pretext for the restriction of certain human rights.

All the international instruments relating to civil and political rights, as do national constitutions, contain clauses providing for so-called states of emergency. It is not possible to ignore the existence of extraordinary conditions which may make it necessary to resort to exceptional means, including the temporary and limited suspension of some citizen rights.

Without going into too much detail on this much discussed topic,[7] it is necessary to point out that states of emergency should neither be easily resorted to nor become a *carte blanche* for the wholesale suspension of human rights.

There should be in the first place a present or imminent peril which threatens society as a whole. The International Convention on Civil and Political Rights and the European Human Rights Convention demand that any such alleged peril should threaten 'the existence of the nation',[8] while the American Convention on Human Rights mentions the 'case of war, public danger or other emergency which threatens the independence or security of the State . . .'[9] Therefore, states of emergency are only justified in situations which endanger the integrity or independence of the nation, or at least, as the European Human Rights Covenant points out, 'a threat to the organized existence of the community of the mentioned State'.[10] The danger which cannot be resisted by ordinary means must threaten the whole community and not just its government, since the exceptional powers are means of social defence and not simply instruments to keep a particular regime in power or to protect some particular interest.

In this sense, the state of emergency procedure has often been abused by justifying its imposition in terms of so-called national security doctrine. These doctrines interpreted the East–West confrontation as equivalent to a war situation and ostensibly involving the whole Hemisphere. And they were used to justify the most drastic measures of repression and contempt for human rights. In contrast to these bogus justifications, there is no doubt that the social convulsions and protests prompted by the crisis may be interpreted as a threat to national security and justify the imposition of a state of exception.

Secondly, strict necessity. The emergency is only justified if it cannot be dealt with by the State's ordinary machinery. And it must only affect those rights which by their nature are involved in the situation; i.e. the doctrine of proportionality must apply. In addition, its duration should not exceed whatever time is strictly required to deal with the particular circumstances. This also is an area open to abuse in interpretation.

Thirdly, certain rights must never be suspended, even during a state of emergency. These include the right to life, the right not to be enslaved or put in servitude, the right to a legal persona, to a name, a nationality, to freedom of conscience and religion, the fundamental political rights, the rights of children and the family, and the proscription on retroactive punishments, as well as whatever is indispensable for the protection of these rights. Emergency measures may not be discriminatory or incompatible with the other international obligations of the State.[11] And the suspension of human rights should adapt to the requirements of the 'general well-being' of a democratic society.[12]

Next, the state of emergency should be officially proclaimed and other Member States informed.[13]

Lastly, the exceptional character of the emergency should require rigorous control systems. The constitution would normally contemplate parliamentary or judicial control, if not both. The absence of reliable domestic control systems and the subjugation of public opinion make the imposition of a state of emergency by authoritarian regimes questionable. Often it is the existence of an illegitimate government itself that sparks off the conditions which are then invoked to suspend human rights guarantees. Besides which, there are no independent means allowed by the government to evaluate whether the suspension was justified. This may make it necessary to resort to the relevant international organs for a review of the situation although this will always be limited in effect since such bodies do not have the power to revoke measures by the national authorities.[14]

As can be seen, the conflicts deriving from the present crisis may be the direct occasion to impose situations in violation of civil and political rights. However, it is not possible, at least within the limited range of this work, to establish the precise relation between the two. In any case, a state of emergency does not seem to be typical of the present crisis.[15]

However, it is important to point out that social conflicts like those related to recession which have taken place in numerous Latin American countries are frequently the occasion of excessive repression and abuse. This may even be the case when the use of extraordinary powers is formally sanctioned by a legitimate government. But the prolonged suspension of public liberties in such a case implies the loss of a fundamental dimension of a democratic society, and may largely reduce the difference between it and a society governed by an overtly authoritarian regime.

Also, it is obvious that the present recession only affects political and civil rights in an indirect manner since they are not the immediate object of the crisis. In the same way whatever policies governments may adopt in this respect are not intended to resolve the situation by themselves. But this is not at all the case with the economic, social and cultural rights; these are involved directly with the present situation and are affected by the measures adopted to overcome it.

Economic, Social and Cultural Rights

Economic, social and cultural rights comprise those rights which protect access to material and cultural goods in conditions consistent with human dignity. For the purposes of this analysis, we will confine ourselves to those listed in the International Covenant on Economic, Social and Cultural Rights.

A first thing which strikes one is why, in spite of the fact that the proclamation of human dignity implies the recognition of a physical, moral and intellectual indivisibility, there exist two Covenants and not one. It is difficult to explain why this distinction was made between civil and political rights on the one hand and economic, social and cultural rights on the other. It is so obvious that, in the absence of economic, social and cultural rights, civil and political rights run the risk of being strictly formalistic, and in the absence of civil and political rights, economic, social and cultural rights could not be guaranteed for very long.[16]

At first, the United Nations had intended to adopt one treaty.[17] Afterwards this changed and the two treaties were agreed, although they were to share the greatest possible number of identical clauses.[18] The reasons for this distinction are still the subject of criticism.[19] They have to do with the idea that the two classes of rights have different methods of implementation and enforcement. According to this view, civil and political rights depend strictly on a legal order which acknowledges and guarantees them, backed up by the competent organs of public power; while economic, social and cultural rights depend on the existence of a social order based on a just distribution of goods, and which cannot be achieved except incrementally as a result of political effort. The first category are rights required immediately and the State assumes an obligation to meet this demand. The latter cannot be met unless the State disposes of the resources to satisfy them, since the obligations which are assumed depend for their fulfilment on the economic and social context. The first category, according to this argument, are true legal rights, susceptible to controls of a legal nature, while the second category are programmatic rights, which can only be monitored politically in the light of the country's socio-economic situation.

Putting aside several inaccuracies involved in this classification of rights,[20] there is one proposition which is true and which is relevant here. As a whole, the realization of economic, social and cultural rights does depend on existing resources, and States cannot be legally obliged to obtain results within a fixed time span; all they can be expected to do is to take the necessary steps so that improvements can follow.[21] This is true in a positive sense, that is, respecting the means which the State commits itself to supply in order to reach the satisfaction to which the right refers. But it is not necessarily correct in a negative sense, that is, where government actions are openly directed at undermining the situation with respect to economic, social and cultural rights. It is one thing not to be able to progress, because of a lack of resources, along the road towards creating a situation where the right is fulfilled. It is quite a different thing for a government to pursue policies deliberately inimical to the fulfilment of such rights. Clearly, the present economic crisis can undermine economic, social and cultural rights in both of these ways.

The Failure to Meet these Rights

The negative growth — i.e. actual contraction — of the Latin American economies has worsened the already difficult living conditions of people in the continent. The increase in unemployment, inflation and the devaluation of currencies have caused acute impoverishment, especially among wage workers and partially employed people, and even among the liberal professions. Many middle-class people are being pushed down into the proletariat and the proportion of those below the poverty line has increased dramatically.

In this situation human rights are not just placed in jeopardy when Latin Americans lose the right to live as full and free citizens, but also because immense numbers of people are being deprived of the possibility of living as human beings at all. It is enough to look at the relevant International Convention to see how far these rights are placed in jeopardy today.

According to the Convention, every person has the right to work. States and political parties commit themselves to adopt adequate measures to guarantee this right. In particular, Article 6 commits them to 'achieving an economic development which will . . . [provide] full and productive employment in conditions which guarantee the fundamental political and economic liberties of the human-being'.[22] But what is the actual situation in Latin America today? In contrast to this goal, there has been a massive increase in unemployment and the contraction of the region's economy has been such that living standards in 1983 had fallen back to 1977 levels.[23]

The Convention also prescribes the right of every worker to fair and satisfactory working conditions, comprising among other things, equal wages for equal work and 'conditions of existence which are dignified for them and for their families' (Article 7). It also declares the 'right of all persons to social security, including social insurance' (Article 9). Yet the working conditions and wages of the great majority of employees in Latin America were already critical before this recession, particularly so in the case of rural workers and the indigenous population. The impact of the crisis, especially with the deterioration of real wages, has made the situation far worse and put back any hopes of solving it.

The same can be said of Article 11 of the Convention, which proclaims 'the rights of all persons to an adequate level of living and for his family, including adequate food, shelter and clothing, and to a continuous improvement in the condition of living'.[24]

Other clauses in the Convention refer to additional activities and services which the State is called on to render or guarantee, but which the declining revenues of Latin American governments render impossible. This applies, for example, to the protection of the family and maternity rights (Article 10), the right to education (Articles 13 and 14), and the right to health (Article 12).

It is not the purpose of this work to measure in all its magnitude the impact of the crisis on these rights, but that does not prevent one from pointing out the social, economic and cultural damage sustained by the Latin American population despite the international guarantees of these rights. Leaving aside for the moment the legalistic question of how far States have obliged themselves to guarantee the effective delivery of these rights, it is irrefutable that the present Latin American situation displays a marked deterioration in most people's enjoyment of their internationally guaranteed economic, social and cultural rights. And it should be recalled that when the United Nations treated civil and political rights separately from economic, social and cultural rights, this did not imply that the latter were in any way of lesser importance than the former.

From its earliest years, the United Nations has emphasized that a 'man deprived of economic, social and cultural rights does not represent the human-being which is defined in the Universal Declaration and the ideal of a free man'.[25] In practice, the human suffering which comes from material misery is just as degrading as that stemming from a loss of civil rights.

There really isn't any true security without effective human rights, because 'the security of a State precisely consists of the exercise of public power in a way that cannot be questioned, either internally or externally, a situation which cannot be achieved without assuring the human rights of those over whom power is exerted.'[26]

We must not forget that the prolongation of the present situation may lead to greater social disturbances than those already witnessed in some Latin American countries, which implies an increase in confrontations and repression and a progressive destabilization of public institutions. President Raúl Alfonsín warned in Washington of what may occur and the way in which the present crisis threatens the democratic rebirth of the continent.[27] He also argued that the economic crisis, the debt situation and events in Central America together constituted a serious threat to the peace and security of the Hemisphere.[28]

Nevertheless, in a strictly legal sense, the current socio-economic situation in Latin America, even though incompatible with the requirements of human dignity, docs not necessarily represent a violation of the International Convention on Economic, Social and Cultural Rights, or of the American Convention on Human Rights. Articles 1 and 2 of the former Convention merely bind States to do their utmost, including by means of legislation, to render these rights fully effective. Article 27 of the American Convention does likewise.

These treaty provisions remind us that these kinds of rights are only realizable in the long run and the obligation of the State to guarantee their full enjoyment is conditional on the availability of resources. For these reasons, the fact that the objectives of the Treaty are not completely achieved cannot be regarded as a violation in itself. Thus, while the State is obliged to demonstrate its determination, as in the application of 'available resources' to move towards the satisfaction of certain rights, the task of showing whether it had reneged on this obligation would require an evaluation of what resources were 'available'. This implies a judgement on the economic policy of a government, which is not always easy. It is exactly one of the difficulties involved in the international protection of this kind of rights, and it begs the question whether the same thing would occur if one was trying to evaluate the outright suppression of those rights by governmental acts.

Their Outright Suppression

The International Court of Human Rights has pointed out that economic, social and cultural rights must be conceived in both a positive and a negative sense. What do these negative acts consist in? Must any act contrary to the content of the Conventions be considered an infraction?

It is generally acknowledged that, besides the suffering which the present crisis involves, it implies the adoption of a policy of adjustment, or austerity and collective sacrifices, as a means for the improvement of the economy. The existence of international obligations with respect to economic, social and cultural rights does not preclude the adoption of certain policies which curtail or reduce them. Article 4 of the International Convention states that those rights may be reduced, but 'only by limitations determined by law, only to the extent compatible with the primacy of those rights, and with the exclusive objective of promoting the general well-being of a democratic society'.

It would obviously not make sense for governments to be deprived of the means to remedy emergency situations like those which could arise from natural disasters or armed conflicts, or even a situation like the present one. In the area of civil and political rights, governments are allowed to declare a state of exception, albeit within predetermined conditions. There exists no immediate parallel in the field of economic, social and cultural rights. However it is possible to find an analogous situation in the provisions which permit limiting those rights since it is easy to imagine that, in situations of exceptional emergency, the general welfare may dictate lower limits.

Nevertheless, the restrictions which may be considered permissible in this field also have to abide by more or less strict requirements. In the field of civil and political rights, one limitation concerns those rights which are considered to be fundamental and, therefore, irrevocable. The primary one of these is the right to life. This means that under no circumstances may any government adopt policies which threaten the physical survival of human beings. This implies not only a prohibition on a government depriving a citizen of his life or physical integrity, but also a prohibition of policies which jeopardize the conditions of subsistence in such a way that may lead human beings to perish through poverty. It is true that in especially critical situations this tragic outcome is inevitable, but from the point of view of the protection of human rights, life is an absolute value which should be respected so far as possible when deciding what economic policies to pursue.

In the second place, limitations to economic, social and cultural rights must respect the nature of the right and be related to the purpose of promoting the general well-being of a democratic society. As with restrictions on civil liberties, the measures adopted should be strictly necessary, proportionate to the situation and temporary.

Strict necessity must be judged in the light of what alternative policies are possible and their consequences. The measures chosen should combine the least possible violation of human rights with the maximum efficacy in terms of bringing about a positive outcome to the crisis. The one thing which, if at all possible, must not be sacrificed is the right of a person to a dignified standard of living.

As for the second condition, proportionality, this demands an acceptable relation between the sacrifice being imposed on the population and the collective benefits which that same population will obtain as a result of the measures taken. This implies that the general sacrifice must have a counterpart in the shape of progress which is both general and tangible, i.e. it must be oriented to satisfying the rights of the majority and not of just one part of society, be it the government or the financial or productive sectors. Proportionality also means that the restrictions do not suppress or remove these rights permanently. For example, a necessary temporary restriction on the creation of new jobs must not be confused with the deliberate adoption of a policy to keep people unemployed.

The third principle — the temporary duration of the exceptional measures taken — is perhaps the least easy requirement to evaluate. Restrictions on economic, social and cultural rights must last for as short a time as possible. It should not be forgotten that, from the point of view of the doctrine of human rights and the international conventions which acknowledge and protect them, the deliberate suppression of those rights is not legitimate, no matter whether it is being supposedly done in the public interest at large or for the ostensible benefit of some specific social sector. The individual autonomy and dignity of every human being, which is the ultimate basis for respect for his rights, rules out utilitarian arguments of this nature. In the same way that is not admissible to impose a tyranny on the pretext of preparing the population to enjoy democratic institutions in the future, it is equally indefensible deliberately to reduce the current social and economic rights of the majority of the population with the excuse that it will guarantee the future well-being or survival of a sector of the economy. This false pragmatism 'pretends to compensate for the damage suffered by one individual with the benefit enjoyed by others, not taking into account that compensation only exists when the person compensated is the same as the one who has been damaged'.[29] It is not possible to 'merge the interests of individuals in a single system, disregarding that they are the interests of different and separate persons'.[30]

General policies, of course, only operate within concrete realities. It is not possible simply to accept a policy at face value, without comparing it with the alternatives. This is all the more important in a critical situation in which the options are all more or less disappointing.

When examining general policies being pursued as a solution to the economic crisis, attention must be paid to the formulas or 'recipes' of the International Monetary Fund, especially when these are tied up with the foreign debt situation of Latin American countries and become conditions of the international banking system for renegotiating that debt.

It has been pointed out that the 'Fund wanted to achieve two objectives: (i) to assure creditors that the debtor country would make the necessary adjustments; and (ii) assure the debtor country that it would have an adequate amount of financing. Even though the Fund was able to achieve the first objective, there is still a long way to go to fully fulfil the second one.'[31]

The 'adjustments' required by the Fund in its 'stabilization packages' have for years consisted of the following measures:

(a) Domestic anti-inflationary policies which require a reduction in govern-ment expeditures, a contraction of financial credit and the freezing of salaries. This implies in turn a reduction in social service expenditure, an economic recession and the bankruptcy of those enterprises which are dependent on public sector spending, all of which results in an increase in unemployment. Since the freezing of salaries is not accompanied by a parallel freezing of prices and taxes (on the contrary, they increase), the overall result becomes a real impoverishment of the population as a whole.

(b) Devaluation of the currency in terms of US dollars and the elimination of foreign exchange controls.

(c) Incentives to attract foreign investment, especially measures to guarantee 'social peace' and tax incentives.

As a whole these measures, even though they may improve the balance of payments in the short term, increase social differences and worsen the situation of the economic, social and cultural rights of the dispossessed classes.

In financial terms, the conditions attached to the repayment of the debt, as well as those which the banking system has been requiring for rescheduling purposes, represent serious, if not destructive, burdens on the resources of the countries concerned. A larger and larger percentage of their exports have to be committed to the payment of interest alone,[32] and an increased proportion of their GNPs go to service the loans and interest due.[33]

This overall picture indicates that there are great pressures being exerted on Latin American countries, in particular the big debtors, for the adoption of policies which, at least in the short run, are objectively contradictory to the objectives of the International Convention on Economic, Social and Cultural Rights. The Convention's universal and legally binding appreciation of the minimal conditions in which each person should live in dignity is being violated as a result of these policy pressures from the IMF and the international private banks. Many of the rights to which we have referred are in jeopardy: the right to work, the right to enjoy satisfactory working conditions (among which are a fair wage, the right to an adequate standard of living, and the improvement in the conditions of existence), the right to health, to education and to social security, the right of the family and the protection of motherhood, and so on.

Is it legally correct for States that are bound by the Convention to adopt economic policies which will inevitably affect adversely the rights proclaimed by the Treaty? While a single easy answer may not be possible because the issue will depend on what alternative options are available, there are several pointers that we need to take note of. The human factor must not be relegated to a secondary position when establishing the terms of adjustment of the economy, not even when the rescheduling of the debt is being arranged. States, no matter what one's point of view, are human communities before being debtors. Secondly, when choosing among alternative policies for the adjustment of the economy to overcome the present crisis, the State should bear in mind the International Convention on Economic, Social and Cultural Rights and select those policies which place the fewest restrictions on the rights proclaimed in the Treaty.

The sacrifices involved must be the least possible with the benefits accruing reaching the greatest number. This means taking issue with the short-term prescriptions of the banks which seek to establish the repayment of the debt as the fundamental priority in the economic policies of the debtors. It means disagreeing with them that the difficulties are only transitory and that the Latin American countries followed erroneous economic policies previously. After all, the banks have only themselves to blame; the risks were self-evident when they chose to extend such massive credits to the Third World.

Starting from this general orientation, we can ask the following questions: What proportion of the GNP shall be committed to the payment of the foreign debt? According to Article 1 of the UN Convention, all peoples may dispose of their wealth, and 'in no case should a people be deprived of their own means of subsistence'. So what is the threshold? And does it constitute a legal limit on the terms which can be agreed for the payment of the debt? And is not this just a risk those who lent almost unlimited resources to the Third World have to live with?

Conversely, what limits are there on those States bound by the UN Conventions in accepting refinancing conditions?

Would it be possible to protect the objective non-fulfilment with the progressive and conditional character of the obligations assumed? It should not be forgotten that the Convention can also be violated in a negative way and Article 5 states categorically that 'no provision of the present Convention can be interpreted in the sense of acknowledging the right of any State, group, or individual to undertake activities or realize acts which be directed to the destruction of any of the rights or liberties acknowledged by the Convention, or their limitations in a measure greater than foreseen by it.'

These questions may not lead us to definitive conclusions. Concrete answers can only be given in the light of concrete realities. But when negotiating solutions to the debt or implementing policies to solve the crisis, the existence of human rights obligations should be taken into account. Indeed these are just as binding on States, or even more so, than their financial obligations. There can be no justification for ignoring them, not only because they constitute international legal obligations, but because they represent an extraordinary advance in how human beings are valued, an advance which it would be inexcusable to ignore or pretend to cancel.

Notes

1. Earlier British constitutional precedents include the Magna Carta of 1215, the Habeas Corpus Act of 1679 and Bill of Rights of 1689. However, these documents differ from those we mention in that they go beyond a recognition of the intangible rights of the person with respect to the State, and also establish duties persons owe to government.

2. Cf. T. C. Van Boven, 'Les critères de distinction des droits de l'homme'. UNESCO, Paris, 1978.

3. Both treaties create true international tribunals to resolve any violation of their provisions in cases which have not been able to be resolved satisfactorily in a previous instance.

4. In the case of Europe, there is a parallel treaty, the European Social Charter, which touches on the economic, social and cultural rights. In the Americas, however, the Human Rights Commission limits itself to an acknowledgement of those rights as the object of 'progressive development' (Article 25). There is at the present time a preliminary project submitted for discussion at the OAS to create an Additional Protocol on the matter.

5. The real nature of these rights has been mentioned in order to clarify the difference between human rights and peoples' rights, since they are confusing to some. Certain people believe that these are the most fundamental of the human rights; for others, the rights of peoples are the essential condition needed to be able to enjoy human rights. This seems to be the approach of the UN General Assembly. Cf. Van Minh, 'Droits de l'homme et pouvoirs privés' in *Multinationales et droits de l'homme*, PUF, Amiens, 1984. However, the truth is that formally they are inscribed in the United Nations Human Rights Conventions and their content corresponds to the effects of these commentaries.

6. Preamble to the Universal Declaration and to both Conventions.

7. Some of the more recent publications on the subject include H. Fáundnez-Ledezma, 'La protección de los derechos humanos en situaciones de emergencia', in *Contemporary Issues in International Law* (Essays in honour of Luis B. Sohn) edited by T. Buergenthal, Engel Publisher, 1984, pp. 101–12; C. O'Donnel Sepulveda, 'Los Derechos Humanos y el derecho internacional humanitario ante la subverción en América Latina', *Boletín Mexicano de Derecho Comparado*, Nueva Serie, No. 49, 1984, pp. 101–52, D. O'Donnel, 'Legitimidad de los estados de excepción a la luz de los instrumentos de derechos humanos', in *Review of the Faculty of Legal Rights*, Pontificia Universidad Católica del Perú, No. 38, December 1984, pp. 165–231; also the Final Report of the Seminar, State Security, Human Rights and Humanitarian Rights, organized by the International Red Cross Committee and the Inter-American Institute of Human Rights, San José, Costa Rica, 1982–1984, in particular the presentation of H. Montealegre, pp. 31–50.

8. Articles 4 and 15 respectively.

9. Article 27.

10. Lawless Case, Series B–1960–61, p. 82.

11. Cf. Article 27(2) of the American Convention. The International Convention on Civil and Political Rights is less restrictive (Article 4).

12. Article 27(1) of the American Convention and Article 4 of the Convention.

13. Article 29(2) of the Universal Declaration.

14. Cf. Fáundnez, op cit., p. 117.

15. There are also structural limitations on the human rights which prevail even where there is no state of emergency. Human rights are not absolute and are subject to restrictions. These include the rights of others, public order, public morals, national security, public health etc.

16. Van Boven, op. cit., p. 54.

17. Doc. A2929 (V) 1–21.

18. Decision 543 (VI) of the General Assembly.

19. Cf. I. Szabo, 'Fondements historiques et développment des droits de l'homme' in *Les dimensions . . .* op. cit., p. 32.

20. Several of the rights normally classified as economic, social or cultural are in fact immediately realizable and do depend only on judicial enforcement. For example, trade union rights, liberty of teaching, the rights of an author or the freedom of work. Parallel to this, there are other rights which are classified as civil and political but can only be gradually realized, such as the rights of the child and the family.

21. In some cases there seems to be an agreement not only to make resources available for the realization of those rights; but to reach positive progressive results, or at least not fall back. This is the assumption behind the right to a 'continuous improvement in living conditions' (Article 11(1)).

22. Article 6.

23. Per capita income (in 1970 US dollars) fell from $1,918 in 1977 to $883 in 1983, a

difference of $1.009. the year in which negative growth began (−5.9% in 1983 alone). Source: CEPAL/SES-20/G. 17/21-2-84, p. 4.

24. The average annual increase in consumer prices, which was 12% in 1970, has gone to 40.3% in 1977 and 84.9% in 1982. See CEPAL, 'Estudio Económico de América Latina y el Caribe', Vol. 1, p. 35.

25. Resolution 543 (VI) of the General Assembly.

26. Montealegre, op. cit., p. 44.

27. *El Nacional*, Caracas, 20 March 1985.

28. *The Daily Journal*, Caracas, 21 March 1985.

29. S. C. Nino, 'Etica y Derechos Humanos', *Paidos Studio*, Buenos Aires, 1984, p. 113.

30. Ibid.

31. Cf. J. A. Silva-Michelena, *Política y Bloques de Poder*, Siglo XXI Editora, Mexico, 1984, p. 93.

32. 35% for Latin America as a whole, with some countries paying more: Argentina (51%), Brazil (43.5%), Mexico (38%), Chile (37.5%), and Nicaragua (3%). Source: E/CEPAL/SES-20/G-17-21-2-1984, op. cit., p. 46.

33. According to the available information, in Venezuela it would reach between 30% and 40% of GNP.

Index

List of Contributors

Atilio A. Boron is an Argentinian political scientist, based in Buenos Aires.

Clovis Brigagão is a political scientist at the University of Rio de Janeiro, and a former adviser to the government of the state of Rio de Janeiro.

Armando Córdova is a Salvadorean sociologist; currently research fellow at the Centre for Interdisciplinary Studies in Humanities of the National Autonomous University of Mexico.

Hector Faúndez-Ledezma is a Chilean specialist in international law teaching at the Faculty of Law and Political Sciences of the Central University of Venezuela.

Pablo González Casanova is a sociologist and former Rector of the National Autonomous University of Mexico and Professor at its Institute for Social Research.

Edgardo Mercado Jarrín is President of the Peruvian Geopolitical and Strategic Studies Institute.

Felipe MacGregor, SJ, is the President of the Peruvian Association for Peace Studies.

Kinhide Mushakoji is the Vice-Rector of the Regional and Global Studies Division of the United Nations University in Tokyo.

Pedro Nikken is Professor at the Institute of Public Jurisprudence at the Central University of Venezuela.

Aníbal Quijano is a Peruvian sociologist and Director of the Centre for Social Research in Lima, teaching at the San Carlos University.

Theotonio dos Santos is a Brazilian sociologist and Professor of Sociology at the University of Brasilia.

José Agustín Silva-Michelena (1934–86) was a Venezuelan sociologist, Professor of the Central University of Venezuela and former Director of its Centre for Development Studies (CENDES).

Heinz R. Sonntag teaches sociology at the Central University of Venezuela and is a research fellow and former Director of its CENDES.

Augusto Varas is a Chilean sociologist teaching at the Latin American Faculty for Social Sciences (FLACSO) in Santiago.